Gatekeeper

The Tactical Guide to Commitment

Shawn T. Smith

Publisher's Note

First Edition: September 2023

Published in Denver, Colorado, by Mesa Press, a division of Mesa Psychological Services, Inc. 4045 Wadsworth Boulevard, Suite 200, Wheat Ridge, CO 80033

Designed by Clockwise Media Group
Edited by Jennifer Jas

ISBN 978-0-9906864-6-0 (paperback)
ISBN 978-0-9906864-7-7 (electronic book)
Library of Congress Control Number: 2023942909

Contents

Introduction **1**

— BEFORE WE BEGIN —

Five Policies for Rational Thinking in an Emotional Arena **17**

1. Purpose Precedes Romance 18
2. The Mind Is Divided Against Itself 39
3. Time Is Your Ally 42
4. Dispassionate Observation Lights the Way 45
5. Playful Experimentation Expands Awareness 53

— BOOK I —

Composure **57**

How the Mind Handles Relationship Patterns 71

Pathways to Chaos 86

The Road to Composure 95

Foundational Skill: Allow Others to Experience Discomfort 106

— BOOK II —

Dignity **111**

Compulsive Self-Policing 115

What Women Cannot Teach Men 123

Pathways to Shame 132

The Road to Dignity 141

Foundational Skill: Act in the Service of Values Before Comfort 152

— BOOK III —

Resilience **157**

Her Relationship to the World 162

The Bright Triad 171

Pathways to Frailty 179
The Road to Resilience 187
Foundational Skill: Embrace the Challenge of High-Functioning Relationships 192

—BOOK IV—

Joy **199**
"Happy Wife, Happy Life" 202
Pathways to Fatigue 215
The Road to Joy 222
Foundational Skill: Respect Intuition 235
Just One More Thing 245

—BOOK V—

Love **247**
Love Is Not Enough 251
Pathways to Torment 259
The Road to Love 266
Foundational Skill: You Set the Speed Limit 277
The Final Word 280

Introduction

This book is for men who want to improve the role of women in their lives and upgrade themselves in the process. For the sake of efficiency, I'll break with custom and begin by telling you what this book is not.

It is not about picking up women. It's not about what women want, how to impress them, or how to please them in bed. While rooted in affection for women, this book is unconcerned with their preferences.

It is instead about *your* life, *your* purpose, and *your* well-being. It's about being a disciplined thinker in matters of the heart and finding relationships that support your destiny.

Let me tell you about the moment on a random weekday when, thanks to an ill-considered marriage to an otherwise wonderful woman, a man named Andre realized his destiny was no longer his own.[1]

Only yesterday, Andre's future was an open highway with no speed limit. Now he stood at a fork in the road, his progress halted.

---

1 I present case studies and examples throughout the book. I have changed details to protect identities, and I have obtained permission where appropriate. I have also ensured that these case studies are composite sketches detached from any particular individual. This places the focus on common relationship dynamics.

He could either stay in a scenario with a miserable but predictable outcome, or he could launch a costly battle of unknown duration and intensity.

His friends said his problem started the day he met Mia. None of them would say she was a bad person, though they disliked the effect she had on Andre's life. I see his situation differently. I wouldn't say his problem started when he met Mia. His problem started when he became entangled with her before he understood what that commitment would bring to his life.

Entanglements are an important concept in this book. An entanglement is any commitment, like living together, that impedes exit from an unworkable relationship. Andre entangled himself with Mia by cohabiting without forethought. He got swept up in her world shortly after Mia's roommate got engaged and moved in with her fiancé. That left Mia with a rent payment she couldn't cover on her own.

Mia had plenty of options. She could find a new roommate, or rent a lower-cost apartment, or even live with her parents. But Mia found it more appealing to move in with Andre. They had flirtatiously joked about it before. She felt it was the perfect time, and she uttered four little words that have been the downfall of countless men: "It just makes sense."

How could he argue with that? The stars were aligned. Within days, her underwear was in his dresser drawer, and her toothbrush was on his bathroom counter.

At first, they were blissfully happy. They enjoyed the intimacy, the shared meals, and the easy access to sex. What's not to like about a new adventure? They bought furniture together, got a puppy, and even bought a house. They developed entanglements galore. Andre couldn't extract himself if he wanted to. Mia soon got pregnant, then they got married.

For reasons that don't matter here, their relationship fell apart. Their infatuation receded as the differences in their values and life goals became oppressively real. That brings us to Andre's fork-in-the-road moment when he realized his future was no longer his own. He was meeting with a client when it happened.

Andre owned an accounting firm in a midsized Midwestern town. He had spent his early thirties pouring his soul into the company, sometimes working eighty hours per week. It was still a fledgling business, vulnerable to disruptions from outside and from within.

The text he received from Mia was more than disruptive. It turned his world upside down. She wrote, "I can't go on like this. You need to put your family first, or we need to divorce." In an instant, he felt his professional ambitions evaporate.

Her message wasn't a surprise. He knew their marriage had problems, and he was already aware of his two options.

The first was to reduce his devotion to a nascent business that still needed his time and attention. This would mean dropping clients, letting employees go, and relinquishing his dream so he could spend more time with a woman he would certainly come to resent over his lost dreams.

His second option was to endure a costly divorce. Now in his late thirties, he had seen friends and colleagues suffer divorce, their lives and ambitions shattered. He knew the family court system was arbitrary, unaccountable, and often biased against husbands and fathers.

He dreaded the effect divorce would have on his child, and being an accountant, he knew his fledgling company might not survive the financial and emotional disruption of even the smoothest divorce.

With that single text from Mia, his future was no longer his own. Though he didn't realize it at the time, his downfall had started years ago with those four little words: "It just makes sense."

The problem was not that Andre entangled himself with a puppy, a mortgage, or a child. Life's most precious experiences come from entangling oneself in meaningful arrangements. The problem was that he recklessly entangled himself before he understood what he would receive in exchange for his commitment. His future no longer belonged to him because, all those years earlier, he had failed to protect it. It's a common error, but it doesn't have to be.

Maybe No One Told You This

Societies throughout time have required men to give more than we take, to produce more than we consume. We can either be of service to our families and our communities or surrender our status as men. As psychologist Roy Baumeister put it,

> "A woman is entitled to respect until and unless she does something to lose it. A man is not entitled to respect until and unless he does something to gain it."[2]

This is not a theoretical point. For example, American men (but not women) must register for the military draft. Men who won't pledge their willingness to kill or be killed are subject to fines, imprisonment, and exclusion from federal benefits granted to other citizens. (They will still enjoy the honor of paying taxes, though.)

I don't worry about the goodness or justice of this arrangement; it is simply a feature of humanity. We rarely expect women to do dirty, dangerous jobs. They face their own burdens. In 2014, a group of researchers conducted a "wide qualitative examination of how the psychology of men and women have been portrayed throughout history in art, literature, culture and science." They found that universally, women are expected to be attractive, to bear children, and to nurture family life.[3]

Women don't get a free pass, but they are judged less harshly for failing to meet expectations. Meanwhile, we men get to have more judgment-free sex and fun. As part of the trade-off, we are

---

2 Baumeister, R. 2010. *Is There Anything Good About Men: How Cultures Flourish by Exploiting Men.* New York: Oxford University Press.

3 Seager, M., L. Sullivan, and J. Barry. 2014. "Gender-Related Schemas and Suicidality: Validation of the Male and Female Traditional Gender Scripts Questionnaires." *New Male Studies: An International Journal* 3: 34-54. In this survey, the authors noted that the contrasting universal expectations for men include 1) fight and win, 2) provide and protect, and 3) exercise mastery and control. The study also examined gender expectation in suicidality. The authors found, in certain circumstances, that failing to live up to the demands of the male script can cause "extreme psychological distress." For example, a man might view himself as a failure if he has difficulty providing for his family.

expected to sacrifice our safety and comfort. When was the last time you saw a woman hanging off the ass-end of a garbage truck, slinging molten tar on a hot roof, or descending into a malfunctioning sewer to make repairs? Women benefit from men's willingness to get dirty and to get hurt. Again: this is an observation, not a complaint. Both sexes make their sacrifices and enjoy their respective benefits.

A great benefit that flows toward any man who takes up the challenge of masculinity is prestige. It is not a trivial commodity. The man with prestige enjoys admiration and social capital. He's the truck driver, the chef, or the CEO who gets to stand tall and look others in the eye because his masculinity is beyond question. He carries an intact man-card among family, friends, and colleagues. Prestigious men are also especially attractive to women.

Prestige is valuable because it's costly. It takes time and effort to cultivate, and it involves risk. Some men pay the ultimate price for prestige, like the men who comprise more than 95 percent of workplace fatalities.

There's another cost that's central to the theme of this book: prestigious, duty-driven men sometimes fail to consider the long-term ramifications of their romantic choices. In my clinical experience, it's especially true for men who pride themselves on being pillars of strength while asking little in return. They're unaccustomed to wondering, *How will my devotion to this woman affect my life? How will this commitment serve my values, my purpose, and my happiness?*

I have yet to meet a man who was explicitly taught to consider those questions. It's not as if men knowingly throw themselves into atrocious relationships with miserable battle-axes. It's more often the case that men think, *This relationship is good enough. She's cute, the sex is fun, and I can tolerate her quirks.* Few men are taught the skills to assess the costs and benefits of a romantic investment.

When a man has no real demands for a relationship beyond good feelings and good sex, then he is a desperate buyer in a seller's market. As one man told me:

"I was raised to think I should be grateful for any woman who considers me worth dating."

Imagine buying a car with that mindset. Unless you're unusually lucky, you're bound to get a lemon. Like so many others, that man offered his commitment while demanding little in return.

Guiding principles like that one usually sit wordlessly beneath our awareness, directing our actions like a silent puppet master. This book will drag such principles into the light of day. We will build flexibility and freedom around them.

Why? Because romantic commitments are our most consequential relationships. A man who invests without intention and self-awareness can only succeed by luck. He can easily end up nagged and abused for decades. He can be financially devastated in family court. He can lose access to his children.

Perhaps the worst outcome is that of the man who feels trapped in a miserable relationship and who has determined that staying is less costly and destructive than leaving. "It's cheaper to keep her," he jokes with his friends as he runs out the clock.

If the barrier to exit is so high, shouldn't the barrier to entry be equally high? I titled this book *Gatekeeper* because I believe the answer is yes. Men of purpose should be highly selective in relationships, and not just in long-term commitments. Sometimes the briefest liaison leaves a man with a lifetime's worth of unwanted mementos and responsibilities.

Yet, according to one study, people who believe they are choosing short-term relationships are more tolerant of anger problems, substance abuse, and dishonesty than those who believe they're choosing long-term relationships. Men are more tolerant of such shortcomings than women.[4]

When short-term flings turn into long-term obligations, people are stuck with all the chaos and poor character traits they should never have tolerated. Plus, the more we tolerate substandard re-

---

4 Jonason, P. K., J. R. Garcia, G. D. Webster, N. P. Li, and H. E. Fisher. 2015. "Relationship Dealbreakers: Traits People Avoid in Potential Mates." *Personality and Social Psychology Bulletin* 41: 1697-711.

lationships, the more comfortable we become. Practice makes us more skilled at rationalizing and managing subpar romantic investments.

The alternative involves an idea that may require a bit of effort to grasp: As men, we are responsible for all the results of a romantic endeavor. That's not to say we are accountable for her behavior. She alone bears responsibility for her actions, but we alone decide who passes through the gate—whether it's a one-night stand or a marriage. That means we are responsible for what we receive in return. And not just the good stuff. Prizes may include gonorrhea, keyed car paint, and stolen dreams.

Here's the upside: When we accept responsibility for our romantic choices, we grant ourselves the freedom to have standards. We give ourselves the power and the duty to reject arrangements that bring misery and chaos.

As for Andre, he had done a lot right in his life. He had been strategic, motivated, and focused. Unfortunately, he made a single tactical error that undermined years of hard work. He was careless with his commitment, but not because he lacked character. It was simply that no one had prepared him for the task of choosing a partner.

He's not alone. Maybe you, like Andre and like me, were never told these truths:

- **Committing to a woman is one of the most far-reaching decisions you will ever make.** It affects all aspects of life, from happiness to career success and physical and mental health. Most men, if they understand the basics of intentionality, learn to simply examine a potential partner's surface characteristics. They ask shallow questions like *Does she have obvious mental health problems or other red flags?* That's not even close to sufficient. This book will give you a more complete strategy.
- **You're allowed to prioritize your purpose, your values, and your future.** Most men learn that their own desires are secondary to the priorities of their fami-

lies, employers, and wives … anyone who lays claim to his time and effort. If that describes you, I hope this book will cause you to question that arrangement.

- **Misaligned values don't make her a bad person, but they make the relationship a liability.** Though it may violate the storybook platitudes we've all heard, it's useful to think of romantic relationships in terms of assets and liabilities. Of course, we should enjoy the more tender aspects of our relationships, but we ignore the nuts-and-bolts practicalities at our peril. It is not only acceptable to view romance through the hard, cold lens of pragmatism; my clinical experience says it is absolutely necessary.
- **You're allowed to judge a woman's character.** A young, gorgeous woman won't be young and gorgeous forever, but a conniving bitch will always be a conniving bitch—and she will probably get worse. Not only is it acceptable to judge a woman's character, but it is absolutely necessary to do so. Every man will eventually realize that character matters. The question is whether he will realize it before he makes a grievous error, or after.
- **A woman may behave as if she wants to control you, but she will resent you if she succeeds.** This ranks high on the list of realities few men are explicitly taught. You are not meant to be domesticated by anyone—including and especially any woman to whom you devote your time and attention. You may think it will please her to sacrifice your values and well-being for her, but doing so may cause her to view you as spineless, and it will create a relationship in which neither partner is happy. No healthy woman wants a man to be her obedient pet.
- **Women do not complete men.** Life is not a Hollywood romantic comedy. Romance is one of the sweetest parts of life, but it cannot be the cornerstone of a man's

world. Men must find purpose outside their relationships in order to be fully present within their relationships.

- **Women's association with us is not an act of charity.** Women are lucky to have us, just as we are lucky to have them. You are an equal participant in that equation, and you're allowed to reject any woman who believes you are indebted to her for graciously bestowing her presence upon you.
- **Women do not belong on pedestals.** Men and women function *together*. Neither side has cornered the market on virtue or iniquity. Idealizing a woman burdens her with a duty to perfection that she can't satisfy.
- **You're allowed to place limits on relationships.** Sometimes a little girl will boldly pronounce that she has a boyfriend. She will claim possession of some unsuspecting little fellow without his permission, and in a most adorable manner. It's less adorable when a grown woman claims possession of a man by inserting herself into his life. There is a long-standing framework for romantic relationships that can help the contemporary man avoid such incursions. That framework, called courtship, places romantic relationships into these categories: prospect, girlfriend, fiancée (or intended), and wife (or equivalent).

  A romantic prospect doesn't become a girlfriend (earning your exclusivity) until it's apparent she possesses an outstanding character and shared values. A girlfriend doesn't advance to fiancée (earning the right to plan a future with you) until her character and values remain a consistently positive addition to your life. A fiancée doesn't graduate to wife (earning your lasting commitment) until she demonstrates her ability to be a devoted, considerate partner throughout the planning and negotiating of your shared future.

  It is the gatekeeper's job to enforce the boundaries commensurate with each category. If she occupies any position other than wife or equivalent, then there is no reason for her to store clothes in your closet or tampons in your bathroom; no reason to share a rent payment, car repair bills, or pets. These boundaries are the keys to your kingdom. Guard them.

- **You're allowed to reject a relationship.** We all have probably known a man who remained in a relationship that should have ended at "hello." You're allowed to reject unhealthy or poorly matched relationships. The earlier you do so, the better for all concerned.
- **You're allowed to establish your purpose and your values before committing to a relationship.** It's useful to know your ship's destination before taking on passengers. Women often want to secure a man's commitment before he has had sufficient time and experience to determine his own values and purpose, locking him into a path he may regret. The desire for commitment is a wonderful feminine trait, but you are not obliged to obey it.
- **You're allowed to revoke your presence from those who don't appreciate you.** It's no secret that masculinity is unpopular in certain quarters these days. You are under no obligation to work for companies, attend universities, or patronize businesses that view masculinity with contempt. It's no less true in the romantic realm. Male attention and devotion are the most valuable problem-solving commodities on the planet. Reserve them for those who value them.
- **Your devotion is not her right.** Your attention is a privilege others must earn. No one is entitled to your presence, your consideration, or your labor. Those commodities are not community property. They are yours to distribute as you see fit.
- **You're allowed to have standards.** You're allowed to reject women who bring misery and chaos. You're allowed to disregard damsels in distress and pursue your purpose without drama or hindrance. You're allowed to choose women of grace and good character.

There's an old aphorism that says women are the gatekeepers of sex, and men are the gatekeepers of commitment. The thinking is that each side safeguards what is, respectively, most costly. Sex, with the possibility of pregnancy, is more costly to women. Commitment, with its foreclosure of alternate mating possibilities, is more costly to men.

It's an imperfect idea because men (like women) value commitment, and women (like men) value sex. Nor are the risks so neatly divided. Men (like women) pay a price for becoming parents, and women (like men) pay an opportunity cost for commitment. Still, the idea is not wrong. Women are generally more protective of sex, and men are generally more protective of alternative mating opportunities.[5]

The first usage of that term—gatekeeper—seems to date back to 1948, when the geneticist Angus John Bateman (a man's name if ever there was one) wrote an influential paper regarding the mating behavior of female fruit flies. Bateman noticed that their limited ability to produce eggs constrains their reproductive potential. However, the reproductive success of males is constrained only by their access to females. Male fruit flies simply don't operate under the same time constraints as females.[6]

That time constraint compels female fruit flies to be choosy about mates. Because their eggs are expensive, female fruit flies are the gatekeepers of fruit-fly sex. As Bateman wrote,

---

5 Although culture shapes the dating landscape, this book assumes the basics of mating remain constant even as its surface features shift. Such features include ever-changing social forces (like birth control), subcultures (various social and ideological movements like feminism and Men Going Their Own Way), and technology (online dating). Despite the shifting landscape, our basic human nature evolves at a glacial pace. Human mating preferences have developed over hundreds of thousands of years, and our species has found reproductive success in long-term pair bonding. That arrangement involves ancient mating behaviors that will remain relatively constant even in an ever-changing cultural landscape. See, for example, Fletcher, G. J. O., J. A. Simpson, L. Campbell, and N. C. Overall. 2015. "Pair Bonding, Romantic Love, and Evolution: The Curious Case of Homo Sapiens." *Perspectives on Psychological Science* 10: 20-36.

6 Bateman, J. A. 1948. "Intra-sexual Selection in Drosophila." *Heredity* 2: 349-368.

> "… the male is eager for any female, without discrimination, whereas the female chooses the male."

The more, the better, if you're a male fruit fly. Bateman made no mention of them being the gatekeepers of commitment. Male fruit flies aren't interested in devotion. I suppose lady fruit flies don't offer much in the way of personality.

We can't generalize from flies to humans, but Bateman noticed a universal concept among complex, sexually dimorphous species: the mating process involves some measure of choosiness from one or both parties.

That brings us to the problem I hope to address in this book. Given the far-reaching consequences of romantic commitment, men should be choosy. Yet, I see little evidence that men reliably act as gatekeepers for commitment. By my reckoning, we are less skillful than women at choosing our mates. Evolutionary psychology backs me up: men experience "love at first sight" more than women do. Men are also quicker to become attached and likelier to have sex with women we barely know. Our own male psychology dramatically increases the risk of unworkable entanglements.[7]

The field of evolutionary psychology may have created the erroneous impression that, like fruit flies, women are choosier than men, and men court women and compete for female attention like peacocks compete for peahens.

Those ideas hold some truth, but as psychology professor and author Steve Stewart-Williams has pointed out, the Males Compete/Females Choose model of human mating is exaggerated and overstated. A more accurate model is what he calls the Mutual Mate Choice (MMC) model. The MMC model recognizes that humans (along with some mammals like lemurs, marmosets, and

7 Buss, D. M. 2019. "The Evolution of Love in Humans." In *The New Psychology of Love*, edited by R. J. Sternberg and K. Sternberg. Cambridge University Press.

gibbons) form pair bonds because the males and females both invest similarly in the survival of offspring.[8]

It boils down to this: unlike fruit flies and peacocks, men should be choosy. There's a lot on the line when we offer our devotion, from our own well-being to that of our future families and children.

It's not my place to advocate for or against long-term commitment or marriage. I'm not a spiritual advisor. I assume any man who has read this far wants to build a shared enterprise with a caring and supportive woman. My only agenda is to persuade that man to be picky. We should be at least as discriminating about our most consequential relationships as we are about the cars we drive.

The Job Ahead

I realize being choosy might reduce dating options in what may seem like an already barren landscape. You might even wonder if raising your standards means you will sit on the sidelines while other men out-compete you in the romantic arena.

That's only true if you're competing for any woman who will have you, which is a bit like rolling dice to determine what food you will eat for the rest of the year. Maybe you'll get lucky and dine on filet mignon and Mom's apple pie. Maybe fate will frown on you and ... well, I'll let you use your imagination.

If you limit your romantic prospects to those who fit your plans and advance your purpose, then you have already excluded most women. That includes many wonderful women who, for various

8 Stewart-Williams, S., and A. G. Thomas. 2013. "The Ape That Thought It Was a Peacock: Does Evolutionary Psychology Exaggerate Human Sex Differences?" *Psychological Inquiry* 24: 137-168. In one illustration of male choosiness, the authors wrote: "The idea that women are the choosier sex is one of the best-known claims associated with [evolutionary psychology]. Ironically, another of the best-known claims associated with [evolutionary psychology] is an exception to this rule: On average, men are choosier than women about the physical attractiveness of a prospective mate." They added men may lower their overall standards about casual sex, but "... when it comes to the most important mating decisions of a man's life—who he will marry, who he will have children with—the difference in choosiness [between men and women] is much smaller and maybe nonexistent."

pragmatic reasons, simply don't belong by your side. Besides, I'm not convinced choosiness diminishes options. As a psychologist, I have worked with many men who noticed distinct benefits from raising their standards.

First, as they raise their expectations for romantic commitment, they simultaneously raise their personal expectations. I have yet to meet a man who says, "I want to improve my relationships, but I don't want to improve myself." It's a parallel process with compounding benefits. Raising their personal expectations necessarily improves their performance in life. That increases their prestige, which in turn gives them more confidence and makes them more appealing both personally and professionally.

Second, as these men scrutinized their relationship patterns and became more discriminating, they noticed a temporary decrease in opportunities with women. The women they once found attractive became repellent, and the women they now desired seemed out of reach. They were in a sort of limbo.

However, they eventually began noticing healthy relationship options that once seemed beyond the realm of possibility. Sometimes getting what we want out of life begins with a leap of faith and closing the door to what we don't want.

Maybe their options increased because they valued themselves for the first time, and hence they carried themselves differently. Or perhaps women noticed their new willingness to reject relationships, and they found it enticing. If that seems counterintuitive, consider this question: Have you ever seen an "everything must go" sale at a Lamborghini dealership? How about a "come one, come all" enrollment drive at Harvard? I have not. Yet people desire these things. High standards don't repel. They attract.

Another factor in these men's success is their willingness to connect with a different group of women—a new willingness to make eye contact, exchange words, and express interest—while simultaneously closing lines of communication with the women they previously pursued. We tend to find what we're searching for when we close avenues of convenience and look past undesirable or ill-fitting options.

Will it happen for you? I don't know. Treat this as an experiment. But I can say this: there's no downside to dissecting your manner of choosing relationships. This book is about putting yourself under the microscope. It's easiest to manage our relationship patterns when we understand how they work.

Choosiness is not always simple for men. It sometimes goes against our nature. It may violate what we learned from our parents and other important figures, and it may contradict what we think people expect of us. What should a man expect in exchange for his commitment? For far too many, that question is barely an afterthought.

That's where this book comes in. While we're dissecting relationship patterns, we will cover a set of bare-minimum relationship qualities few men are taught to look for.

1. **Composure.** A healthy relationship helps a man advance his reason for being. We'll look at how to establish and refine purpose, and how to choose relationships that advance that purpose rather than saddle us with chaos.
2. **Dignity.** A healthy relationship doesn't constrain a man. It's rocket fuel. It helps him thrive in good times and grow during bad times.
3. **Resilience.** A healthy relationship makes a man tougher, more flexible, and more resourceful against the problems of the world. The wrong relationship does the opposite; it drains his strength.
4. **Joy.** Happiness comes and goes, but a joyful relationship is a source of comfort even in hard times.
5. **Love.** This is necessary for any healthy romantic connection. However, it must be the gatekeeper's final consideration in allocating his commitment, not his first consideration. Prioritizing love over more pragmatic concerns has caused the downfall of too many men. That's why I won't use that word again until we have concluded more important business. Until then, it is The Word Which Shall Not Yet Be Spoken.

These five qualities are, in my clinical opinion, the bare-bones ingredients for a successful relationship. We will look at the function of each one and why it matters. We will tease apart the reasons so many men—perhaps including you—reject some or all of these qualities. Crucially, we'll discuss strategies for choosing these five qualities over their counterparts, which are chaos, shame, frailty, fatigue, and torment.

The gatekeeper is no sleepy night watchman overlooking an empty warehouse. He's a discerning sentinel protecting the abundance born of his character and his labor. He chooses the members of his inner circle with deep deliberation. He doesn't bow to shame or the pressure to lower his standards. He understands that good sex and a pretty face aren't enough to justify a relationship that hobbles him.

The gatekeeper accepts the painful task of dismissing unworkable relationships with otherwise good women, though principled decision-making tempers that pain. He also understands not all women are qualified for romantic relationships. Among those who are, only a few possess values and character traits compatible with his own. He doesn't allow himself to become so enthralled with the particulars of any woman that he is blind to the effects the relationship will have on his purpose and his goals.

Men have endless reasons for choosing relationships that drag them down. That's why the bulk of this book is about *you* and the unwritten principles that shape your relationships with women. If you are up to the task, then let's get to work.

— BEFORE WE BEGIN —

Five Policies for Rational Thinking in an Emotional Arena

Prioritize purpose over romance • Manage a divided mind • Subdue emotional impulse • Master the art of dispassionate observation • Create room for new and better relationships

What separates the gatekeeper from other men? It's his unique ability to think about the white-knuckle romantic arena in a self-possessed, disciplined manner. His superpower is the capacity to employ intellect where other men succumb to hormones, recklessness, and desperation.

Before we discuss the matter of women and commitment, let's build a rational framework around the topic. Most of us need a bit of intellectual protection against our emotional vulnerabilities toward women. We need a protective border around the peculiar processes of our own emotional minds. Here are five mental policies to set the tone for the task ahead.

1. Purpose precedes romance.
2. The mind is divided against itself.
3. Time is your ally.
4. Dispassionate observation lights the way.
5. Playful experimentation expands awareness.

Let's take them one at a time, like any serene gatekeeper would.

1. Purpose Precedes Romance

Purpose will be a theme throughout the book. A man's purpose is central to every aspect of his life. It forms the contours of his day and determines his standing in the community. It is the wellspring of his prestige and self-regard. Purpose can sustain a man's spirit when other assets fail.

The wise gatekeeper ensures his relationships align with his purpose in order to protect all that flows from it. Does that mean he must know precisely why he exists before he is safe to establish a romantic commitment? No, and we'll sort that out as we go along. The point is that he can't afford to neglect his purpose when choosing relationships.

Purpose can be an intimidating topic. Let's demystify it and, for those who struggle with the matter, put strategies in place. We'll begin with a man's most basic purposeful activity: work.

In 2018, British psychologist John Barry set out to uncover the factors behind good mental health in men. He found job satisfaction is the strongest predictor of positive mindset among men, being around three times higher than the next strongest predictor.[9]

---

9 Barry, J. A. 2020. "Job Satisfaction, Relationship, Stability, and Valuing One's Health Are the Strongest Predictors of Men's Mental Well-Being." *Psychreg Journal of Psychology*, 4(3): 4-27. Other strong predictors of a positive mindset among men in the US and UK included physical health, income, age (men generally get happier with age, with men in their fifties being at "peak positivity"), being married, participation in sports and friendship, and current or prior military service.

Men who work are men at peace. It's not merely about income. Dr. Barry found that employed men are more optimistic, happy, motivated, emotionally stable, confident, and in control. The values men associated with meaningful work included honesty, reliability, and dependability. Men are most satisfied when they have a direct impact on the success of a business.

He found the inverse effects to be equally true. Dr. Barry wrote:

> "… joblessness erodes the effectiveness of every significant protective factor and makes it harder for men to sustain a healthy, happy lifestyle … Give a man a job he finds satisfying and you give him not only hope, but sometimes even a reason to live."

For men, work is not merely about punching a clock each day. It is about being part of an endeavor larger than ourselves. Our health, longevity, happiness, and standing in the community flow from purpose.

To understand our purpose is to know why we exist and how we should spend our days. A clear sense of purpose focuses our decisions and intensifies our efforts. As Robert Greene wrote in *The Laws of Human Nature*,

> "In military history, we can identify two types of armies—those that fight for a cause or an idea, and those that fight largely for money, as part of a job. … Fighting for a cause is known as a force multiplier—the greater the connection to the cause, the higher the morale, which translates into greater force. Such an army can often defeat one that is much larger but less motivated. We can say something similar about your life: operating with a high sense of purpose is a force multiplier."

A man's sense of purpose is an ever-present compass guiding the way, and there will always be someone or something trying to pull him off course. It can be the distraction of a broken-down car or the efforts of competitors who want to defeat him.

And then there are unhealthy relationships with women. Talk about an impediment to purposeful action! The wrong relationship can bring chaos, shame, frailty, fatigue, and torment. The quality of a man's relationships might be the single largest influence on his effectiveness.

Purpose is tough to pin down. There is no instruction manual, so how is a guy to decide the course of his life? This is a challenge for younger guys, and it can be equally difficult for older men, especially during life transitions like divorce, or when they reach a level of financial independence that allows new freedoms.

Most men struggle with the question of purpose. Perfect clarity isn't necessary. What's necessary is movement in a meaningful direction. Sometimes any direction that's consistent with your values is better than standing still.

In *The Tactical Guide to Women*, I suggested breaking purpose down into manageable components: status, responsibility, and effectiveness. Here's a summary of each component.[10]

Status

We men get a bad rap about our relationship abilities. We're told we are too stoic, too competitive, or insufficiently empathetic. This is a misunderstanding of men. It judges us by a feminine sensibility that doesn't easily translate to the masculine heart and mind. While women may be more efficient in some modes of communication, like verbalizing thoughts and emotions, men are more efficient in others.

Of great significance is our innate ability to navigate hierarchies smoothly and wordlessly. Men participate in multiple hierarchies ranging from the workplace to the softball team, switching roles and status effortlessly. That involves first-rate nonverbal communication skills and nuanced relationship abilities.

That uniquely male capacity is tied to our status-tracking ability. Purposeful men know where we sit in our local hierarchies. We know who we answer to and who answers to us. As children,

---

10 For citations associated with this summary, please see Chapter 3 of *The Tactical Guide to Women*.

boys organize themselves in hierarchical groups as early as age five, with plenty of physical and mental contests to establish the pecking order.

Girls tend to organize themselves into dyads and flat, leaderless groups with more verbal communication and more bickering. To criticize men for being overly competitive is to overlook the cooperation that comprises the bulk of our interactions.

Status is about relationships with supervisors, mentors, subordinates, contractors, mentees, teachers, students, and even the stranger on the street. If we take care of those relationships, we operate well within our various hierarchies.

I'm not sure women truly grasp the nature and subtlety of relationships and status among men. Nevertheless, healthy, mature women aren't threatened by a man's professional and collegial commitment outside their romantic relationships. Only in unhealthy relationships do women try to damage our status by interfering with our professional and personal interactions.

Responsibility

Men die roughly five years earlier than women across all age groups. The reasons for that include unintentional injuries, heart disease, and a suicide rate nearly four times higher than for women.[11]

A man can extend his life simply by taking on responsibility for an initiative larger than himself, whether it's a meaningful career; a commitment to the community; or any other weighty, values-driven responsibility. We take better care of ourselves when we embrace these responsibilities. We're happier and healthier, but every advantage comes with a trade-off.

Responsibility requires us to partition our time and effort. The women in our lives sometimes bristle during those moments when they aren't our top priority. The only way to completely avoid making others uncomfortable is to shun obligations to anything larger than ourselves.

---

11 Heron, M. 2019. "Deaths: Leading Causes for 2017." *National Vital Statistics Reports* 68(6): 1-76.

Women often find a man's obligations to be simultaneously attractive and frustrating. This is a minor dilemma for men: we complicate our lives and our relationships when we take on responsibility, yet we are less healthy and less prepared for relationships when we avoid it.

Effectiveness

The late teens and early twenties are a challenging period for most men. We're too young to know where we're going or how to get there, yet we're too old not to have a plan. A carefree young guy wakes up one day, and suddenly the world demands that he do useful work and contribute to society.

For Western men, there is no single rite of passage (such as a successful hunt) to mark a transition from boyhood to manhood. Those ancient rites of passage have been replaced by the demand for ongoing professional, academic, or military success. Today, a man must demonstrate his continual ability to influence his surroundings.

Once we gain prestige, we can easily lose it. Man-cards are revokable. All you have to do is get soft and rest on your laurels. Stop producing publicly verifiable demonstrations of effectiveness before retirement age, and suddenly people murmur about your worth.

Men can opt out of this expectation. Any man can be lazy and entitled, and he will survive. It's not as if society will feed him to the lions for refusing to pull his weight. He will simply be considered less than masculine. Men of purpose will disregard him, and his romantic prospects will decline. Some men find the lack of status to be a reasonable trade-off for a life of inactivity.

For most men, however, there is no better feeling than wielding agency and affecting the world. It is a sublime experience to walk with our head held high and some well-earned money in our pocket.

The ability to have some manner of positive effect on the world is a bare-minimum requirement for any man who wishes to enjoy the perks of manhood, including satisfying relationships with healthy, high-functioning women.

❄ ❄ ❄

Status, responsibility, and effectiveness. This is just one framework for thinking about purpose, but any reasonable framing of the problem focuses on action and creation. Purposeful living is hard work, but as Dr. Barry's research shows, the burden is the blessing. The only thing worse than the hard work of cultivating purpose is *not* doing that hard work.

If we don't cultivate status, responsibility, and effectiveness, then we surrender a portion of our masculinity in a world that estimates our worth by precisely that which we have relinquished. Status is like a credit score. We get one whether we like it or not, and people judge us by it. The good news is that the world doesn't demand perfection from men. It merely demands honest effort.

Herein lies another minor quandary for men. We must simultaneously respond to the pressures of society if we wish to be taken seriously, yet to be taken seriously, we must be at least partially insensitive to the demands others place on our time and attention.

To live happy and fulfilling lives, we must each be simultaneously selfless enough to recognize cultural demands, yet selfish enough to pursue those demands in a personally meaningful way. The latter part of that equation requires our occasional willingness to disappoint those who are close to us. They may not like the way we execute our purpose, but anyone worthy of our inner circle will respect our devotion to it.

Where does that leave us? Whatever your aspirations, your purpose is foundational to your well-being. It is not to be compromised any more than sleeping, eating, or exercising. And you certainly do not need to apologize for it.

Purposeful living requires us to follow our own compass and to surround ourselves with people who support us even when they must occasionally take a back seat. The purpose-driven man doesn't thrive on external validation. Doing so will deprive him of status because wise judges of character don't trust the guy who needs to be liked. They know his loyalty will always be for sale.

Sometimes women are correct when they ask us to take a break from our mission. Purposeful men can get so involved that we lose perspective and impede our own performance, or even harm our health. Good women sometimes remind us when we need to compromise, but they never ask us to relinquish activities that nourish our soul.

One of our most destructive activities—for ourselves and our relationships—is to apologize for pursuing our purpose. Doing so trains people to believe our purpose isn't worth defending. How can we expect others to respect our pursuit of purpose if we implicitly reject it by begging for forgiveness? And how can our closest relations trust we will stand up for them when we won't even stand up for our own values?

The man who refuses to apologize for his purpose will attract those who find his purpose appealing. He will also repel those whose values don't align. Good. Wish them well. The ones who depart create room for those who belong.

Of course, that looks easy on paper. The willingness to prioritize purpose can feel selfish to men who were taught to ignore their own needs. If that describes you, I'll ask you to explore the possibility that solid relationships can withstand the occasional disappointment. A healthy woman doesn't fall apart when it's time for her man to go to work.

Cultivating and Refining Purpose

Ask any prosperous, older man how he arrived at his success, and he will probably describe a winding road with unexpected turns. Even the rare man who has a singular passion to become a surgeon, a commando, or an artist must contend with forces trying to knock him off course. Just ask Odysseus or Rocky Balboa how many ways the world can impede a guy's journey.

One's purpose doesn't need to be a grand vision to cure cancer, revolutionize an industry, or live the Lamborghini lifestyle of social media charlatans. When I think of my purpose, I think of the day-to-day challenge of living according to my values. Giving more than I take. Building something larger than myself. It's a simple recipe as old as humanity, and it's a reliable path to satisfaction.

Most of us know where our general interests lie, but we don't have a precise destination in mind. Luckily, we don't need a perfect roadmap. All we really need is to move in the general direction of our values.

The key is to *move* and give ourselves a bit of grace for an imperfect journey. The world will let us know if we're making a useful contribution. When we succeed, we get money, admiration, and prestige—although they can lie at the end of a long and arduous road. That long, hard road is better than wandering under a dark cloud of aimlessness.

Finding purpose is every man's million-dollar quest. Young men must discover it, and older men must continually refine it. The following is a list of techniques to help a guy clarify his purpose, no matter his stage of life. I wish I could say I invented these techniques. At best, I can say I collaborated with other men as they cultivated their missions. If you find this list useful, they are the heroes.

Check your rearview mirror.

A couple of common refrains exist among men who have difficulty pinning down their values and their purpose. One is that it's difficult to isolate what matters because so many areas seem important. The other is that nothing seems important enough to pursue with any intensity.

This type of cloudiness can evaporate when we check the rearview mirror—that is, when we examine how we have spent our time in the past. Often, the clues to what we value are all around us. For example, consider the man with a penchant for photography. If he looks back, he will see an unmistakable trail of creative endeavors, along with a history of investments in equipment and time spent building his skills. The man with a passion for literature will find books in his midst and classes and writing in his past.

Men often discount purposeful activities when we also happen to enjoy them. It's as if having fun renders an activity frivolous. At times, it's necessary to be willing to suffer for one's purpose, but there's no rule that says we can't enjoy the pursuit of purpose.

Cultivate effectiveness.

Of the three building blocks to purpose—status, responsibility, and effectiveness—the last one is the simplest to develop. Any man can build a skillset simply by starting. Pick a direction consistent with your values, and begin building skills.

This is probably a good time to define the term "values." I have been using that word, but I haven't given you my sense of its meaning. I have shamelessly pinched a definition from behavioral psychologists who frame values as behaviors more than beliefs. To them, values are how a person behaves when they're living a meaningful life.

Values are about the man you want to be at work, within your community, among your friends, and within your intimate relationships. If a man values fatherhood, for example, his behaviors match what he believes an ideal father would do, even before he has children.[12]

Values are like directions on a map. You can always move westward, but you can never arrive at "West." There is no such place. The journey is simply one step after another, one day after the next, making course corrections along the way, finding the humor when we stumble, and picking ourselves up when we fall.

Relationship quality flows from compatibility of values. Couples who have conflicting values will fight over trivialities—paint color, dog food, petty cash—with no idea they are arguing over the

12 See, for example, LeJeune, J., and J. B. Luoma. 2019. *Values in Therapy*. Oakland, CA: Context Press. The authors define values as "freely chosen, verbally constructed consequences of ongoing, dynamic, evolving patterns of activity, which establish predominant reinforcers for that activity that are intrinsic in engagement in the valued behavioral pattern itself." Translation: values are self-reinforcing behaviors.

more malignant problem of opposing worldviews. More on that throughout the book.

Getting back to the topic of effectiveness, we can cultivate it simply by trying to be useful in any values-consistent endeavor. Work is central to that.

I held many jobs as a young man, beginning at nine years old working for my father as a dishwasher and barback. I learned how to sweat and how to prioritize tasks. The first job that required actual skills came in my late teens when I talked my way into a trainee position as a mechanic in a bowling alley. I valued being able to fix things, so I found a job to develop that skill.

Back then, I could not have articulated my motivation. I didn't yet possess the ability to express myself. I simply knew that I liked machines, so I asked for a job at the closest business that had them.

I didn't pursue that line of work, but I gained knowledge that serves me to this day. I learned about isolating variables, working with balanced systems, and becoming a team player. Best of all, I learned how to dismantle, repair, and reassemble a machine. It's one of the most useful skills I have ever learned. (At the end of this book, I'll tell you about one of the most interesting characters I met at that job, and what he inadvertently taught me about vetting relationships.)

When a man is stuck in purposelessness, or if he is thinking about changing paths, expanding his skillset might be the simplest and most powerful game plan. Live in different places; take different jobs; try different hobbies. Sample new options and cultures while you're doing useful activities. Be prepared to change direction, and embrace failure. Even if you pursue an endeavor only to discover it's not your cup of tea, the new skills will come in handy at some point.

It's easy to overthink and overcomplicate this question of purpose. A man can meditate on his direction in life, but nothing is more instructive than getting his hands dirty. You never know which experiences will be the most formative.

Take on responsibility.

Here's one way to learn whether the purpose you are pursuing is consistent with your values: put some skin in the game. Take on responsibility. Make yourself accountable to someone outside of yourself.

For example, most universities offer promising graduate students positions as teaching assistants. These positions give aspiring instructors the opportunity to try the job.

Not only do they get to sample what it's like to teach, but they also get to manage student complaints, write and grade tests, and deal with bureaucracy. They even get an inside glimpse of office politics. Whatever purpose you are pursuing, you can find a way to dive deeper and become more than a mere participant. Taking on responsibility to others in the realm opens a window to reality.

A bit of responsibility will also test your spirit for the tasks involved in your purpose. You will find your strengths and weaknesses, and people will push buttons you didn't know you had. (As I'm sure any teaching assistant can attest.) Putting skin in the game will help you determine whether the upside of the endeavor outweighs the downside.

Set time-bound goals.

Values and purpose are never "complete." Still, they require specific, time-bound goals.

Say a man's values include becoming self-employed. A short-term goal might be to set aside a specific amount of startup money each week. A medium-term goal might be to make a specific number of sales by a certain date. A long-term goal might be to own a building for the business within a specified number of years.

Values tell us what kind of man we want to be. They guide our actions moment by moment and day by day. Purpose tells us why we drag our asses out of bed each morning. Progress is easiest to monitor when it's tied to measurable outcomes.

Be strategic about options.

I once met an older businessman who had succeeded with various investments and enterprises. When I met him, he was liquidating his holdings to the tune of several million dollars. He planned to retire to an island paradise and take on fresh adventures.

This man had enjoyed an exhilarating career with many forks in the road and plenty of tough decisions. I asked him what he had done during his career when he was forced to make a decision but couldn't identify the best course of action.

He said that in those moments, he took whichever action preserved the greatest number of options. That gave him time to gather information. It also allowed events around him to unfold and reduce uncertainty on their own. Then, as the situation became more clear, he could make his decision on his own terms.

A man's purpose is an ever-evolving asset. A crucial component of good risk management is to simply avoid mistakes when possible. Prematurely closing off options is an easy one to avoid. It's winning by not losing.

Follow your aptitude.

When it's time to zero in on a career, "follow your dreams" is brilliant advice—provided the marketplace values what you dream of doing. The boy who dreams of being a software engineer or auto mechanic will have little trouble getting paid for doing what he enjoys. However, the boy who dreams of being a professional bassoon player better have a backup plan (like software engineer or auto mechanic).

The more pragmatic "find a job that needs to be done and do it" is also solid advice, if what the marketplace needs doesn't make you miserable or conflict with your values. Maybe your community needs truck drivers, the job pays well, and you come from a family of long-haul truckers. The stars are aligned for a lucrative career, but why torment yourself if the thought of that lifestyle makes your skin crawl?

Plenty of men are stuck in limbo between these two extremes. They know their dream of bassoon groupies is a long shot, but they don't want to drive a truck or whatever is the local job equivalent. Some men remain stuck there for years, wondering, *What do I want to do?*

A different question might break the stalemate: *What am I good at?*

Having never met you, I'm certain the answer isn't "nothing." Moving toward our aptitude is a good-enough way to get unstuck when purpose seems elusive. The aptitude you choose may not be your ultimate destination, but it's better than marinating in uncertainty.

Embrace the pain.

We have all seen the hero's journey in books and movies. First, a man feels the call to adventure. Then he finds a mystical mentor who teaches the skills to navigate trials and temptations. He descends into the abyss, then he emerges transformed and successful. Huzzah.

I suppose that occasionally happens in real life, but sorting out values and purpose is usually messier and more discouraging than in the movies. For starters, the people and things we value have the power to hurt us. For example, it's miserable to lose a job that provides meaning.

Pursuing purpose also means we might disappoint people we care about when they want more of our time and attention, don't understand our decisions, or want our choices to be more like theirs.

Then there's the sometimes-miserable realization that our chosen direction isn't what we thought it would be. I have met professors who were passionate about their work until they discovered their positions were governed more by bureaucracy than teaching or research. Pursuing their purpose left them jaded.

Even in ideal circumstances, being on track with one's purpose can leave a man feeling incompetent. I never felt more inept than during my training to become a psychologist. The best supervisors were relentless about pointing out my errors. Failure isn't optional when refining our purpose. It's a requirement.

It got even worse when I became skilled enough to recognize my own mistakes. To this day, my mind torments me over my missteps as a psychologist—and every day, I rack up a few more.

Lying awake at 3:00 a.m., ruminating over the errors we've made or the people we've disappointed, doesn't get much coverage in romantic tales of the hero's journey. Yet those moments are the unavoidable discomforts of a values-driven life. They are more instructive than any book or classroom lecture. Those bumps and bruises are evidence we are on the ever-winding path to our ideal selves. Learning to embrace them is the mark of a master.

Embrace urgency.

Let's assume we're all lucky and we get to live ninety years in good health. That's a mere 4,680 weeks, roughly 1,500 of which we will spend in childhood and old age. What remains is precious little time for the pursuit of purpose. There will come a time when we are all out of distant horizons, a time when the urgent pursuit of goals is mostly behind us.

What will you want to look back on? Who will you want to be surrounded by? What legacy will you want to reflect on as you take those last few steps toward your own funeral?

The human mind operates on two timelines: short-term and long-term. The short-term is the terrain of the emotional mind. It is always and only interested in what will bring immediate safety and comfort.

That emotional part of our mind is headquartered in evolutionarily ancient structures deep within the brain, like the limbic system we share with all other warm-blooded creatures. One job of these structures is to monitor reward and punishment and to use emotions like joy to motivate us toward safety and comfort *right now*. They create emotions like fear and disgust to motivate us away from danger or discomfort *right now*.

If you have ever seen a dog eat so much it got sick, or give itself a parasite for the third time by drinking filthy ditch water, or hang its head in shame after once again destroying its owner's shoes, then you have seen behaviors approximating our emotional mind's sense of future consequences. Given free rein, our emotional minds will act just like that dog: *Full steam ahead. Tomorrow be damned!*

If your emotional mind is like mine, it would have you spend every moment playing video games, surfing the web, or pounding down potato chips. It will procrastinate and meander just to avoid a moment's discomfort.

Meanwhile, months and years can slip away.

We all have our predilections, and it is useful for you to know how your emotional mind prefers to squander your future. It's a rare dog that gorges itself to the point of vomiting *and* revels in a good draft of ditch water *and* eats shoes. Each dog has its quirks, and so does each of us.

Maybe your mind likes the sweet abandon of liquor or pot (always followed by a harsh rebound into reality), or it can't get enough online gaming (the double-motivation of avoiding pain and enjoying immediate gratification). Perhaps it's just lazy. It will search for any excuse to avoid work (which is reliably followed by a hefty dose of guilt).

If you know how your emotional mind prefers to squander your time, then you know where it will take you if you let it drive the bus. During those last few months and years before your funeral, what legacy will your emotional mind have given you if you let it spend a lifetime calling the shots?

The mind's second timeline is the long-term terrain of the rational mind. It is so uniquely human that it doesn't need much explanation. It's what allows us to shape the world according to our wishes.

The rational mind is headquartered in the prefrontal cortex—that area of the brain above our eyes—and far away from the limbic system. Unlike the emotional mind, it can peer into the future, organize activity, and embrace discomfort for the sake of values and purpose.

Between the emotional and rational minds are intermediary structures that help decide which will win out in any given situation. One such structure is the anterior cingulate cortex. (Don't worry, there won't be a quiz.) Among other functions like empathy and error detection, it appears to be involved in impulse control. To put it in imprecise but useful terms, it uses input from the rational mind to overrule emotional logic, or vice versa.

We need both sides. They compete for our focus, and they cooperate to keep us from self-destruction. We don't need to deny the emotional mind at every turn. Our task is to strengthen our ability to override it when necessary; for example, by putting down the game controller when it's time to get to work. Each time we practice discipline, we strengthen the ability of areas like the anterior cingulate cortex to help us override emotional impulse.

We pay a price when we don't exercise that mental muscle. You may have met someone who is brilliant but can't seem to accomplish anything. They're too vulnerable to immediate gratification. As smart as they are, they haven't overcome their emotional mind's insistence on short-term comfort.

Most of us don't need strategies to silence the emotional mind. Instead, we need the ability to disregard it when it's not serving us. If there's a muscle that is all too often atrophied in people who fall short of their potential, it lies in structures that mediate between logic and emotion. The good news is we can strengthen that muscle.

Knowing our values and purpose is half the battle. The other half is our willingness to heed that part of the brain that says, *Just start. Do it. Step away from the distraction and go. Now.*

When we are stuck in inertia, we have the option of doing something—anything, no matter how small—that moves us toward our values and our purpose. For example, if I need to go to the gym but doing so seems like an overwhelming task, I can start with the small step of standing up ... then putting on my shoes ... then walking out the door. Maybe I *feel* like I can't go to the gym, but I can still get there one step at a time.

Those small steps can be the most important, not because they have a monumental effect but because they work the muscles of focus and choice. We may be unable to control the impulses our emotional minds throw at us, but we can control where we place our attention and how we move our limbs. The more we work those mental muscles, the stronger they get.

One source of fuel is urgency. The clock is ticking. We each have little time. This week will be behind you in the blink of an eye. This year will vanish before you know it. Before long, your entire life will be behind you. A guy can turn away from that fact, or he can embrace it, have some fun, and make a splash one small, disciplined step at a time.

Don't waste problems.

Most men crave a cause to fight for like most women crave a being to care for. Almost every problem presents an opportunity to fight and to refine one's values and purpose.

When Apple executives fired Steve Jobs from the company he built, he used the opportunity to create the computer company NeXT, which ultimately put him back at the helm of Apple.

When Mark Twain lost his fortune, he began to write and speak prolifically until he had regained his financial standing.

When George Foreman was a floundering, aging boxer, he lent his name and his charismatic persona to a kitchen grill, and he made millions.

Their problems impeded none of these men. They were brawlers who fought back with strategy and hard work. They each recalibrated or redefined their purpose, and they prevailed.

So things aren't going your way? Fine. Now you have a mission. You may feel insecure, broke, misunderstood, or alone, but at least you are a warrior with a cause.

Thrive among men.

Male rites of passage are a muddled process in the modern world—we can't all go out and kill a lion—but initiation into manhood still matters. Whereas our ancestors may have needed to prove themselves in a test of bravery or competence, men today are expected to demonstrate ongoing achievements over years and decades. There is no single rite of passage for the Western man.

Social psychologist Roy Baumeister wrote this about modern rites of passage:

> "In a fragile young tribe surrounded by enemies, it may emphasize valor and battlefield heroics as the test of manhood. In an isolated tribe where food is scarce, hunting may become the way to prove oneself. In an advanced industrial democracy, it may come down to making a substantial amount of money."[13]

Baumeister also points out that modern societies have little concern for the man or his welfare. It is strictly a "what have you done for me lately?" arrangement in which a man can lose his standing the moment he falls short of expectations.

That pressure to perform is yet another reason it's imperative for each of us to be driven by our own purpose so we aren't absorbed into serving the ambitions of others. To that end, men are well served by a primary feature of rites of passage: to refine our purpose outside the company of women, away from the temptation to win their favor or supplant our interests with theirs.

When we separate ourselves even occasionally from women, we open ourselves to the inspiration, feedback, and mentorship of other men. When we fail to individuate from the world of the feminine, we make ourselves vulnerable to unwitting conscription without ever discovering our own purpose.

Think of the man who never overcame his obedience to a controlling mother. He's the same man who seeks other overbearing and controlling women to whom he can submit. (That will be a theme throughout this book. If you have ever "clicked" with a woman who is a terrible fit for you, there's a good chance she is behaving toward you in a way other important women have. If we aren't careful, we chase the comfort of familiar patterns.)

Men tend to devote ourselves to the agendas of women. That isn't a weakness in men. It is simply how most of us are built. Men

---

13 Baumeister, R. 2010. *Is There Anything Good About Men: How Cultures Flourish by Exploiting Men*. New York: Oxford University Press.

evolved alongside women as their protectors and providers. The challenge is to protect and provide on *our* terms.

Succeeding in the world of men is crucial if we hope to define the terms under which we will protect and provide. Why? Because women cannot teach men the finer points of masculinity. They can teach us how to be "good men" who treat them well, but they cannot teach us how to be "good at being a man," to borrow a phrase from author Jack Donovan. He wrote:

> "Being good at being a man is about showing other men that you are the kind of guy they'd want on their team if the shit hits the fan."[14]

For all that women offer, this is one lesson they cannot teach men. Luckily, no matter a man's age, we can each cultivate a network of male mentors and role models who help us push beyond our reach and who teach us how to be good at being men.

If those mentors aren't immediately available, we can at least study the choices and behaviors of men we admire, those who have achieved some approximation of what we hope to accomplish.

We can learn plenty about our values and purpose in the company of women. Disregarding their wisdom would be foolish. However, it's equally foolish to believe we can fully serve our values and purpose without surrendering the comfort and approval of women. We must be able to thrive among men in the workplace, the dojo, the football field, or anywhere men band together toward a task. Men—at least the trustworthy ones—offer feedback women never could.

Cultivate pride.

I recently helped a friend move. Someone's son, a boy of about twelve years old, was running a dolly for the first time. No one asked him to. He wanted to help, and he probably thought the dolly looked fun.

---

14 Donovan, J. 2012. *The Way of Men.* Milwaukee, Oregon: Dissonant Hum.

He was tentative at first. He mostly moved small objects and got in the way. Soon, he learned to use the mechanical advantage of the dolly, he merged his efforts with the surrounding adults, and he was more helpful. By lunchtime, he walked like he was ten feet tall. He was proud of the amount he had moved and organized. (He may have been a little too proud, but he didn't need to know that.)

Men need this experience throughout life. We need to know we can do difficult tasks, and do them well. Luckily, there's always a new challenge we can master, from learning a language to rebuilding carburetors. Pride is a compass that tells us where our values lie.

By the way, if you're the kind of man who is squeamish about displaying your pride, consider a 2011 study that found "happiness was the most attractive female emotion expression, and one of the least attractive in males. In contrast, pride showed the reverse pattern; it was the most attractive male expression, and one of the least attractive in women."[15]

❄ ❄ ❄

Every red-blooded man probably wonders, *Will purpose make me more attractive to women*? Undoubtedly. As the evolutionary psychologist Steve Stewart-Williams wrote,

> "Men and women start pairing up long before they're old enough to accumulate significant wealth or status. Even then, though, women find traits that predict wealth and status more alluring than do men: traits such as confidence, competence, and raw, unbridled ambition."[16]

From a woman's point of view, the most attractive man has ambition, the personality to manifest his plans, and a willingness to invest in a family. So, yes. Purpose makes a man more attrac-

15 Tracy, J. L., and A. T. Beall. 2011. "Happy Guys Finish Last: The Impact of Emotion Expressions on Sexual Attraction." *Emotion* 11: 1379-87.

16 Stewart-Williams, S. 2020. *The Ape That Understood the Universe: How the Mind and Culture Evolve*. Cambridge: Cambridge University Press.

tive—but you may have already gathered that this fact is irrelevant to the gatekeeper.

Your purpose and your execution determine your standing in the world. You reap the benefits; you pay the price. It therefore belongs to *you*. In my clinical experience, the most useful question is not *How can I devise a purpose that will please women?* but *Which women and relationships fit with my purpose?*

I can't ignore the flip side of the coin: aimlessness will absolutely damage your attractiveness to women. Men who appear incompetent, domesticated, or harmless simply have fewer and lower-quality options than men who are lively and productive. Living in pursuit of our purpose is the opposite of living to get laid. Once we go down that path, our purpose is no longer our own. We've outsourced it to women. Healthy relationships with women involve their admiration, not their matronly approval.

The anxiety most of us experience at the prospect of female disapproval is no trifling matter. But that's not a battle to be fought against women. It's a battle within ourselves, which we will discuss throughout the book.

However we wish to frame it, women who successfully browbeat and domesticate their men invariably come to resent those men for their lack of resolve. That's not an original observation. The actress Marlene Dietrich said, "Most women set out to try to change a man, and when they have changed him they do not like him."

We can interpret Dietrich's comment as saying that men are at their most attractive when we are uncompromising in our values. Once again, we're at the inescapable conclusion that each man's purpose belongs to *him alone*.

We also reach what I hope is the increasingly obvious conclusion that a woman has no place in your inner circle if your relationship with her conflicts with your purpose or values. She may be a wonderful person, but any man who shoehorns himself into a relationship built on conflicting values will create resentment on both sides.

2. The Mind Is Divided Against Itself

This theme will appear throughout the book: the mind is always divided against itself in one way or another, and some part of that conflict lies beneath the threshold of awareness. These inner conflicts can lead us into the wrong relationships.

The divided mind is not a metaphor. It's a biological reality. The brain is a modular organ that spends much of its metabolic effort mediating and inhibiting itself. That seems by design. One task of the prefrontal cortex—that area of the brain just behind your forehead—is to inhibit impulses from more primitive areas of the brain. For example: you want that second beer (emotional impulse), but you decide against it (rational override).[17]

The conflict between emotion and rationality may be the most visceral experience of the divided mind. We can feel it anytime we desire something we know will harm us. Counterproductive emotional impulses correspond with structures involved in motivation and memory. The limbic system, situated deep in the brain, is famously implicated in these tasks. Sometimes it's the drunken cousin shouting, "Go for it!" against all common sense.

The emotional components of our minds are so persuasive because they have direct access to our bodies. The limbic system can make our hearts race and our stomachs sink. Our rational side can't make us feel a thing.

Here's a demonstration. Think back to the first girl you had a crush on. Remember the butterflies in your stomach? The sweaty palms? The racing heart? That was your emotional mind directly affecting your body.

---

17 For a fascinating example of internal conflict at a low level of processing, see: Garner, A. R., and G. B. Keller. 2022. "A Cortical Circuit for Audio-Visual Predictions." *Nature Neuroscience* 25: 99-105. In this study on visual perception in mice, the authors found that a mouse's previous auditory learning can literally shape and suppress what its eyes see in the present. The competition between auditory and visual perception appears to exist in the service of sharpening a mouse's overall perception.

Now think about this: 28 + 35 = 63. Go ahead, think about it *real hard*. Does it give you a tingle? Is your heart racing with sensuous anticipation? Do you find it the least bit intriguing? Probably not. (Though numbers can be emotionally compelling. The figures 36-24-36 might trigger a minor primal response if they caught the attention of your emotional side.)

Because our rational side can't really feel anything, our emotional side has a serious advantage in directing our behavior during emotionally charged situations—and for most men, few topics are more emotionally charged than women and sex.

Rationality is at a disadvantage when the emotional side floods us with sensation. Sometimes we are utterly defenseless against it, as when people fall into addictions or anxiety-driven compulsive behaviors—or, to the point of this book, relationships we know will harm us in the future, but which feel so damn good in the present. The renowned psychiatrist Bessel van der Kolk wrote, "No matter how much insight and understanding we develop, the rational brain is basically impotent to talk the emotional brain out of its own reality."[18]

The emotional mind, for all its intentions at keeping us safe, doesn't know what constitutes a healthy relationship. It only knows what feels good, whether it's booze, chocolate bars, or sex with an alluring woman who is absolutely wrong for us. When we cave to the emotional mind, it can leave us with that familiar feeling of being our own worst enemy. That feeling of shame and regret, perhaps more than any other, epitomizes the mind divided against itself.

All this leads to one inescapable conclusion: The emotional mind requires supervision. However, it's not the enemy. It simply operates under a unique set of rules. As for relationships, almost every emotional habit was adaptive and functional earlier in life. When it appears the emotional mind is trying to run us off a cliff, there's a good chance it's simply trying to solve a problem that no longer exists.

---

18 van der Kolk, Bessel. 2014. *The Body Keeps the Score*. Penguin Publishing Group.

For example, a mind that was burned by girls in high school can spend the rest of its life trying to prevent it from happening again, even long after we improve our skills and relationships with women. Where rational logic can say, "That was then, and this is now," emotional logic insists, "That was then, and *this* is then." It can be deceptively convincing.

That term—emotional logic—sounds oxymoronic, like "negative growth" or "intense apathy," but the emotional components of our minds are impeccably logical ... from a certain point of view. Emotional logic solves this problem: How can I get what I need for comfort and survival *right now*?

To the point of this book, the emotional mind gets mighty pushy about women. Anything we can do to create a bit of distance from our own drives and passions helps liberate us from counterproductive patterns. Consider this popular saying in behavioral psychology:

> "Between stimulus and response, there is a space. In that space lies our freedom and our power to choose our response. In our response lies our growth and our happiness."

One of my favorite quick-and-dirty techniques for expanding that space between stimulus and response involves labeling our thoughts as mere thoughts and our feelings as mere feelings, no matter how strongly they appear to reflect reality. For example, suppose you are angry with yourself because you forgot a deadline, and your mind produces an emotionally charged thought like:

> "I'm an idiot."

It might *feel* 100 percent true, but it's not an objective reality, and it's only helpful in that it gives us a little pain to remember next time we face a deadline. It doesn't solve the current problem. Labeling it as merely a thought, rather than a fact, looks like this:

> "*I'm experiencing the thought* that I am an idiot."

With practice, many people notice a subtle shift. They may still be angry at themselves, but they also experience a bit of detachment from the anger. That frees them to respond strategically rather than simply marinating in pain and aggravation. It's as if they are observing their own minds from across the room, which gives the rational side a chance to enter the picture. The goal isn't to silence the emotional side but simply to put the rational side in the driver's seat when necessary. There's plenty of room in the back seat for the emotional mind.

I'll expand on this idea throughout the book, and I'll challenge you to observe your own emotional logic with patience and curiosity. We may not get to turn it off, especially around women, but we can choose how we respond to it.

3. Time Is Your Ally

The emotional mind is impulsive. Whatever it wants, it wants it *now*. Personally, I have never found much success in arguing against my mind. The more I try to avoid a thought, the more my mind throws it right back at me. Fyodor Dostoevsky noticed this problem. He wrote:

> "Try to pose for yourself this task: not to think of a polar bear, and you will see that the cursed thing will come to mind every minute."[19]

In 1987, three psychologists tested Dostoevsky's observation by asking research participants to avoid the thought of a white bear for five minutes. Here's what they found:

> "… these subjects showed significantly more tokens of thought about the bear than did subjects who were asked to think about a white bear from the outset. These observations suggest that attempted thought suppression

19 Dostoevsky, F. 1985. *Winter Notes on Summer Impressions*. London: Quartet.

has paradoxical effects as a self-control strategy, perhaps even producing the very obsession or preoccupation that it is directed against."[20]

Yet trying to avoid thoughts and control the mind is second nature. One reason is that sometimes it works. When we are annoyed by a thought and the stakes are low, we can often move our mind in a different direction. For example, if you have a song stuck in your head, you can usually dislodge it by listening to and replacing it with a new song.

A more important reason is that we are accustomed to controlling or avoiding problems in the real world, outside the mind. If I am anxious about riding in airplanes, for example, I can avoid them.

It's different when we're anxious about that which comes from within. We can't always step away from our thoughts and feelings, especially when the stakes are higher than simply ridding our minds of an annoying song. If the white bear study and the ensuing line of research are correct, then fighting the mind is a losing battle.

To the matter at hand—romantic commitment—suppose a man's mind fixates on an attractive woman. It says, in its own nonverbal way, *She's perfect. Don't let her get away*. (That phrasing is too charitable toward the man's mind, which is more likely saying, *I need to bed that woman immediately!*)

If your mind is like mine, trying *not* to think about her is as tiring as thinking about her. Plus, there's the added distraction of wishing we weren't thinking about her at all. Thinking about her, and wishing we weren't, is like thinking about her twice as much. I'm unaware of any technique that's more than a temporary distraction when a man's mind has latched onto a sight as stirring as a seemingly perfect woman.

---

20 Wegner, D. M., D. J. Schneider, S. R. Carter, and T. L. White. 1987. "Paradoxical Effects of Thought Suppression." *Journal of Personality and Social Psychology* 53: 5-13.

That's okay. We have two important tools at our disposal; the first being time. (The other is relinquishing the battle within, which we'll touch on throughout the book.)

Even though we can't control the thoughts, feelings, and impulses our minds throw at us, we can control whether we obey them. At the very least, we can pause and take a breath. We can sit through the emotional tension and give our rational minds a chance to engage alongside the impetuous emotional side. Don't worry. You have a big brain with plenty of room for both.

I encourage you to consider the possibility that you don't need to immediately eliminate discomfort associated with women, whatever form it takes. Throughout the book, I will suggest moving toward the discomfort and even cultivating humor and gratitude for it. There's no harm in speaking back to the emotional side of our own minds, especially in the service of buying time when it overwhelms us with impulse: *Thanks, mind, I know you're just trying to help, but there's no emergency here. I'm going to cool my jets before I respond.*

If this way of thinking about your mind seems unfamiliar or counterintuitive, then you're right on track. If it's old hat, then you're ahead of the game. Either way, we will continue to sort it out as we go along.

We men have a way of becoming desperate around women. We can become so consumed with a particular woman that we forget to ask what effect she might have on our lives. The element of time—the simple act of slowing down—is a tremendous tool for reining in impulsive emotional logic.

You have probably already used time to manage impulses. Maybe you saw a gadget you thought you couldn't live without, but you waited and noticed the urgency subsided. Or perhaps you had an overwhelming impulse to berate a boss or friend, but you let yourself cool off before approaching them.

The most challenging and dangerous impulse concerning women (aside from the impulse toward unprotected sex outside a carefully vetted relationship) is the drive to secure her commitment before we know her. Andre, from the introduction, is a great example. He rushed in and devastated his life plans by creating entanglements—a dog, a mortgage, a marriage, and a child. He unintentionally conscripted himself to her life plan, rather than his own, and they both paid the price.

That pressure doesn't merely come from within. It may also come from her, from your friends and family, or from your community. They might all urge you to *Hurry. Commit. Do it now.*

The gatekeeper's first responsibility has almost nothing to do with women. It is to study his own unique impulses and master his response to them. He begins by giving the slow-moving rational mind enough time to evaluate lightning-quick emotional impulses. In the meantime, his emotional mind, and everyone else, will just have to wait. They will survive the inconvenience.

4. Dispassionate Observation Lights the Way

How do we get the rational mind off its haunches and involved in our decisions? By acting like scientists and approaching relationships with dispassionate, objective data collection. As Yogi Berra said, "You can observe a lot by watching."

A gatekeeper must observe women—along with the effects of his commitment to them—in a counterintuitive manner. The skilled, rational gatekeeper thinks *inductively* about women (which is rare) rather than *deductively* (the typical way men and women think about each other).

Inductive thinking involves gathering information about a situation before producing an explanation. *Deductive* reasoning is the other way around. It involves explaining a unique situation by applying an existing theory to it.

For example: You notice your new girlfriend has many male friends. Inductive reasoning says, *I don't know what this means. I'll collect more information before I try to make sense of it.* Deductive reasoning says, *I already know what this means because I have an existing theory about women who have many male friends.*

Each approach has strengths and weaknesses. Any well-functioning mind needs to possess both skills. However, as a psychologist, I have learned that assessing the character of any person or relationship is mostly an exercise in induction. Why? Because individuals don't always fit neatly into existing theoretical frameworks. When trying to understand someone, you can't go wrong by starting with the assumption that you know nothing about them.

I'm not saying we shouldn't use existing theories to evaluate relationships. I'm not even sure how to avoid theorizing. Our minds are pattern-noticing, theory-generating machines. Good luck turning them off. I'm simply suggesting that theories are too blunt an instrument to help you fully understand the complexities of any individual. When making decisions about a romantic commitment, deductive reasoning can be dangerously misleading.

Suppose a man considers committing to a particular woman. Like Andre from the introduction, he has known her for a few months, and he wants to move in with her (though he's not entirely sure why).

He needs to know if he can trust her, but he doesn't really know her yet. Patient observation would give him the information he needs, but this hypothetical man is impatient and unwilling to wait. Instead of taking time to gather information, he uses theories about women *in general* to fill in the blanks about her character *in particular*.

His theories, developed over a lifetime, give him the illusion that he knows what to expect from her. If he is in a hurry to shack up, and if they share mutual infatuation, then he will compare her (briefly and with blinders on) to his favorite theory. He will tell himself, "She checks all the boxes." In reality, he knows little about her character or the costs and benefits he will receive in exchange for his commitment. He simply hasn't had time to cultivate an understanding. That's why he relies on theories.

Theories aren't evil. We notice patterns and build theories because doing so usually advances our survival.

For example, let's say I eat a can of expired salmon, and shortly thereafter, I'm hospitalized with a fever and unbearable stomach cramps. It's only reasonable for me to develop a theory about expired salmon. My mind will automatically devise an explanation having to do with bacteria, or parasites, or rusty cans.

It doesn't matter if my theory is correct. It could save my life in the future because it casts a wide net. From now on, I will be suspicious of all cans of salmon, disregarding the fact that almost none of them are tainted. It doesn't matter if my theory is wrong. It doesn't even matter if something other than the salmon made me sick. There's no cost to my theory being wrong because there's no real cost to avoiding cans of salmon.

As a result, I will view all cans of salmon through the lens of food poisoning. My new theory is correct in the sense that any can of salmon *can* be contaminated, but it is incorrect in the sense that any can of salmon *is likely* to be contaminated. And it's possible the one I ate was not contaminated nor the cause of my illness.

After all that cogitating, I have learned a fact about cans of salmon in general (they can be tainted), but I have learned nothing about any can of salmon in particular. My theory saves time and effort—a meaningful advantage in a world full of decision points—but efficiency comes at the cost of accuracy.

Let's forget about salmon and get back to romantic commitment. Speed is not the goal. It can't be. In romance, as in driving in the rain, speed kills.

Accuracy is the goal, and accurate assessment of relationships is difficult enough without saddling ourselves with the inherent disadvantages of deductive reasoning. It's useful elsewhere, but in the task of vetting romantic commitment, deductive reasoning is mostly downside with minimal upside.

Here's what I mean. Suppose a man discovers a quirk in his girlfriend's personality: she gets unreasonably jealous about his past relationships.

Let's also say this woman is wonderful in other ways. She's kind, attentive, and polite to his family. But whenever the specter of an old girlfriend appears, he simply cannot mollify her insecurity. Her anger lasts for days.

It's a confusing situation for our man. The relationship is an asset during pleasant moments, but occasionally, it's a miserable burden. He's ambivalent. Since ambivalence is uncomfortable, he turns to his favorite theory to relieve him of confusion and indecision. Rather than taking time to collect more information (induction), he uses a theory to speed things up (deduction).

He doesn't even have to use his own theory. His friends and family will be more than happy to share their favorites. If he asks five people to explain her behavior, he'll get five different explanations, each based on a different theoretical framework.

- His best friend, who still feels injured by his parents' bitter divorce, might deduce that she fears abandonment and she's afraid of being vulnerable. (People often use vague filler words like "vulnerable" to avoid a more precise description.) He believes she is sublimating her fear with the more empowering emotion of anger. He read it in a book while trying to sort out his own feelings, and it made sense to him.
- His Uncle Ted, who has been happily married for thirty-eight years, will explain that it's simply a woman's nature to bring a bit of hysteria to a relationship. "Just get her some flowers, and you'll be fine," he says. Ted bases his theoretical framework on his experience that things always work out. Ted is fortunate. He has not yet encountered the need to revise his framework.
- His mother, having recently listened to an informative podcast about infidelity, will explain that his girlfriend is suffering from vicarious neglect, or some such thing, and it's her son's responsibility to walk her through it. His mother's theoretical framework regularly shifts to reflect her most recent foray into pop psychology. "The poor girl just needs to know she's wanted," she explains.
- Mike, his golf buddy, will tell him the situation will only get worse. "Trust me," he says. "I married a jealous woman. I'm lucky she lets me play golf at all. Hell, she probably has one of her bitchy little friends spying on me from behind a tree right now." Mike's abusive and controlling wife defines and dominates his theoretical framework.

- Sandra, his supervisor at work, will explain that his girlfriend has unrealistic expectations for the relationship. "I took a management seminar last year," she says. "We discussed employees who feel unsettled and dissatisfied with their jobs. The key is to clarify roles and expectations." Sandra enjoys exploring new theoretical frameworks and imposing them on her employees.

Theorizing is plenty of fun if you don't care about accuracy. None of these theories gives us a reliable path forward.

What do we know with any certainty? We know this man has a jealous girlfriend. That's it. That's all we know. And in reality, we may not even know that for certain. People don't always say what they mean, and they almost never recount the facts accurately.

Leaning on a convenient theoretical framework—deduction—can give us that cozy little feeling that we know what's going on. But theories and fancy explanations can be fatally misleading in ambiguous situations with other plausible explanations. Here's the fundamental defect in any theory regarding women: the set of explanations it can detect is smaller than the set of explanations that might exist. Worse, once we buy into a theory, it can change the way we perceive the world. That's called theory-ladenness, and it's a problem when you're trying to get a clear view of a complex situation.

Way back in 1949, an elegant experiment exposed the way theoretical frameworks alter our perceptions. During the experiment, the researchers flashed brief images of playing cards on a screen and asked participants to report what they saw.[21]

However, like many researchers of that era, they had a trick up their sleeves. Most of the playing cards were normal: six of hearts, eight of clubs, and so on. But some were trick cards: a black five of hearts or a red six of spades. (Normally, spades are black and hearts are red.)

---

21 Bruner, J. S., and L. Postman. 1949. "On the Perception of Incongruity: A Paradigm." *Journal of Personality* 18: 206-223.

The participants had probably seen thousands of normal playing cards in their lives but never encountered cards with the wrong colors. As a result, their theoretical framework was that hearts and diamonds are red; spades and clubs are black. It's a dependable framework in nearly every case.

When the participants saw the brief images of trick cards, they didn't have time to think about the images. The experiment moved too quickly. So how did their brains resolve the discrepancy between their theoretical framework and the images on the screen? They transformed what they *actually* saw (a black four of hearts, for example) into what they *expected* to see (a red four of hearts). Theory-ladenness changed their perception.

What does this have to do with a jealous girlfriend? It shows that a great deal of perceptual processing takes place before we consciously evaluate a situation. Our minds often show us what we expect to see. It applies to our perception of women, too.

With practice, the participants in that experiment learned how to recognize the trick cards. The experimenters alerted them to the trick, which allowed the participants to revise their frameworks. However, our own pet theories rarely supply accurate feedback, so it's hard to know when they're wrong. Each of us can look at the jealous girlfriend and see precisely what our theoretical frameworks tell us to see. Worse still, we can each walk away feeling 100 percent correct, even if we missed the truth by a mile.

But it gets worse. The more we use our theories, the stronger they become, even if they have been giving us the wrong answers. A couple of years after the playing card experiment, the same researchers wrote another paper in which they said,

> "The greater the strength of a hypothesis, the less the amount of appropriate information necessary to confirm it."[22]

22 Bruner, J. S., L. Postman, and J. Rodrigues. 1951. "Expectation and the Perception of Color." *Journal of Psychology* 64: 216-227.

That might be the most important sentence those researchers ever wrote. They weren't saying a theory is easily *correct*. They were saying it is easily *confirmed*.

Think back to that expired salmon. If I walk away from a can of salmon because my theory tells me to, then my theory gets reinforced. It doesn't matter if the theory is wrong about nearly every can of salmon on the planet. If my mind watches me avoid a *particular* can of salmon, and if I don't get sick, then my mind concludes that the theory was correct, and the theory grows stronger.

Our theoretical frameworks solidify in the absence of feedback. Each time we fail to detect an error, we incrementally strengthen our theoretical framework, no matter how ass-backwards it might be. Imagine what a lifetime of uncorrected theorizing does to our perception. Maybe you know someone who has turned himself into a crackpot by avoiding feedback and reinforcing his own goofball theories.[23]

My theoretical frameworks have caused me to grievously misread people and situations. I was once cheated by a contractor who reminded me of the dependable, hardworking people I had grown up around. He looked like them and spoke like them, but his character was far from theirs. My theory about hardworking people may be correct in general, but it was wrong about him in particular.

I'm not suggesting you should ignore your theories about women. We each need a framework to guide us. An imperfect theory is better than no theory because it represents an attempt to gain understanding.

The problems arise when we use our frameworks to explain or predict the behavior of individuals. That error cost me thousands of dollars when I misjudged the character of my crooked contractor.

---

23 Lord, C. G., L. Ross, and M. R. Lepper. 1979. "Biases Assimilation and Attitude Polarization: The Effects of Prior Theories on Subsequently Considered Evidence." *Journal of Personality and Social Psychology* 37: 2098-2109.

Inductive reasoning doesn't replace deductive reasoning, but it is insurance against the downsides. In my book *The Tactical Guide to Women*, I suggested adopting standards for the women you allow into your world. I offered a set of standards I call the Bright Triad, which I'll summarize in Book III: Resilience.

Measuring her character against established standards, whether it's the Bright Triad or a different framework, involves observing behavior over a long period and noticing patterns. That dispassionate observation is the opposite of theory-based explanations and predictions. It's more work, it takes more time, and it requires tolerating uncertainty rather than basking in the comfort of artificial understanding.

There are lots of useful questions you can ask about a woman's character and her values. Emotional maturity is one criterion I suggested in *The Tactical Guide to Women*. Her level of maturity, or any other aspect of her character, is not immediately apparent. People can hide their shortcomings in the early stages of a relationship. To discover her true nature, you become a patient observer in multiple contexts, from different points of view, using independent sources of information ... and you do this over an extended period.

That means you watch how she treats her family and her coworkers, the wait staff on vacation in Cabo, and employees of the airline that lost her luggage. You watch her in public and behind closed doors. You watch her on good days and bad. You listen to how *her* friends and family speak about her, and you listen to how *your* friends and family speak about her.

You listen to the way she speaks about others when they're not around, what offends her, and how she handles conflict. You listen to your intuition, your intellect, and your inner circle. You do it all with patience and detachment.

A perfectly accurate set of observations doesn't exist, but to approach accuracy, you look *backward* at her actual behavior rather than forward at a theoretical prediction. There's no guarantee her past behavior will predict her future behavior. Nor are there guarantees against ugly surprises. Consider physical violence, for example. Just because she hasn't been violent in the past doesn't mean she won't be violent in the future.

That's one of the blind spots of this inductive approach. Absence of evidence is not evidence of absence. Inductive thinking can create false certainty. But tracking her actual behavior is a damn sight more reliable than whatever near-random guess your average theory can offer.

Inductive thinking requires more patience and effort than the alternative. It's also less fun because it doesn't offer clever-sounding predictions. But this is your future we're talking about. It's worth the extra effort.

By the way, this inductive approach is an old idea among psychology researchers. If you're trying to measure a variable that's difficult to pin down—like whether a potential partner is likely to improve your life or to wreck it—you want sufficient information, from multiple sources, with checks and balances against the mind's automatic errors.

The bottom line is that it can be costly to theorize about people in the same way you might theorize about cans of salmon. Theoretical frameworks give single-variable answers to multivariate questions. But over a long enough timeline, and with enough information, what you see in a person is pretty much what you get.

5. Playful Experimentation Expands Awareness

Here's one last request before we jump into our five relationship standards. If you choose to approach romantic commitment differently based on the ideas in this book, I hope you will treat those changes as an experiment requiring patient testing and observation.

It takes time to institute even a minor change with any consistency—especially challenging tasks like raising our relationship standards and rethinking how we allocate commitment. It takes even longer to observe and compare the new condition with the previous one.

It also takes effort to overcome resistance from others who are uncomfortable with our changes, and to bounce back from relapses. (Relapses are part of any change, and they are a wonderful source of information if we can face them with curiosity rather than shame.)

Here are two reasons to treat change as an experiment.

First, don't believe a word I say. It's your life, not mine, so please check my words against your experience. You alone bear the consequences of your romantic commitments. You should, therefore, treat these words with skepticism.

Second, treating ideas as experimental reduces the emotional investment in outcomes, as well as resistance to trying new thoughts and behaviors. Most men can afford to raise their standards for women, relationships, and commitment, but it's an arduous task because it challenges the assumptions we hold about ourselves and others.

As you dive into the work ahead, you might reasonably wonder, *Who am I if I'm not the man people have become accustomed to?* This book can help you find out.

It's difficult to act in ways that contradict our view of ourselves. Treating new standards and behaviors as an experiment, and not an obligation, eases the task. You're always free to return to your old ways if the new ones somehow make your situation worse. On the other hand, revising your standards and updating your self-perception might generate opportunities you hadn't considered. Only time and observation will tell.

I suggest that for the duration of the experiment—however long you wish to conduct it—you obey your intellect first and your heart second, and never let your hormones call the shots. Hormones are idiots.

FLIGHT CHECK

Each section of this book will conclude with a few open-ended questions to bring your inner workings into the light of day. I encourage you to ponder them as long as necessary. Even better, journal about them. Letting the mind wander on the written page is a great way to shine a light on influences and thinking patterns we otherwise don't notice.

I suggest sipping these questions like fine wine rather than guzzling them like cheap beer. There is no deadline, and there are no wrong answers.

- **Values and purpose.** Think back on your romantic commitments. In what way have those relationships aligned with your values and purpose? In what way have they conflicted? If you continue the trend, will your romantic relationships move you closer to what you hope to accomplish in life, or will they carry you in a direction you don't wish to travel? What is it about those relationships that leads you to your answers?
- **The divided mind.** Recall the times you have felt conflicted about major decisions. How have you resolved those conflicts? Has your approach served you well, or has it undermined your success and happiness?
- **Theories about women.** What theoretical frameworks have you developed about women and commitment? Where did those theories originate?

– BOOK I –

Composure

Align romance with purpose • Expose the roots of destructive relationship patterns • Choose commitments that bring composure rather than chaos • Allow others to experience discomfort

You wouldn't play chess on a trampoline. You wouldn't prepare your tax return during a child's birthday party, or run a marathon with a drum kit strapped to your back. Those tasks require composure, which I'll define as the capacity to execute sustained, focused effort with minimal distraction. To be composed is to be calm and in control of one's actions.

Yet some of us choose relationships so jumbled and tumultuous they thwart composure. They cloud our values and interfere with purposeful execution of values-driven action. We've all done it. Who among us isn't vulnerable to the corrosive effects of chaos, provided it comes in a sufficiently attractive package?

Romantic relationships usually bring some measure of chaos into a man's life, though chaos is not necessarily a bad word. A roller coaster is chaotic, but it's designed to stay on the rails. A touch of constructive chaos awakens our vitality. It strips away the stultifying routine that can invade a man's life. It wakes him up and shakes a bit of life into him. The right kind of chaos, in the right kind of relationship, offers that gift. It's a sad thing to see a couple subsisting on a flavorless routine of bland dinner, mindless television, and occasional dutiful sex.

At the other extreme lies destructive chaos. It diminishes a man's vitality; it stifles him. It clouds his purpose and diverts his efforts. It's the type of chaos that ends in debacles like family court, physical violence, or the numbing escape through booze and other addictions.

Life gives us enough destructive chaos. Friends and relatives get sick. Responsible people get laid off. Accidents of all varieties can alter life in an instant. A healthy relationship adds to our composure and thus our ability to manage these problems. An unhealthy, chaotic relationship only serves to complicate life's normal challenges. Plenty of men, for reasons we'll explore, have difficulty seeing the difference between constructive and destructive chaos.

Chaos or composure: this is the first of our five vital relationship assessments that we'll discuss in each "Book" or chapter (composure, dignity, resilience, joy, and The Word Which Shall Not Yet Be Spoken). We'll start our composure discussion with three case studies—Alonzo, Elliot, and Samuel —each illustrating a different path to destructive chaos, and each showing varying degrees of success as gatekeepers. Next, we'll dig into our first set of organizing principles, which are internal forces that drive our relationship choices. Then we'll examine strategies for choosing composure over chaos, as well as one of the most important skills every gatekeeper must possess.

Here's Alonzo's story.

Alonzo's Reckless Entanglement

In matters of the heart, you can usually predict where a person is going if you know where they came from. To whatever extent

Alonzo invited destructive chaos into his life, he came by it honestly. He was simply recreating what he saw as a child.

His parents were the embodiment of destructive chaos. His mother was a relentless nag, and his father was a retreating ninny who hid at work rather than face her. At least that's how Alonzo characterized them.

Alonzo recalls continual bickering between his parents. They shared the sort of relentless, low-grade hostility that pushes higher values and purposeful action into the background. It's difficult to imagine how Alonzo's father could ever reach his full potential when he spent so much time ruminating with his friends and coworkers about the latest conflict with his wife.

Eventually, thankfully, they divorced. Alonzo was a high school sophomore at the time. Naturally, the divorce was every bit as chaotic and contentious as the marriage. He often had to fend for himself because his parents were so preoccupied with their personal and financial disintegration. He lived with whichever parent was functioning best during the extended legal battle, and he bunked with friends and relatives whenever he could.

Alonzo barely graduated from high school as a solid D student. The personal distractions simply overwhelmed his focus. Throughout high school, he gravitated toward part-time jobs where he could be physically active and make money. He enjoyed his camaraderie with coworkers, as well as the distraction from family chaos. He found peace at work.

His first proper job was with a friend's father who had a small general contracting business. Thanks to his inquisitiveness and his congenial nature, Alonzo's supervisors were happy to teach him marketable skills. By his midtwenties, he was becoming a jack-of-all-trades. He could tile, frame, drywall, and do basic plumbing and electrical work.

By his early thirties, he was buying shabby houses, repairing them, and flipping them for profit. He was also savvy with money. While many of his former high school classmates were climbing out of student loan debt, Alonzo was amassing real estate and an investment portfolio. He came from chaos, but he was building an empire.

Then he met Maura.

Maura wasn't his first girlfriend, but she captivated him like no other. He saw a spark to her personality. She brought the excitement Alonzo felt was missing from his disciplined world. He was bored with his life of structure and self-control. Maura made him feel alive, and the sex was great. They were infatuated … but infatuation always fades.

In their case, it faded quickly. It was about six months into the relationship when he noticed Maura was often angry with him. With increasing frequency, he had to calm her because she had taken outsized offense at a trivial incident. For example, he once ate a late lunch when they were planning an early dinner. For several days, Maura felt as if Alonzo had betrayed her.

She also felt that he spent too much time working, especially when she was troubled by her own work problems, family disagreements, or other life events that consumed her.

Alonzo was quick to point out that it wasn't all bad. He enjoyed her company, but he always knew the next crisis was imminent. Being a dutiful man, he felt it was his responsibility to help her manage her emotions. That meant, in part, walking on eggshells to avoid upsetting her. He learned to avoid discussing his challenges at work because she frequently responded by accusing him of sullying the mood.

The more he helped her remain calm and feel cherished, the more dependent she became on his presence. She came to fear minor disappointments and disagreements within the relationship because she took such benign events to mean they were in distress. In those moments, if Alonzo were to have any peace, he had to reassure her enthusiastically that their relationship was fine.

Keeping Maura happy grew into an emotional roller coaster for Alonzo. "When it's good, it's great," he would tell friends. He meant it. She never lost the spirit that so infatuated him, and she was never outright mean.

Yet, a storm was always brewing on the horizon. She could fall apart at any moment, for reasons he couldn't predict. Putting her back together, as time-consuming and draining as it was, was easier than dealing with the fallout of, in her words, abandoning her.

What started as a relationship that brought liveliness and joy to his world was now a chaotic distraction, much like his father's marriage had been. It was interfering with his work. It made him distracted and irritable. He was on constant alert for the next crisis, and he had long since lost contact with friends and hobbies.

He knew this relationship was carrying him down a destructive path and that it had the potential to undermine what he had worked so hard to build, yet he was intent on saving it. When I asked him why, he was silent for a moment and then said, "I guess that's what men do."

It's a common quandary: How much effort should a man put toward a relationship that grows worse with each attempt to repair it? How long should he swim against the current?

I don't think Maura is the bad guy here, nor do I find it useful to frame this situation in those terms. Doing so misplaces the focus and leads to questions that serve little purpose. *Can she change? Should I adjust?*

More useful questions include *What is this romantic commitment bringing into my life?* That question—and the willingness to answer it honestly—can cut through the fog of emotion. What a man does with the answer is up to him alone. Alonzo chose to keep fighting.

Opportunity cost is what you give up in the pursuit of an outcome. To keep Maura, he would have to give up a large measure of focus and achievement. Is their relationship worth the cost? Only Alonzo can answer that question because only he knows the value he places on each. My best advice in such situations: be honest about what you're sacrificing and what you're getting in return.

If it sounds unromantic to frame it that way, then good. We men are vulnerable to the emotional folly of misplaced romantic sentiment. In my professional opinion, sentimentality belongs in healthy relationships with high-functioning people, not in chaotic relationships that ruin our composure.

Relationships like Alonzo and Maura's are worth repairing, if possible, but there comes a point of diminishing returns. Men who are unwilling to admit when a relationship fails can get drawn into misery, sometimes for life. Propping up a malfunctioning relationship becomes their only purpose. Alonzo is not the first man to say, "I guess that's what men do."

Suffering through these relationships is like being broke. It puts a man in a reactive position with no margin for error. When a man lacks money, every proverbial flat tire is a crisis. Similarly, minor problems become major distractions in a chaotic relationship. When there's no margin for error, no problem is too small to become a big deal. Once a man opens the door to chaos, chaos calls the shots.

Alonzo not only embraced the lack of composure brought by his relationship with Maura, but he also refused to relinquish it in the face of overwhelming evidence that it impeded his purpose. He overlooked the fact that every attempt to eliminate destructive chaos only magnified it; each act of reassurance had to exceed the previous one. Maura wasn't a bad person, but his commitment to her ruined his composure. My bias is showing: I think he sacrificed too much. He lost his way.

Our next case study is another in which purpose and romantic desires conflict, though it has a more productive ending.

Elliot's Temporary Lack of Clarity

This case involves a high-functioning woman who is nearly perfect. She's not the one who brought chaos to the relationship. His lack of foresight was to blame.

This sort of case reminds me of the power of compound interest. If you're an investor, interest can amount to free money. If you're a borrower, it can accrue to an insurmountable debt. Some lenders, for example, add unpaid interest to the original loan amount. Even with diligent payments, the balance of the loan can increase over time. Predatory student loans are notorious for this, and they can keep borrowers indentured for decades.

A similar process can play out in romance. The man who chooses relationships consistent with his values and his purpose gets propelled forward. Success compounds on success. The man who chooses relationships that conflict with either his purpose (his reason for getting up each day) or his values (the man he wants to be) is fighting a battle on two fronts. Not only must he contend with the naturally occurring forces that try to undermine his efforts, but he must also overcome resistance from within the walls of his own kingdom.

Elliot, the subject of this case study, was still wrestling with the question of his purpose and values when he entangled himself in the wrong relationship. Like the hapless student loan borrower who never emerges from his debt, some men never emerge from the compounding resistance of their romantic endeavors. Fortunately, he reversed the downward trend before it was too late, though not without causing a good deal of heartache for himself and others. Here's what happened.

It wasn't until his midtwenties that Elliot decided to pursue a military career. Prior, though he didn't know his ultimate calling, he had laid the groundwork for it. He knew he wanted a structured career in which he fought for a cause he believed in.

He began his journey by earning a bachelor's degree in history with a minor in computer science. That poised him for either the military or law school. To add to his marketability, he had always made physical fitness a priority, and he had volunteered for leadership positions at school and in the community.

Elliot had instinctively grasped a guideline from this book's section on purpose: *be strategic about options*. He was smart, motivated, and focused. Unfortunately, he made a grave error: he moved in with his girlfriend, Chelsea, before deciding which path he would take.

Elliot and Chelsea had met in college, fallen for each other, and leased their first apartment together when Elliot was only twenty-three. It would prove to be a reckless decision. Sometimes young men who are exceptionally self-possessed overestimate their emotional wisdom. Whatever the cause, his recklessness didn't stop with cohabitation. They each became close with the other's family, and shortly after moving in together, he and Chelsea got a dog. The dog stole their hearts, as is a dog's way.

Chelsea understood the two career options Elliot was considering. She was willing to relocate for a few years during law school, but the thought of an itinerant military life filled her with dread. She and Elliot lived in her hometown, close to her family and friends. Maintaining those connections was a core value for Chelsea, and she had no intention of abandoning her home. She pressed him to opt for law school.

Elliot had set up consultations with military recruiters and practicing lawyers, and a few months after he turned twenty-five, he realized he needed to pursue a military career, even with all the uncertainty it entailed. That's when his life got complicated.

This man who had planned so strategically to live according to his values and purpose was now in the grips of that age-old trap: entanglement. He was not free simply to embark on his path. He had a live-in girlfriend, the expectations of their respective families and friends, a lease, and a dog to consider. (The dog might seem trivial compared to the other entanglements, but pets complicate breakups with surprising frequency and intensity.)

Chelsea was no innocent bystander in this debacle. She had made her own decisions. Nevertheless, she couldn't help feeling that Elliot had offered false promises. She had a valid point. He had always known the importance of family to her. Yet here he was, revoking an implicit offer to settle down in her hometown.

Chelsea had presumed she was en route to marriage and children near the family and friends she treasured. She had no interest in following a military husband around the globe. Nor did she want to remain behind, essentially a single parent, if he were to be stationed in faraway places. Both possibilities conflicted with *her* values.

Elliot had his tit in a wringer, as my father used to say. He had two unappealing options.

The first was the most immediately difficult: he could break up with Chelsea. This meant severing the entanglements they had created and ending the life they were building together. It also meant putting her at odds with her family. He had always known her traditional parents viewed cohabitation as a prelude to marriage, as did Chelsea. He knew he was dating a traditional woman who believed she was on a course toward marriage, and he welcomed it.

Her family had been warm and generous with him in return, and he had accepted their kindness. His family had also become attached to Chelsea.

To compound the pain, Elliot wanted family and children as much as Chelsea did. He thought she would make a wonderful wife and mother. If he broke up with her now, he would do so knowing he had wasted two years of her life and narrowed her window on motherhood. She might have used that precious time to find someone with more compatible values.

Option #1 was quite unattractive to Elliot.

He had a second option. He could "do the right thing" and "make an honest woman of her." He could stay the course, marry Chelsea, forgo his military career, and start applying (halfheartedly) to law schools.

This choice would spare him Chelsea's resentment—for a while. However, it would not spare *him* of resentment toward Chelsea for having sacrificed his true ambition. Nor would it spare her the knowledge and experience of his bitterness toward her.

This is, unfortunately, a position far too many men place themselves in. Many select option #2. They forgo their aspirations in favor of the entanglements they created. For the lucky ones, it works out fine. Others experience a disturbing and irreparable drift away from what they were meant to pursue in life. Many unfairly resent the women who end up directing their futures.

You have seen this if you've ever met a depressed, angry man who has no proper explanation for his misery. He complains about the boss, the bills, and "the old ball and chain" as if it all just mysteriously appeared. In reality, he built that life one concession at a time. If he finds that too painful to admit, he's likely to sulk and complain as if the situation had been imposed on him by some malevolent force.

There's no shame in it if you have been there yourself. It's terribly easy for a good man to obey the external imperative to commit ourselves, even against our will. Conscientious, dutiful men are the most vulnerable to that trap.

No matter the outcome—adequate or miserable—these men end up wondering, *What if …?* The choice to compromise or surrender their purpose creates a feedback loop that can carry him increasingly further from his values.

Here's what I mean. Suppose Chelsea had followed him in his military career. Each time they moved, he would have to manage both the relocation *and* her unhappiness about it. He would have to face her growing resentment with each holiday, birthday, or family get-together they couldn't attend.

Imagine how that emotional overhead would affect his professional decisions, her happiness, and each of them as parents. It's hard to be our ideal selves when we're fighting daily emotional fires.

Elliot has a third option, and it belongs in the realm of fantasy and sarcasm. He could build a time machine. Then he could travel back in time and say to Chelsea, "I can't build a life with you yet because I'm not yet clear about my plans."

There would be no shared apartment, no dog, and no heightened familial expectations. There would be nothing to impede his purpose beyond the pain of saying goodbye to someone he cared for.

Ultimately, he and Chelsea split up. For whatever my opinion is worth, it was a wise decision. In such situations, today's pain is a known and tolerable quantity. Tomorrow's pain is the emotional equivalent of compound interest. It knows no limits.

This might be the gatekeeper's most onerous duty: saying goodbye to wonderful women who happen to have incompatible values. The task is even harder when staring into the eyes of an adoring labradoodle.

Resentment can color every interaction in relationships built upon forgone desires. And what color is that, exactly? It's usually whatever color helps the man avoid his woman's ire for the moment. Men who begin their relationships by trying to avoid discomfort usually spend the rest of their relationships in the same mode. If a man is not willing to defend his values at the outset, then there's no reason to think he ever will.

A friend once told me about a male relative in such a relationship. On one occasion, while car shopping with his wife, they found two identical models of the car she wanted. One was red, and the other was a premium shade of cobalt blue. She preferred the premium blue.

The husband, who was the sole provider, protested because the blue car cost $2,500 more than the red one. She was unconcerned; he relented. He knew buying the less-expensive car would mean tolerating months or years of complaints and passive-aggressive jabs.

She didn't care that he had to work for the extra money. She regarded his time and effort as commodities that belonged to her alone. And who taught her that such an arrangement was acceptable? He did, by compromising his values and purpose early and often.

That man wasn't purchasing blue paint. He was purchasing momentary respite from the continual flow of griping. She would be grateful for a while, after which she would return to her baseline dissatisfaction. The worst part? There was not a chance she respected him. I have yet to meet a woman who admired her man for being spineless.

No man sets out to create a relationship in which misery compounds like a high-interest loan. No man says, "I want to spend the rest of my life in an emotionally abusive, soul-crushing combat zone." Yet, men can follow countless paths to such relationships.

As for Elliot, he was late to the role of gatekeeper, but he rose to the occasion before it was too late. His resolve undoubtedly prevented ongoing misery for all concerned. Whereas Alonzo remained in an unhealthy relationship out of his sense of duty, Elliot chose to leave a healthy relationship to avoid inevitable chaos.

Let's turn now to our third case study. This one is an exemplary illustration of successful gatekeeping. Samuel's story shows it is not the woman in question who poses a threat to our future but how we view ourselves in relation to women.

Samuel's Hard-Earned Victory

Samuel began encountering Mickie at the gym on Wednesday and Friday afternoons. It was as if she had memorized his schedule and planned her workouts to coincide with his.

As is often the case in private gyms, he had heard a bit about Mickie before she began flirting with him. Rumor had it she was seeing a software engineer who was unaware she was flirting with other men. She had a reputation at a nearby pub for being, as one of Samuel's friends put it, "the town bicycle" and a heavy partier.

She was also the type of woman Samuel historically pursued: wild, quick-witted, and passionate, with the perfect physical attributes to trip his emotional trigger. He described her as "short and stacked."

Samuel had a history of alcohol abuse and turbulent relationships. After a brief marriage that ended in bankruptcy and an onerous bout of depression, he changed his life. He replaced his drinking with twelve-step meetings and a disciplined approach to diet and physical fitness. Alongside his personal development, he found new joy and purpose in mentoring others who were starting their recovery from substance abuse.

He also worked hard to understand what drew him to unhealthy relationships with chaotic women. Part of the attraction was simply the excitement. Part was an age-old belief that he was both unworthy and incapable of calm relationships with emotionally mature women.

Despite creating a healthful, purposeful life, he couldn't help being drawn to women like Mickie. She stirred his spirit, and he had missed the action-packed relationships he once had. After a steady diet of chaos and disorder, he found healthier relationships to be a bit boring at first.

However, the composure he found in healthier relationships made his life much easier. He liked that. He could see Mickie more clearly than he could see women in his past. More importantly, he saw himself clearly.

His new insight gave him a crystal ball of sorts. He could foresee how easy it would be to enmesh with her. *The old me would have shacked up with her in a month*, he thought. He could also foresee the path to destruction that lay before him. It was familiar territory that he hoped not to revisit.

Mickie's manners around the gym were coarse, and Samuel noticed she was prone to drama. He saw how she charmed the other men but also how she distracted them. He sensed her tension and conflict with other women in the gym, along with the erratic workout routine that reflected a distractible and impulsive mind.

The old Samuel would have described her as alluring and thrilling. Now he saw her as alluring but dangerous. His emotional impulses hadn't changed, but his rational side was now fully engaged. He saw her as precisely the type of woman who could drag him back to his old, self-destructive ways.

Naturally, she noticed him too. She singled him out for special attention. It was as if she recognized a kindred spirit who appreciated the grittier side of life.

Her overtures toward him were anything but subtle. They included such direct hits as "When are you going to take me out?" She even conspicuously ogled him throughout his routine. He could feel her eyes lingering on him while he tried to focus on his workout.

The new Samuel went to the gym to train, not to flirt, though in his weaker moments, he had given her just enough reinforcement to pique her interest in him. He regretted that. Now she was an unpleasant distraction. *It would be so easy to give in to her*, he thought. He could abandon his discipline and return to the familiarity of chaos. He could drop out of his twelve-step program and stop working so damned hard.

That familiar chaos was like a warm fog just waiting to envelop him. Mickie felt familiar, and the emotional mind prizes familiarity. All he had to do was follow her lead, and he could drift into his old, blissfully heedless ways.

For reasons he had difficulty articulating, that simply wasn't an option. His rational side was winning, but he didn't know how long he could hold out. He had to draw the line before temptation overtook him. His twelve-step work had taught him that he would experience moments of weakness when he was too hungry, angry, lonely, or tired to resist dangerous temptations. He didn't want to succumb when one of those moments arrived.

He tried to discourage her flirtation with gentle, humorous redirections. "I'm a monk, and my monastery only lets me out to lift. Gotta be back by six!"

His retreat only encouraged her, so he became more direct. "It's not in the cards, Mickie, but Dave was asking about you." He met her with good humor while trying to send a clear signal of his disinterest.

Still, she was undeterred. Mickie pressed on past his rejections. She continued to flirt with and ogle him. The more he retreated, the more she pursued.

Notice an important subtext to their interactions: Mickie was giving Samuel a problem to solve. Rather than respecting his wishes, she pressed on as if to say, "What are you gonna do about it?" She kept pushing each time he said *no*. Ignoring *no* is a serious warning sign of questionable intentions. Imagine what the refusal to accept *no* looks like in a long-term relationship. Imagine telling your wife, "We can't afford a new car," only to have her buy it anyway with your name on the note.

Samuel's options dwindled. He could reject her more aggressively, ask for the gym owner's help, or continue tolerating the tempting distraction. He could also cede the territory and find another gym.

He lost sleep over the situation. He felt as if a demon was taunting him to return to his old ways. After exhausting other options, Samuel decided to ignore her. He didn't return her greetings or interact with her at all. While that sounds simple enough, it was distressing for him. He was unaccustomed to refusing a woman's demands, and she punished him by acting as if *he* were the one who lacked manners. She complained about him to anyone who would listen, trying to damage his friendships and his reputation.

Samuel felt as if the universe was punishing him for doing the right thing, but he persevered, and eventually Mickie moved on.

As an aside, Mickie's tantrum—her attempt to damage his reputation—was what psychologists call an extinction burst. That's an increase in unwanted behavior when the behavior no longer pays off. As Samuel discovered, the unwanted behavior eventually subsides if a person rides out the extinction burst. This is handy knowledge for parents of young children during meltdowns.

Mickie's initial interactions were probably more nuanced and alluring than I portrayed here. A different man, with a different background, may not have noticed her chaotic nature. But Samuel spotted the danger like a recovering alcoholic can spot someone making a weak justification to get wasted. He wanted no part of her messy, thrilling chaos.

Most of us, at the right time and with an attractive-enough woman, will open the gate to turmoil and mischief. Sometimes that moment of weakness can dog us for decades or even a lifetime. Samuel avoided that trap. He knew himself, and he understood his default relationship patterns. Chaotic relationships were part of his past but not his future.

How the Mind Handles Relationship Patterns

Samuel understood his weakness concerning women, much more so than either Elliot or Alonzo. That insight is a superpower—one that every gatekeeper must possess. It allows a man to see around metaphorical corners and avoid painful traps.

This is where we start uncovering the ways in which your mind approaches relationships with women. In this chapter, we tease out whether, how, and to what extent your mind seeks chaos rather than composure. In future chapters, we'll give similar scrutiny to dignity, resilience, joy, and The Word Which Shall Not Yet Be Spoken.

I'd like to take a moment to define a term I will use throughout the book: *organizing principles*. It's shorthand for the roles we have learned to play in the lives of others. What I'll discuss here isn't the only way to think about relationship patterns, but it's a useful and efficient way to think about how and why we choose some women and overlook others.

The thinking goes like this: We each have an unspoken, instinctual understanding of how relationships work and how to conduct ourselves in a way that keeps them predictable. Organizing principles are more than beliefs. They're fundamental assumptions about our roles in the social landscape; the rules of the game formed by our earliest interpersonal experiences and shaped over a lifetime.

We instinctually seek relationships that conform to our organizing principles, and we avoid those that don't. We can't act on our organizing principles by ourselves. We need others to play along and satisfy the other side of the relationship equation.

Here's an example of an organizing principle that might resonate with Samuel: *I only have value in chaotic relationships*. That principle dictates both the type of woman he will seek and how he will conduct himself within the relationship.

Like the "old" Samuel, we're prone to blindly act on our organizing principles when we lack the words to describe them. Counterproductive principles drive our decisions when our rational side doesn't know what the emotional side is up to. However, there's good news. Like the "new" Samuel, we gain freedom from our least productive principles when we put them under a microscope and study how they work.

A large part of the gatekeeper's job is simple but harsh: discriminate and disqualify those who have no place within the walls of his kingdom. Each man's greatest challenge to that task comes from within. It's his own emotional mind with its sometimes counterproductive organizing principles.

We have touched on emotional logic. Let's pin it down further, starting with this premise: We control some parts of the mind, and other parts we don't. For example, if I give you a math problem, you can choose to calculate the answer or you can tell me to pound sand. You're in control.

However, if a woman walks by who possesses every physical quality you find attractive, and if your mind works like most men's, you have no control over your emotional reaction. Luckily, we get to control our rational response to our emotional reaction, as Samuel did.

As for controlling the emotional reaction itself, I've never found much success, nor do I see a necessity. Even if I try to put an attractive woman out of my mind, I'm not escaping the thought. I'm not smart enough to fool me.

Maybe you've experienced the same when you have tried to avoid dwelling on the curve of a woman's hips, or the way her hair tumbles over her bare shoulder, or her adorable little overbite—or, as in Samuel's case, the way she pushes just the right emotional buttons. Good luck eliminating that feeling. Sometimes the emotional mind likes what it sees, and we can't do much about it.

That's not to say emotional impulses are foolish. Emotional logic is always rational—to a degree. Samuel's emotional mind tried to push him toward Mickie, despite his knowledge that a relationship with her would be dangerous. How can that possibly be rational?

Part of the answer is that emotional logic prizes predictability and routine. Suppose, for example, a child learned to hide from conflict because his parents turned simple disagreements into dangerous feuds. That child's emotional mind is apt forevermore to believe, *Hiding kept me alive back then, so hiding will keep me alive now.* It will speak in emotional impulse rather than words.

His emotional logic doesn't know or care that situations are different now that he is an adult. His emotional side will insist, *That was then, and this is then*, even if his rational side knows better. The wordless, emotional impulse will amount to behaviors like the urge to run away whenever the possibility of conflict appears.

The emotional mind lacks some of the information the rational mind possesses. Brain structures like the limbic system don't have direct access to the eyes and ears (though interestingly, they have direct access to smell, which is why a familiar aroma can instantaneously conjure emotional memories). Emotional logic operates on timeless, visceral impressions rather than current reality. It understands experience, not words. Patterns, not math. Reaction, not reason.

Part of the gatekeeper's challenge is to avoid anger at that side of ourselves. The emotional mind is only doing what it thinks is best. If we understand what it's trying to achieve, then we can supervise it. That involves putting words to previously wordless impulses and principles. Sometimes we uncover painful ones, such as:

- I'm unworthy of healthy women, so I settle for unhealthy ones.
- Kind women have no interest in me, so I tolerate cruelty.
- Women will crumble if I abandon them, so I stick around even if it hurts me.
- I'm damaged goods, so I put up a front to prevent women from discovering the truth about me.

Emotional logic usually appears more clearly in what we see ourselves doing and feeling than in what we overtly think. Because organizing principles are all about relationships, relationships are where we act out those behaviors and feelings.

As a rough example—and rest assured that we will fine-tune this type of discussion as we go along—a man who believes women find him unattractive will behave toward women *as if* it were true. He'll avoid women in order to avoid the judgment he expects to receive from them.

That's his emotional mind driving his interactions with women. It doesn't matter if the perception is accurate. Inflexible emotional logic will play out in real time: *women find me unattractive, so I will avoid their scorn by avoiding them.*

Under that organizing principle, resentment is a tool that prevents him from approaching women, just as fear is a tool that prevents him from approaching alligators. From an emotional point of view, it's perfectly logical.

The strategy I find most effective is not one of suppressing or controlling emotional logic but of understanding it and disregarding it when it's counterproductive. Why not fight the emotional mind? Why not beat it into submission? Because, to revisit the white bear research, trying to suppress an emotional impulse often backfires and strengthens it instead.

Luckily, this strategy of allowing the existence of emotional logic—acceptance—isn't as tricky as it might seem. Consider a painful thought (or feeling) like *I'm damaged goods*. To accept the thought doesn't mean accepting it as a *fact*. It simply means accepting, without judgment, that the mind had a *thought*. Nothing more. The heart beats, the lungs breathe, and the mind thinks.

The alternative to acceptance is avoidance and suppression, but trying to evade painful thoughts and feelings requires strategies that can get destructive. They might range from avoiding women altogether to substance abuse or to more sophisticated means such as projecting anger or resentment onto others in order to hide it from ourselves.

To repeat my earlier request, I'm not asking you to believe me. I'm only asking you to experiment with holding lightly whatever you might notice about yourself as we go forward. The emotional mind might insist it's speaking truth, but you're under no obligation to believe it.

I'm also asking you to consider the possibility that your emotional mind is not the enemy. Even though it can lead you by the joystick into disastrous relationships, it has its reasons. Our job is to uncover those reasons and build flexibility around them.

Sometimes our emotional minds are like guard dogs that don't know the difference between a harmless passerby and an assassin climbing the fence. Why not give that part of ourselves a bit of grace and understanding? It's trying to help; it just can't see the big picture, and it relies heavily on habit.

Shortcuts and habits are a feature of the human mind. For example, a 2006 study about eating patterns examined the ways we conserve cognitive resources and revealed that we have eating habits within our eating habits. The routines may not always be healthy, but they save time.[24]

The authors noticed two types of eating habits. *Carryover* habits derive from previous choices; for example, the degree to which this morning's breakfast choice affects this evening's dinner choice. *Baseline* habits are repetitive behaviors influenced by context.

Breakfast tends to operate on a baseline habit. People are generally consistent about breakfast choices because contextual cues are similar from one morning to the next. Most people wake up around the same time each day and follow consistent morning rituals. That sets the table for consistent behavior. Dinner meals have less consistent contextual cues and fewer time constraints. It's more influenced by what we have eaten recently.

Eating habits—like mating habits—run on autopilot because habits reduce effort around repetitive decision-making. In the study's summary, the authors wrote:

> "Our central argument is that habits help in the efficient management of limited cognitive resources. When behaviors become habitual through repetition, they consume fewer resources and make it possible to engage in thoughts unrelated to ongoing behavior."

Eating habits are relatively straightforward, but imagine the complexity of social habits. We need shortcuts—organizing principles—to spare us from what would otherwise be overwhelming mental calculus.

Here's an example: Suppose you meet a woman you find attractive. She has a strong, directive personality. Without shortcuts, you would have to assess her behavior as if you'd never encountered a strong, directive woman.

---

24 Khare, A., and J. Inman. 2006. "Habitual Behavior in American Eating Patterns: The Role of Meal Occasions." *Journal of Consumer Research* 12: 567-575.

You would face questions like: *Do I enjoy letting women make decisions for me? How do others perceive her behavior, and how will it reflect on me? Will I be able to hold my own when we have opposing desires?* The questions created by any meaningful interaction with her could be endless. A guy could spend years sorting it out.

Thank goodness for time-saving organizing principles. Our history with domineering women will guide our interactions so we don't have to agonize over every choice we make in her presence. Organizing principles aren't mere habits, like eating patterns. They are pervasive, reflexive motivators for complex social behaviors. They are usually so primal and ingrained that they lack words until we do the work of excavating and describing them.

If we don't do that work, our own principles are as invisible as the air we breathe. In fact, we can usually see organizing principles in *others* more easily than in ourselves. ("She really goes for the daddy figures," or "I think he hates his boss because he fears authority.") Our eyes point outward, not inward. Sometimes that's to our detriment.

Learning how to relate to others is a bit like learning to tie our shoes. It takes a lot of up-front effort. Then, at some point, we go on autopilot. We don't think about our interactions (with the shoestring or with people). It's only a problem when old relationship rules don't fit the current situation. Remember, emotional logic is prone to inertia: *that was then, and* this *is then.*

Putting our own behavior under the microscope illuminates principles we didn't know were operating in the background. For example, a man who studies and catalogs his behavior around domineering women might notice this type of organizing principle:

I choose domineering women because I feel safe with them.

That man might choose domineering women so he can avoid mistakes by avoiding decisions. If he doesn't make mistakes, says his emotional mind, then he can't get in trouble. Maybe as a child, he experienced outsized and irrational punishment for mistakes. That could easily lead to this kind of organizing principle. Even though he doesn't like domineering women, he knows how to operate within the standards they enforce.

Or consider this one:

I fear domineering women because they have hurt me in the past.

This man has gathered, through experience, that women who are controlling are also abusive. That's not every man's experience, but let's say it was his experience. His emotional mind might reasonably conclude that he's safer if he calls the shots, so he pursues meek women who crave leadership. This man's mind automatically avoids any woman who reminds him of his past. His mind will give him a visceral reaction of contempt for such women, even though they are not the same women who mistreated him.

These two men may have had similar experiences with domineering women and yet they arrive at very different reactions. Organizing principles are as unique as every man who reads this book.

Throughout, we'll focus on organizing principles concerning women, even though we harbor principles for all types of relationships. As a bonus for doing this work, once you identify your principles in the realm of romance, then you will notice similar principles in other kinds of relationships. Our principles follow us to work, to the gym, or anywhere we interact with people.

By the way, I didn't invent the term "organizing principle." It's an archaic term that has fallen out of use, and that's a shame. I'm resurrecting it for this book because it captures relationship motivations more accurately than popular terms like "core beliefs."[25]

25 Heinz Kohut was one of the first to use the term. He studied neurology in 1930s Germany, then fled to Chicago to escape Nazi persecution. Kohut was interested in the interplay between self and others during development. In particular, he believed the way we come to view our role in relationships was shaped by the ability of our parents and other authority figures to understand and respond to our childhood drives and urges. See: Flanagan, Laura Melano. 1996. "The theory of self-psychology." In Joan Berzoff, Laura Melano Flanagan, and Patricia Hertz (eds.). *Inside Out and Outside In*, Second Edition. Northvale, New Jersey: Jason Aronson.

Organizing principles describe a deeper motivational force than do mere beliefs about ourselves and others. They describe how we view ourselves *in relation* to others. They're about the interplay between people; the repetition and recreation of relationship patterns we may not even notice. That's what makes the notion useful in our discussion about romantic commitment. A belief is merely about *us* or *them*. An organizing principle is about *us in relation to them*.

The upside to our stealthy organizing principles is the efficiency they bring to the act of navigating complex relationships. The downside is that they blind us to nuance, and they often recreate what we're trying to avoid. For example, consider principles having to do with trust.

Trust is so central to our organizing principles that we can pass it from one generation to the next, echoing the experience of parents and grandparents. In a 2009 paper on attachment style, Peter Kilmann and his colleagues found:

> "[P]ositive associations were found between mothers' fearful attachment scores and the fearful, preoccupied, and dismissive attachment scores of daughters. Daughters of matched secure parents were more likely to report a secure attachment style, while daughters of matched insecure parents were more likely to report an insecure attachment style."[26]

The researchers speculated that parents' attachment styles affect the way they interact with their children. The parents' behavior transmits part of their view of relationships to the next generation. Organizing principles are so prone to recreation that we can even recreate them in our own children.

As another example, in an older study on the intergenerational transmission of divorce, researchers found "the likelihood of

---

26 Kilmann, P. R., J. M. C. Vendemia, M. M. Parnell, and G. C. Urbaniak. 2009. "Parent Characteristics Linked with Daughters' Attachment Styles." *Adolescence* 44: 557-568.

divorce was especially high if both spouses came from divorced families of origin."[27]

Among the variables accounting for the increased risk are issues you might expect, like cohabiting before marriage, marrying too young, and a tolerant attitude toward divorce. One of the most important reasons, however, was "problematic interpersonal behavior," which the authors describe as "problems with anger, jealousy, hurt feelings, communication, infidelity, and so on."

Those "problematic interpersonal behaviors" flow directly from the way people organize their relationships. Take jealousy, for example. If experience teaches a person that he should not trust others, then he's prone to treating others as if they are untrustworthy. His suspiciousness will lead others to question *his* trustworthiness. Others will approach him cautiously, which in turn causes him to question their motives.

It's a self-fulfilling organizing principle that says, *My role in the lives of others is to be the target of their deceit and aggression.* If we can't find the experiences we expect, we will recreate them.

There's a reason organizing principles are so powerful: they are usually functional at first, when we are young and depend on them to get our needs met. The man who operates under a principle such as, *If I don't make mistakes around women, then I won't get in trouble*, probably arrived at that belief because a domineering mother, or another authority figure, was unforgiving. His organizing principle helped him navigate that tyrannical relationship.

Unfortunately, that organizing principle keeps operating (and replicating) long after it outlives its usefulness. When he becomes an adult, his principle might alienate women by causing him to behave in the same subdued manner that kept him out of trouble as a boy. He might then resent women for failing to notice him, even though he actively cultivated their disinterest. Our organizing principles usually start out as useful strategies, but the more

---

27 Amato, P. 1996. "Explaining the Intergenerational Transmission of Divorce." *Journal of Marriage and the Family* 58: 628-640.

self-protective ones can grow into painful self-fulfilling prophesies right under our noses.

The man who believes women are domineering, for example, will often find domineering women to date. It's not necessarily because he finds them attractive. It's that he finds them familiar. His personality fits with a domineering woman like a key fits in a lock. If he can't find a domineering woman, he will transform an otherwise reasonable woman by behaving so ineptly that she can only tolerate him if she becomes the nagging battle-ax he expected all along.

We seek romantic partners who fit our deepest insecurities. If we can't find them, we build them. That's the power of our organizing principles, and that's why it's so important to unearth them. Our history predicts our future unless we understand ourselves enough to make different choices.

The task involves understanding the environment we came from, our most hurtful relationship experiences, and our most helpful ones. We don't need to wallow in the past; we just need to understand it. It's difficult to choose the role relationships *will* play in our lives without dissecting the role relationships *have* played in our lives. Writer Aleksandr Solzhenitsyn was fond of an old Russian proverb that warns, "Dwell on the past and you will lose an eye. Forget the past and you will lose both eyes."

Playing the Slots

We will periodically return to one more important psychological concept throughout the book. It's the slot-machine effect, and it has to do with the self-fulfilling characteristic of organizing principles. When we hit a periodic jackpot after a string of losses, we're compelled to keep trying for the next jackpot, even if we're slowly emptying the bank account. It works in relationships the same way it works in casinos.

For example, suppose a man views women through the lens of this organizing principle:

I must work to earn approval since women don't offer it freely.

His role with women has been to serve in exchange for praise or acceptance. That kind of principle doesn't develop in a vacuum. Maybe he had a mother who was stingy or unpredictable with affection, or a string of overly critical female teachers.

His experience says women dole out approval as if it were gold doubloons. That scarcity led him to believe female approval was precious and necessary. (In his earliest days, it was.) His organizing principle will lead him toward women who feel familiar: aloof and disapproving.

He will choose women who offer kindness and appreciation inconsistently, at best. Sometimes it's a little; sometimes a lot. Plus, he can never be certain he'll receive any validation at all. Sometimes these women will reward a particular behavior, and sometimes they will rebuff it.

To use a term from behavioral psychology, this is the *reinforcement schedule* behind slot machines. They rarely pay out. When they do, it will likely be a pittance. The combination of variable intervals and amounts keeps a person pulling the lever in pursuit of that next elusive payout.

Most people are fairly consistent and don't behave precisely like slot machines. But our hypothetical man is not interested in consistent women. They're unfamiliar. He gravitates toward unpredictable, inconsistent women. He doesn't always enjoy their company, but at least he understands the rules of the game.

Unfortunately, like the little old lady sitting at a slot machine with a cigarette and an old-fashioned in her hand, he *always* goes back for more. He's so focused on the occasional payout of validation that he's blind to the organizing principle he keeps reenacting. We've all been there: so busy being busy that we'd be hard-pressed to identify precisely what we're trying to accomplish. It's part of the human condition.

It's also why our organizing principles can be easier to detect in our feelings and behaviors than in our thoughts. When our behavior goes on autopilot, as it does with slot-machine situations, we don't think about our actions. Our hypothetical man, desperate for approval, is thinking about how to achieve the next minor victory—like getting a hug after fixing her computer or moving her couch. He doesn't wonder *why* he looks for a hug any more than the little old lady wonders *why* she pulls the slot-machine lever.

However, he might be able to notice his feelings and behaviors if he chooses to watch for them. What he *feels* around women is like the excited desperation one feels while approaching a slot machine. What he is *doing* is staying busy while avoiding his own values and purpose. If he's attuned to his feelings and behaviors, then he can notice them, turn off the autopilot, and engage his rational mind.

This example is not extreme, nor is it uncommon. It illustrates what happens when we aren't intentional and selective about our relationships. If we won't drive the bus, then our emotional mind is happy to take the wheel and reenact old principles, even if doing so drives us over a cliff.

Identifying those old principles takes work, and it's not always comfortable. Just think how difficult it will be for our hypothetical man to deny his inclination toward female validation. For him, validation has been like intermittent meals to a starving inmate. His emotional mind will not be pleased if he forgoes that familiar slot-machine reinforcement. It will hit him with a hefty dose of anxiety.

Luckily, the discomfort of denying the emotional mind hasn't killed anyone yet. Nor does it last forever. But the pain of being ruled by it? That can last a lifetime.

A woman once told me a story that illustrates the point. A cousin of hers—who came from a stable and loving family—was on the verge of marrying a woman who behaved badly during wedding preparations. She was moody rather than joyful; demanding rather than gracious; confrontational rather than cooperative. Her mother behaved similarly.

These are bad omens for a marriage. Her temperament was unsuitable for the role of spouse, which requires selflessness and collaboration. Of course, her behavior was not new; it was simply elevated. She had been impatient and demanding throughout the relationship. He might have been willing to acknowledge it sooner had he not entangled himself by moving in with her months earlier.

Yet here he was, despite her behavior, standing on the tracks of that oncoming wedding train. You could almost watch the new organizing principles forming in real time:

> *Marriage is tense and volatile. My role is to endure the hostility of an unstable and disrespectful wife.*

His male relatives noticed his helplessness and confusion as the wedding fast approached. They foresaw how unpleasant the marriage was likely to be. On the weekend before the wedding, they intervened by separating him from the tumult of the preparations.

They took him golfing and bought him dinner. They talked to him, they listened, and they helped him make sense of what was unfolding. They challenged him to consider the long-term implications of his fiancée's behavior. If she behaved this way when she was supposed to be at her happiest, how might she behave years down the road, in private? He would be trapped, and she would have no reason to contain her hostility.

It was only after consultation with older and more experienced men that his best option became clear: he canceled the wedding at the last minute.

It was a difficult decision, especially with so much time and money already invested in the wedding by so many people. He felt ashamed and embarrassed, but he undoubtedly spared himself years of misery. He avoided the role of the downtrodden good egg who would be forever at the mercy of an overwrought and explosive woman.

Once he had broken away from what would undoubtedly be a train wreck of a marriage, he was free to write his blueprint for future relationships. It might have looked like this:

> *Romantic commitment must bring composure, dignity, resilience, and joy. My role is that of a man who serves himself and others by pursuing his values and his purpose.*

In the best circumstances, our organizing principles reduce social complexity and help us make healthy decisions. More commonly, our organizing principles give us mixed results. Most people grow up in decent circumstances among people who cherish them, but they still pick up a few principles and patterns along the way that serve them poorly. Such was the case with our man at his wedding.

In less-than-ideal circumstances, our organizing principles become self-fulfilling prophecies as we repeat the same miserable patterns—not just with women but with coworkers, family, friends, and strangers. For good or bad, we tend to treat ourselves the way others have treated us.

The following section is a sampling of organizing principles that lead men to chaotic relationships: principles that cause them to reject composure. Each of our five Books (chapters) will have a similar list titled "Avoid These Traps," which presents examples of counterproductive organizing principles. I have compiled these lists from my clinical notes after having worked closely with hundreds of men, women, and couples.

You won't find statistics here, population norms, averages, or standard deviations. These lists simply distill my observations about male motivations for tolerating substandard relationships. These are my field notes, and I offer this peek into what has transpired in my office over the last fifteen years.

Your organizing principles are as unique as your fingerprints. I don't know if any of the principles I offer will precisely capture your experience. But I believe most men will encounter a few throughout the book that make him think, *That feels familiar.*

When that happens, I hope you will stop and spend some time with the organizing principle that caught your attention. Refine it. Sharpen it. Put words to the role you have learned to fill in relation to women. Describe the heartache, the passions, the fears, the desires, and the victories that have shaped your relationship patterns. Be the dispassionate observer of your own inner workings, and bring that cloudy image into focus.

Pathways to Chaos

Imagine the world from the emotional mind's point of view. It's a dangerous place, and your job is to write the rules for navigating it. However, updating the rules to fit current circumstances isn't in your job description. That means the rules you wrote as a youngster are still on the books now that you're an adult.

Not all organizing principles are counterproductive; most serve us well. But in this book, we'll focus on the ones that predispose us to accept less than we should in exchange for our commitment. I encourage you to think of them as old, out-of-date rules written by an overprotective mind. Our first sampling of counterproductive principles are those that invite chaos rather than composure. Let's dive in.

Chaos is normal in my life.

The man who operates under this organizing principle grew up with chaos and drama. His parents were a mess. His siblings were the neighborhood soap opera. His family culture is one of upheaval, hostility, money problems, substance abuse, divorces, infidelities, gossip, or intrigue. There is no limit to the ways parents and families can create instability.

Children absorb and adapt as they have no alternative. Try to imagine the six-year-old who calls a meeting with his parents to explain his need for a more stable environment. "Mom, Dad, I will need to find a new place to live if you can't create a more tranquil and predictable environment. It's nothing personal. My developing mind requires more sensible and dependable behavior from the adults in my life."

Seems an unlikely scenario for a child. Yet, the man who comes from chaos may be no more capable of creating stability in his life than he was as a boy. He repeats the patterns he saw; his expectations match those of the people who raised him.

It's not that he lacks agency or intellect. It's that his emotional logic lacks alternatives. He either doesn't see the possibility of calmness and composure, or they seem foreign and out of reach.

Such relationships are not part of his emotional equation because they were not part of his history. Nor are they part of his future plans.

If he lives by this organizing principle, then he finds women who are chaotic, even if he resents their effect on him. Like all of us, he seeks the familiar until he chooses otherwise. Unfortunately, he has an incentive to remain in chaos: he knows how to navigate it. He's an expert at swimming against the current. He can solve, or at least tolerate, everyone else's goofy problems and conflicts. Eventually, with enough repetition, he will conclude there is no other role for him.

Even for men who escape the pull of chaos, the siren call remains. It is strongest when his defenses are down. As Samuel discovered (our case study from the gym), healthy, peaceful relationships can feel boring at first. It takes time to adjust to the slower pace and appreciate the beauty of tranquility.

An old metaphor among psychologists is about horses returning to burning barns. It's said that a horse who sees its barn on fire will run inside it rather than run away. To the horse, returning to the barn is an act of self-preservation because the barn has always represented safety and shelter.

I don't know whether horses actually enter burning barns, but people return to their metaphorical burning barns with frightening frequency. It's especially true for people who have been mistreated. Psychiatrist Bessel van der Kolk, describing how people with traumatic histories face new threats, wrote, "Many traumatized people simply give up. Rather than risk experimenting with new options they stay stuck in the fear they know."[28]

Van der Kolk noted that it's also true for non-humans. Many unsavory experiments show that traumatized animals linger in painful situations, provided they previously learned there is no escape. Frankly, that sounds like too many marriages I've seen involving men who find shelter in their ability to function in a crisis or lose themselves in it.

---

28 van der Kolk, Bessel. 2014. *The Body Keeps the Score*. Penguin Publishing Group.

I have no purpose without chaos.

The man operating under this principle senses that he needs a purpose, but he doesn't know how to find it. If his early training required him to function well amid chaos—if he experienced the feeling of being resourceful and effective during crises—then it is easy for his mind to mistake the busyness of chaos for the soul-nourishing work of masculine purpose. He is too busy fighting silly fires to notice how he allows his plans to be hijacked by other people's chaos and shenanigans.

This man is primed for the trap of catering to chaotic women. He will find women in need of his world-class chaos-containment services, which he volunteers free of charge. He will manage to find the woman who hates her job, who has perpetual conflicts with friends, who has money problems, whose dog is a holy terror, or who has messy relationship boundaries with bosses, associates, and strangers. He doesn't tie his self-worth to his pursuit of his values and purpose. His self-worth comes from his ability to manage catastrophes in the lives of chaotic women.

He may look selfless to outsiders, but he reaps a dark benefit. His relationships mask his own lack of focus. He gets to be the high-functioning one in his low-functioning circle. This man's mind has solved the problem of purpose, though it has done so in a way that serves him poorly.

My role is to rescue.

Some women, having failed to overcome their histories of mistreatment or neglect, begin relationships with their stories of trauma. It's the first meaningful detail they tell you about themselves because it's central to their identity.

They don't start a relationship in the normal fashion: getting to know you, enjoying experiences together, and having give-and-take conversations in which each of you reveals your character and ambitions. Instead, they showcase their pain, their anger, their disappointments, and sometimes their bitter pronouncements of personal or sexual boundaries—which they themselves soon violate.

The man operating under this principle is a sucker for sob stories. Having grown up in chaos, distress is his siren song. This man knows how to rescue. In fact, the closer he is to a woman, the less he can operate in any other capacity.

Like the woman who leads with trauma, the man who leads with a compulsion to rescue has yet to come to terms with the experiences that left him in this condition. He doesn't understand what he brings to the table as a potential boyfriend or husband, so he shines like a new penny when he is rescuing. He knows how to play the role of rescuer, and he is good at it.

Sometimes these saviors are engaged in what psychologists call *reaction formation.* That's an exaggerated outward response that is the opposite of what a person really feels. For example, a guy might resent women for the cruelty they have inflicted, but he finds his resentment unacceptable. To mask it from himself and others, he rescues women instead of taking responsibility for his anger. He gets to say to himself, *See? I'm not angry at women. Would an angry man render this much aid?* Simultaneously, he generates an endless supply of new reasons to resent women by immersing himself in their worst conduct.

When a woman who leads with trauma meets a man who leads with a compulsion to rescue, the two of them will build an alliance based on misery. He can never fill her bottomless pit of need, and she can never afford to be happy. (She might lose him if she stops serving as his train wreck.) They will enjoy each other's company, in a way. They will both experience short-term relief from their insecurities but always at the expense of long-term success.

I don't trust myself with the big questions, so I focus on trivia.

Procrastination comes in many forms. Some are immediate, like my favorites: surfing social media or hunting for snacks when I should be working.

Other forms involve habits like perfectionism (it's difficult to complete a project when you're obsessing over the details), plugging away at low-priority tasks (replying to every little email as it arrives rather than carving out time for email so you can focus on more important objectives), and replacing meaningful activity with work-like activity (compulsively making lists, worrying, or planning instead of acting).

Procrastination becomes an art form when we don't even realize we're doing it, like when a man allows relationship chaos to consume time and energy he could put to better use.

The man operating under this principle doesn't trust himself to pursue what matters. Maybe he fears he will fail or that his goals are hopeless. Maybe he simply hasn't clarified his values. Whatever the genesis, chaotic relationships are his way of avoiding the important questions. What man has time to look inward when his girlfriend needs rent money? What man is planning his next professional conquest while holding his girlfriend's hair as she vomits after too much booze?

He may not *look* like he's procrastinating. He may not *feel* like he's procrastinating. Nevertheless, he sets aside his values and purpose each time he rescues a damsel in distress.

An open secret is operating alongside this principle. That damsel in distress is perfectly capable of fighting her own fires, but she doesn't do so because she wants to be rescued as much as he wants to be the hero. They're a perfect imperfect match.

Chaos excuses my losses and failures.

I don't know about you, but my immature side prefers to blame my failures on external factors. Taking responsibility for losses is bitter. It requires a willingness to grow and adapt, even if we don't believe we can do it.

The man who lacks that faith (or the willingness to fake it) will live his life blaming externalities. He may even cover his failures by indulging in chaotic romantic relationships, which give him a "good reason" for every missed meeting, dropped commitment, or late delivery. His alliance with a chaotic woman is a symbiosis of the most depressing kind; she provides him with crises so he can avoid fully engaging with his purpose, and in return, she gets a servant and a savior.

I am incapable of discipline.

Whether it's poor self-confidence or underdeveloped self-discipline, the man operating under this principle lacks commitment to an agenda. His aimlessness allows others' chaos to spill into his life. He is unclear about what he is trying to accomplish, so most of his decisions are untethered from a larger purpose. And since he has no plan of his own, he's vulnerable to sliding into the wrong romantic commitments with women who have their own plans for him.

This is a serious existential problem. He's aimless and drifting, and he hasn't defined the terms under which he knows whether he is succeeding or failing. This man's sense of purpose is in shambles, which opens the door for chaos and failures to accumulate and compound.

In case no one told you, it's normal to struggle with discipline. The emotional mind constantly tries to assert its yearning for comfort. Short-term emotional logic hates long-term discipline like a dog hates a bath (the same dog that loves rolling in roadkill). The upcoming strategies section will aid in keeping chaotic relationships at bay while sorting out this problem of self-discipline.

Life is boring without chaos.

Let's be honest: chaos isn't all downside. Even destructive chaos has its charms. It can be titillating, and it can spark sexual passion. Some men have a robust appetite for stimulation, and chaotic relationships make them feel alive. It's hard to sleepwalk your way through adventures and emergencies.

The man operating under this principle doesn't merely tolerate chaos and drama; he organizes his relationships around the thrill of fire drills and train wrecks. He may even mistake turmoil and disarray for meaningful connection.

An odd aspect of anxiety reminds me of this organizing principle. When people worry, especially about events they can't control, the mind can believe it's being productive rather than merely burning calories to no real-world effect. Ruminating over a problem can and does generate solutions, but it quickly reaches the point of diminishing returns. That's when the mind can mistakenly believe the internal act of worrying is equal to the external act of fixing.

This is partly due to the same slot-machine payoff discussed earlier: once in a while, worrying beyond the point of diminishing returns pays off. If a mind ruminates and tries to predict every possible outcome, it's bound to stumble onto an accurate prediction occasionally. Jackpot. *I was right!* it shouts. It is a victim of its own variable reinforcement schedule. If you keep pulling the lever on the worry machine, it will eventually pay out.

Evidence even exists that a brain system implicated in anxiety intertwines with a system that manages motivation and reward. Worrying doesn't feel good, precisely, but it is comforting. For example, people can fall into a pattern of checking locks or light switches in a way that's counterproductive and uncomfortable, yet simultaneously reassuring. As much as they dislike seeing themselves checking a lock for the third time, it temporarily calms the mind. (Ask me how I know.)[29]

For some men, the thrill of chaotic relationships seems to function similarly. These men might be fully aware their relationships are depleting them, but the chaos is also comforting. In the privacy of my office, more than a few men have acknowledged that their appetite for train wrecks serves them poorly, yet they feel anxious and uncomfortable in stable relationships.

I can't help noticing the parallels between the self-reinforcing aspect of worry and the self-reinforcement of relationship thrill-seeking. The rational mind can see each as self-destructive, while the emotional mind craves the reassurance and comfort these familiar activities provide.

If that's true, it means the relationship thrill-seeker isn't merely a victim of his own poor judgment. That's an unhelpful and oversimplified stance, especially when he recognizes what's happening

29 Zarrindast, M. R., and F. Khakpai. 2015. "The Modulatory Role of Dopamine in Anxiety-like Behavior." *Archives of Iranian Medicine* 18: 591-603.

but has difficulty stepping away. Biology itself may make the relationship pattern difficult to relinquish.

It is far from hopeless, though. In my experience, once people articulate the discrepancy between their rational and emotional logic, they have won the first battle. Making different choices—that is, establishing new patterns—is unfamiliar and difficult at first, but like any other skill, it gets easier with practice.

I can't connect with others in the absence of chaos.

One of the largest factors that brings chaos into a boy's life is fatherlessness. According to the US Census Bureau, roughly 20 percent of American children live in fatherless homes.[30]

In his 2018 book *The Boy Crisis*, Warren Farrell listed seventy ways in which boys benefit from the presence of fathers—and conversely, seventy ways in which boys suffer in their absence. Boys raised without fathers in the home are at higher risk for substance abuse, academic failure, suicide, interpersonal conflict, psychiatric problems, physical illness, bullying or being bullied, unemployment, poverty, aggression, lack of impulse control, homelessness, legal problems, imprisonment, and reduced life expectancy.

In a word: chaos. Fatherlessness is only one path to chaos starting in childhood. Other homes are governed by substance abuse, mental illness, or any number of factors that cause chaos to spread like weeds in a poorly tended garden.

Whatever the source of the chaos, the boy who is immersed in it can become the man who has never experienced interpersonal stability. He organizes his relationships around the perfectly understandable belief that stability doesn't exist.

A man once told me about finding himself in his own kitchen with a carving knife pointed at his face. The knife was held by the woman he previously thought would be the loving mother to his children. Now she was his unhinged live-in girlfriend, irate over a conversation he had with another woman.

---

30 US Census Bureau. 2020. *Living Arrangements of Children Under 18 Years Old: 1960 to Present*. Washington, DC: US Census Bureau.

"It was the scariest moment of my life," he told me. "I didn't know what she was going to do with that knife. I calmed her down—I don't really remember how—and she backed off. I spent a lot of time that night thinking about how I got myself into the situation." (He admitted part of the problem was the same old story of entanglement. He had moved her into his house before he knew her character.)

The incident offered him a moment of clarity, and he didn't squander it. He forced her to move out of his house the next day. Her exit did not go smoothly, but eventually, she left. Some men aren't so lucky. A time comes in many unhappy marriages when a man finally reckons leaving would be costlier than staying. He remains married and runs out the clock. It's a heartbreaking fate.

However, when chaos characterizes the relationship, especially violent chaos, the cost of staying can outweigh even the most painful exit. In that moment in the kitchen, the man staring at the point of a knife was paying the price of chaos. He wasn't pursuing his purpose, and he certainly wasn't having fun. His entire being was focused on the crisis. One wrong move could have left him maimed or dead.

That crisis was not a game. Yet how many men, after similar moments have passed, renew their commitment to dangerous and disorderly relationships? These men surrender the lives they might have had, instead conscripting themselves to an endless stream of danger and disruption.

❄ ❄ ❄

If any of the organizing principles just described ring true, even a little, then I encourage you to explore them more deeply. Do whatever is necessary to shine a light on your relationship patterns. Journal about them. Talk to a psychologist. Smoke a cigar while you watch the sun set. Invest time in contemplating the roles you fill in relationships. Lift those murky organizing principles from the depths of wordless compulsion and into the harsh light of naked precision.

Don't let it rest until you have named it and described it. Don't stop until you know how the principle came to be, who taught you this way of relating to the world, and where it will take you if you don't intervene. You might even pause here and sort that out.

Once you're ready, let's talk strategy. How can we keep chaotic relationships beyond the walls of our kingdom? We'll start with one of my favorite psychological terms: agency.

The Road to Composure

"Agency" is an underappreciated word from old psychological literature. It refers to the ability to plan and act. There's not much of a point in having a purpose if you can't make it happen.

One of the major figures in psychology who wrote about agency was Albert Bandura. He described it using terms like intentionality, forethought, self-regulation (by which he meant monitoring and managing thoughts and behaviors), and self-reflection (examining our own functioning and progress). He also wrote about the necessity of adapting to changing demands.

Agency is fragile, easily damaged by suboptimal circumstances. Consider poverty, for example. It's a brain drain and a destroyer of agency. It taxes the mind by forcing people to deliberate over decisions that otherwise wouldn't require much attention, like whether to top off the gas tank or buy a few more groceries at a time when you can't afford to do both. Poverty consumes mental resources, leaving less energy for questions like "How will I act on my values and make my mark on the world today?"

Poverty also leaves little room for error because a mistake made in poverty has a greater impact than a mistake made in financial security. Errors magnify the pressure of poverty, paving the way for impulsive, emotion-based decisions like renting furniture rather than making do with less glamorous options.[31]

---

31 Mani, A., S. Mullainathan, E. Shafir, and J. Zhao. 2013. "Poverty Impedes Cognitive Function." *Science* 341: 976-980.

At the same time, poverty reduces the margin for error; it also hobbles the problem-solving ability by preoccupying the mind. It increases a person's rate of error precisely when they can least afford to make mistakes.[32]

Poverty requires a person to spend an inordinate amount of time fending off the effects of poverty. You have probably already guessed the point I'm building to: relationship chaos has similar brain-draining effects. Like poverty, romantic chaos causes preoccupation, which leads to inattentiveness, and inattentiveness creates errors. Errors compound, which increases the cost of new errors. And so on.

A man can solve the problem of poverty by working toward wealth. It's also entirely possible to be happy while poor, especially when interpersonal relationships are running smoothly. However, the man in a chaotic relationship isn't working his way toward a more stable life. Even if it feels like today's crisis is the last, tomorrow will bring fresh surprises. Instead of digging his way out, he burrows further in with each passing day.

The man who is lost to chaotic relationships lives in the service of someone else's agenda, and he outsources his source of validation to external forces and people. He's not wondering, *How well did I serve my purpose today?* He's wondering, *Did I keep her calm? How can I avoid the next crisis?* Or worse, he isn't thinking at all. He is merely reacting like a cornered animal. That man has surrendered his agency and replaced it with the impotent masturbation of managing endless turmoil.

Please don't beat yourself up if you have done it. We men are prone to it—particularly conscientious men. Still, the hard truth remains: If we allow it, then we encourage it. The drama and chaos we allow don't belong to *her*, they belong to *us*.

Here are a few strategies for avoiding that fate and creating relationships that are calm, cool, and collected.

32 Schilbach, F., H. Schofield, and S. Mullainathan. 2016. "The Psychological Lives of the Poor." *American Economic Review* 106: 435-440.

Distinguish between imported and domestic chaos.

US senators and military personnel swear an oath to defend the country against threats both foreign and domestic. The oaths recognize the fact that existential threats sometimes come from within one's borders.

I know little about threats to a country, but I know that within the human mind, internal threats can be harder to recognize than external ones. For instance, I can easily spot a coworker trying to undermine me, but it's more difficult to see how my job performance threatens my employment.

Similarly, some men don't distinguish between the normal chaos from the outside world—like unhappy bosses and irrational neighbors—and chaos generated in their own homes by their own relationships.

For example, sometimes women "vent" about problems rather than immediately fixing them. For many women (and plenty of men) venting about a problem creates clarity *so that* they can fix it. For them, venting reduces chaos, even if it feels chaotic to a man on the receiving end. It's a strategy you might struggle to understand if complaining isn't your style.

However, some women, and some men, never transition from the venting phase to the fixing phase. They just gripe endlessly and helplessly.

Whether a partner is venting or displaying related behavior, the question to ask is simply this: Is she solving problems, or is she creating them? Is she fending off foreign chaos, or is she the kingdom's leading producer of it? If you help her to her feet, does she try to walk, figuratively speaking, or does she simply collapse into a heap? There's a world of difference between a woman who actively recovers from a bad day by venting about it and one who is a bottomless pit of need. The man who grew up in constant chaos may not yet understand how to distinguish between the two. If he only ever witnessed endless griping, or other impotent capitulations to problems, then he is the fish who doesn't see the water in which he swims.

One way to determine whether you're that unfortunate fish is to check your history for constantly thwarted plans and goals. Maybe you wanted to go to college, start a business, or travel to a foreign land, but there was always some sort of family drama that prevented it. If you can identify several such data points, then perhaps chaos was part of the foundation of those relationships.

If that's the case, it's useful to find a skilled therapist to help establish a compass for normalcy. A man can also choose to surround himself with people who enjoy calm, productive relationships—much like the recovering alcoholic must ditch his old drinking buddies and find sober friends.

Of course, every relationship is co-created. Sometimes we, not them, stir the drama. You may hear yourself gossiping, complaining, or reveling in victimhood. (I'm ashamed of the number of times I catch myself in the act.) If you're bold enough to take a hard look at that side of yourself, try keeping a ledger in which you track your chaos-inducing behavior. It's an eye-opening exercise.

Another hint that you may be the one inducing drama is the type of sensation-seeking that backfires, such as drinking out of boredom or picking arguments out of vague emotional dissatisfaction. Again, you might be bold enough to track the number of times your emotional mind urges you to stir the pot. Sometimes emotional logic says you have an urgent problem to solve, when rational logic says you're better off holding your tongue.

The world gives us plenty of external threats to our purpose. There's no good reason to allow chaos to undermine us from within.

Beware of infatuation's ability to undermine purpose.

Mutual infatuation with a woman is tremendous fun. I highly recommend the experience at least once in life. The downside is that it can relieve us of our senses and our rationality. Infatuation is not merely blinding; it's misleading. It boosts our energy and tricks us into believing we have the world by the tail, when really, we're just high on hormones.

Without a clear sense of purpose and a clear mind, we risk rearranging our lives in a way we will regret after the infatuation wears off. (Entanglement is just one of the risks. I'd wager we have all met someone who got a tattoo as a permanent expression of temporary passion.)

At this nascent stage of a relationship, the stolid gatekeeper is especially attentive to:

- Her character and values.
- The quality of the relationship, and what this commitment might bring into his life.
- His own organizing principles and whether he is repeating an outmoded relationship pattern.

Infatuation by itself can hurl us off track, but the man who keeps his eye on the objective indicators of relationship quality—the man who is a disciplined thinker in romance—won't suffer disappointment after the infatuation wears off. (We'll discuss more about the inner workings of infatuation when we reach The Word Which Shall Not Yet Be Spoken at the end of this book.)

Look beyond the most obvious relationship options.

Sometimes the most obvious options are the least desirable. An expensive car can be costly to maintain. An impressive house can be a money pit. And a gorgeous woman can be a high-maintenance nightmare unworthy of your commitment. Knockouts are overrated.

Each of us has our own version of a knockout, and it's not just about physical attributes. Sometimes the knockout is the woman who fits our old relationship patterns like a glove. That was Samuel's experience with Mickie at the gym. Not only did she fit his physical predilections, but she felt like a kindred spirit. Their connection was unspoken and instinctual. It's hard to look past that level of knockout.

When it's time for a man to try a new approach to relationships because the old approach kept blowing up in his face, I suggest he try this highly underrated screening technique: look beyond women who seem most familiar and appetizing. Pay attention to the women standing quietly on the periphery ... the ones he might normally overlook.

If you can relate to stories like Samuel's, this technique can be like cleaning up your diet after years of living off beer and pizza. It's not what your emotional mind wants, but the man of purpose plays the long game and reaps the long-term rewards.

If you're trying to escape drama and chaos, don't overlook the stable, "boring" woman who doesn't immediately command your attention. She may only seem boring because you don't yet know what she offers.

Avoid relationships built on tales of woe.

We all know women (and men) who start relationships by sharing their history of abuse, neglect, mistreatment, and connections gone bad. That's their small talk. It's their getting-to-know-you banter, and it's rarely a good sign.

Everyone has a dark chapter in their history, and healthy couples trust each other with that part of themselves. It's not the place to start, though. People who have come to terms with their past suffering have more interesting topics to discuss. Dwelling on their worst experiences usually means they haven't come to terms with them—which means they may be on track to repeat them. They may be positioning themselves as the victim and you as the savior or oppressor.

Some people only know how to connect by complaining, while others can only connect by indulging complaints. The wise gatekeeper doesn't allow himself to take up residence in either of those positions. A relationship consumed by the past has little hope for a future.

Avoid leading with a compulsion to rescue.

Every relationship pattern has at least two sides. The complement to the woman who leads with trauma is the man who leads with a compulsion to rescue. This man is on chaos autopilot, propelled by a counterproductive organizing principle, such as *I have no purpose without chaos. Life is boring without chaos.* Or *I can't connect with others in the absence of chaos.*

After a lifetime of fighting fires, these men can solve almost any problem. It's no surprise they put themselves at the beck and call of women who offer a never-ending source of crises. Women depend on his competence, and he depends on their alleged helplessness. This man is busier than a borrowed mule, and he's going nowhere.

Again, I hope you won't buy into feelings of shame if this describes some part of your relationship history. Nature and socialization predispose good men to put ourselves at the service of others. I'll wager most of us have strayed too far down that path at some point.

Being the occasional shoulder-to-cry-on is part of any mature relationship. Being a handkerchief that absorbs all her ugliness is not. On paper, the line might be obvious; in reality, it can get blurry.

The good news is that drawing that distinction gets easier with practice. If you struggle to know the difference, reflecting on your history is a great way to start. You might begin with a simple inventory of the times you have come riding to the rescue in any type of personal or professional relationship.

Literally make a list. With the datapoints laid out, you can then begin the search for patterns and motivations. Did those incidents occur on your terms, in accordance with your values, and in a way that's compatible with your purpose? If not, what call were you answering? Were you flying on emotional autopilot? Did the situations stir up anxiety that you felt compelled to eliminate? Were you being manipulated? Were you reenacting an outdated relationship pattern?

Journaling on those questions can yield insight and flexibility, as can working with a competent, male-friendly therapist. Leading with a compulsion to rescue is one of the most fundamental ways in which men invite chaos into their lives. It's worth close examination.

Monitor the effects of the relationship.

The Tacoma Narrows Bridge was built in 1940 to span Puget Sound. It was thin and graceful. It also lasted only four months before a mild, steady wind destroyed it.

The sustained wind, while hardly extreme, was the perfect speed to cause harmonic resonance within the long band of suspended road. It was like a child on a playground swing. It only takes a minor push, properly timed during each cycle, to propel the child higher and higher. Online videos show the bridge whipping up and down until, after an hour, the center span crumpled and collapsed into the river below.

The incident seems an apt metaphor for the insidious effect low-grade destructive chaos can have on a man's life. One minor incident can build on another until life is out of control.

I'm reminded of a man who was laid off from a job he disliked. Given his distaste for the job, it should have had little effect on him. However, his job loss was preceded by his wife quitting her job in a huff, which was preceded by her conflict with a supervisor, which was preceded by years of poor budgeting and impulse-buying, which was preceded by … you get the idea. A steady wind. Harmonic resonance.

By the time the man lost his job, his relationship had exhausted his margin of error. What should have been a mild breeze turned catastrophic because chaos was already rocking his world.

Some men can't resist tumultuous women. Any man who has a taste for turbulence must make sure he has enough margin to absorb both the effects of such women and the normal chaos of life without being thrown off his purpose. That's a lot of margin. Whether you're the man who chooses tumult or the man who is learning to avoid it, there is a way to monitor the effects of the relationship on your life: attend to life's little barometers.

We all get feedback from friends, bosses, coworkers, and colleagues, if we're willing to listen. When chaos from home interferes with work and friendships, important people will offer feedback. Bosses will grumble. Friends will say they miss us. Family will ask if we're okay. Customers and clients will become annoyed and eventually take their business elsewhere.

Little numerical signs are also present, like bank accounts shrinking, sales numbers declining, and an increasing amount of time and money spent on distraction devices like pot or booze. Those little numbers can grow into an avalanche of big numbers. In *The Sun Also Rises,* Ernest Hemingway wrote that there are two ways to go bankrupt: gradually, then suddenly. It pays to mind trends during the "gradual" phase.

If you'll pardon the circularity, the best way to monitor and predict the effect of the relationship is to honestly acknowledge the effects of the relationship by tending to the little barometers. Dispassionate observation lights the way.

Reject relationships that bring misery.

Imagine yourself in this scenario. You're at work. Your job is to oversee a large project, like a construction site or a software product. Your team is counting on your guidance, and important pieces of the project converge toward a looming deadline. It's stressful and thrilling. You feel alive.

Amid the action one exhilarating morning, your cellphone rings. It's her. You let her call go to voice mail because you can't afford the interruption at the moment.

She calls again. And again. You're no longer feeling so alive. You're beginning to feel burdened and cornered. This isn't the first time she has intruded on work.

A colleague notices and asks if some emergency requires your attention. "Everything's fine," you say. You don't tell them she has cried wolf so many times that you no longer trust any sign of urgency from her. It's probably just another conflict with a coworker, a fight with her sister, or hairballs from her cat.

Yet, at the same time, you know there will be a price to pay for ignoring her. You can already see how it will play out: another late-night argument that will leave you fatigued tomorrow. Your exhaustion will be your punishment for neglecting her during a crisis. She won't call it punishment, but she will torment you with an interminable midnight conversation about the state of your relationship.

You would rather she just kicked you in the groin. All these colliding thoughts and feelings distract you from the job. You just want the relationship drama to stop. Your focus is no longer on your exhilarating project; it's on reducing the emotional blowback from her.

Such scenarios simply don't happen in relationships that bring composure. There are no contrived emergencies in a healthy relationship. She doesn't cry wolf, nor does the relationship collide with your purpose.

Most men in chaotic relationships will tell you they had many opportunities to leave, and their failure to do so flooded their lives with chaos and capsized their ability to function effectively. Those men would advise the rest of us to notice the earliest signs of destructive chaos and to nip it in the bud. If you're like most men, no one told you this truth: you're allowed to reject soul-sucking relationships.

Pump the brakes.

In romance, speed kills. It kills your purpose, your goals, and your agency.

Neither women nor men have cornered the market on bad relationship choices, but there is one way in which we men outperform women in the race to screw up our lives: We are quicker than women to get attached. We're faster to become possessive over a woman before we understand what we will receive in exchange for our commitment.

In 2011, researchers asked women how quickly they would know they had chosen the right man, and how quickly they would know whether his feelings were mutual. The women speculated they would know within a few months. Men, however, reported "knowing" within a few weeks. It's absurd to think we can understand a person, or a relationship, in such a brief period. Blame the emotional mind. It wants what it wants, and it wants it *now*.[33]

The findings of that experiment line up with my clinical experience. Men are quick to get attached and to declare their devotion. That increases the risk of making bad decisions. However, I have also noticed a bright side. Men are also quicker to pump the brakes once the commitment takes hold. In my experience, it's women who want to escalate the relationship quickly after they feel committed.

That contradiction in our behavior—we come on strong, then we back off—can be a jarring experience for women. Yet there is wisdom (even if it's accidental) in our hesitance to escalate too quickly. Research from the University of Denver found men and women who cohabit out of convenience are likely to marry even if the relationship is subpar. Momentum is a powerful factor in relationship decisions. If a man isn't intentional, he can put his future on an entirely new trajectory with little more than the joint purchase of a couch.[34]

Family, friends, and community also add to the pressure to commit. Parents want grandchildren; married couples want married friends. We even hear it from movies and entertainment where only the courtship matters. The message seems to be: get to the altar and ignore whatever might come later.

Well-intentioned friends may insist you should play house to test the strength of the relationship. Or she might pressure you to capitalize on the conveniences of living together by offering the tempting illusion of a simplified life and easy access to sex. (In reality, you each get the responsibilities of marriage without the benefits or the commitment.)

Chaos often hides itself until the infatuation phase wears off. That means the relationship might be peachy when you move in

---

33 Harrison, M. A., and J. Shortall. 2011. "Women and Men in Love: Who Really Feels It and Says It First?" *Journal of Social Psychology* 151: 727-736.

34 Stanley, S. M., G. K. Rhoades, and H. J. Markman. 2006. "Sliding Versus Deciding: Inertia and the Premarital Cohabitation Effect." *Family Relations* 55: 499-509.

and sour a few weeks later. The less you know about her when you make major commitments, the easier it is to write a story about the relationship, and the harder it is to notice your story is wrong—until it's too late.

The remedy? Pump the brakes. Wait until infatuation wears off—when you're no longer idealizing each other and you see her as a three-dimensional person with both charms and peccadilloes. Time and shared experiences will show you the true nature of the relationship and what this commitment might bring into your life.

Of course, other people might not appreciate you taking your time. They might feel disappointed or angry. Should you care? That brings us to the first of our five foundational gatekeeping skills.

Foundational Skill: Allow Others to Experience Discomfort

Every gatekeeper must possess a few foundational emotional skills, a sort of relationship armory. In the service of avoiding destructive chaos, one of the most important gatekeeping skills is the ability and willingness to tolerate the discomfort of others; to let them be sad, angry, or disappointed with our decisions.

It sounds easy on paper, but it's difficult for duty-driven men.

When we try to protect others from discomfort, it's often our own discomfort we're avoiding. Conscientious, duty-driven men usually don't enjoy the anxiety *we* feel in response to other people's discomfort. We're avoiding our own emotions more than theirs. Men can reach this condition by various paths.

Consider the man drawn to damsels in distress. He sees a woman suffering (often at her own hand), and he feels anxious about it. He may even become confused and believe he is the source of her discomfort if he doesn't rescue her.

Or consider the man who is tormented by the presence of any unhappy woman. In his experience, a woman cannot merely be unhappy. She must also be angry, rejecting, abusive, or scornful.

His sense of worth becomes fused to his ability to calm the women in his life.

Or how about the man who has simply fallen prey to the nice-guy syndrome described by Dr. Robert Glover in his book *No More Mr. Nice Guy*. This man fantasizes that others will treat him well if he caters to them. He operates on hidden, unspoken agreements. *If I work hard, my boss will promote me. If I give my coworker credit for my work, he will return the favor. If I wash the dishes, she will want to have sex with me.*

Unfortunately, the world doesn't play along with those covert contracts, as Dr. Glover calls them. These men are then primed to become indignant when others neglect the obligation they never even knew about. Lacking another strategy, the nice guy then compounds his problem by trying harder to be "nice."

The dirty little secret is that they're not really being "nice." They're trying to get what they want in an indirect and manipulative way. Keeping others comfortable, while unworkable, is a survival strategy for these men.[35]

Living in the service of values means suffering for them. It requires sacrifices, disappointments, setbacks, heartbreaks, fatigue, failure, and of course, the pain of disappointing others or losing relationships. The man who is unwilling to tolerate others' discomfort will struggle to make necessary sacrifices for his values.

Whatever the various motivations for keeping others comfortable to their own detriment, these men all rely on external validation. Their own values take a back seat to the fleeting comfort of approval, thanks to a common false dilemma: *Either people are happy with me, or I am failing.*

There is a third path: tolerating our own anxiety about disapproval. Like most anxieties, allowing others to be uncomfortable is almost never as bad as we think it will be. As psychologists Steven

35 Glover, R. 2000. *No More Mr. Nice Guy: A Proven Plan for Getting What You Want In Love, Sex, and Life*. Philadelphia, PA: Running Press. According to Dr. Glover, this is one of the central beliefs of the nice-guy: "If I can hide my flaws and become what I think others want me to be, then I will be loved, get my needs met, and have a problem-free life." Eventually, it backfires.

Hayes and Kirk Strosahl wrote, "Unwillingness to have anxiety predicts having anxiety in many different forms." The inverse is equally true: we can steal anxiety's power by settling in with it, by defying it, and by knowing that facing it won't kill us. If we can learn to laugh at our own anxiety, like learning to laugh at a schoolyard bully, then it doesn't stand a chance against us.[36]

If a relationship can only exist in the complete absence of tension, or in our unquestioning allegiance to the other party's agenda, then that relationship needs to be excised like a tumor.

36 Hayes, S. C., and K. D. Strosahl. 2004. *A Practical Guide to Acceptance and Commitment Therapy*. New York: Springer.

FLIGHT CHECK

- **Organizing principles.** Think back on your childhood relationships with girls and women. Did you develop behaviors toward them that once protected you but which now serve you poorly? What might they be?
- **Composure.** Would you describe your upbringing as mostly stable? Were your parents present and reliable? Or was your upbringing characterized by instability, chaotic events, or uncertainty? How would you say this aspect of your earliest relationships has shaped your romantic decisions?
- **Agency.** What's it like when women are unhappy with your decisions? Have you ever sacrificed your values or purpose to avoid female disapproval, anxiety, or unhappiness? Up to this point, what have you believed to be your role or responsibilities toward women?

— BOOK II —

Dignity

Identify the role of shame in romantic choices • Choose commitments that fuel dignity • Act in the service of values before comfort

Dignity and shame are opposing sides of the same coin. To be dignified is to be worthy of respect: stately, noble, and reserved. Dignity puts steam in a man's stride, to borrow a phrase from my grandfather.

To be riddled with shame is to feel degraded, small, and foolish. Shame is immobilizing. A man can't thrive in that condition. Why, then, do people experience shame? What's its purpose?

The purpose of primary emotions—happiness, sadness, fear, anger, disgust—is pretty straightforward. They exist to motivate us toward comfort and survival and away from discomfort and threats. Primary emotions cause us to act in response to the physical environment.

Shame is different. Rather than calling for action, it calls for inaction. It's an emotional system—along with guilt, gratitude, grief, depression, and compassion—that evolutionary psychologists consider "recalibrational." These states of emotion exist in relation to our social environment rather than our physical one. They compel us to slow down and check our behavior so we remain in good graces with others.

Shame's particular function is to make us small and silent so we create as few waves as possible and don't repeat whatever behavior causes others to disapprove. It makes us think, *I better sit down, shut up, and figure out why I'm in hot water*.[37]

The closer we are to someone, the likelier we are to experience shame when they are unhappy with us. Shame protects the relationship by motivating us to adjust our behavior. Crucially, the more committed we are to a relationship (or trapped in it), the more affected we are by shame—or manipulated by it, as the case may be.[38]

The power behind shame lies in the threat of exclusion. No one wants to get kicked out of the clan. That means the person who knows he has done the right thing might be as vulnerable to shame as someone who has committed a transgression. The threat of exclusion can be misused and weaponized. Under the right conditions, a man can be shamed into compliance even when he knows he has done nothing wrong.[39]

---

37 Cosmides, L., and J. Tooby. 2016. "The Theoretical Foundations of Evolutionary Psychology." In *The Handbook of Evolutionary Psychology, Volume 1*, edited by D. M. Buss. Hoboken, NJ: John Wiley and Sons.

38 Sznycer, D., K. Takemura, A. W. Delton, K. Sato, T. E. Robertson, L. Cosmides, and J. Tooby. 2012. "Cross-Cultural Differences and Similarities in Proneness to Shame: An Adaptationist and Ecological Approach." *Evolutionary Psychology* 10: 252-370. This cross-cultural study found some cultures (East Asian cultures, for example) are more shame-prone than others (such as the United States and the United Kingdom). People experience shame when they learn their reputation may be diminished in the minds of others. Across cultures, shame proneness was higher among friends than strangers, and we're more likely to feel shame in important relationships when we don't feel we can easily form new ones. The study did not discuss marriages or romantic relationships, but these relationships, by definition, are difficult to replace, making them fertile grounds for shame.

39 Robertson, T. E., D. Sznycer, A. W. Delton, J. Tooby, and L. Cosmides. 2018. "The True Trigger of Shame: Social Devaluation Is Sufficient, Wrongdoing Is Unnecessary." *Evolution and Human Behavior* 39: 566-573.

Men who have an insufficient ability to experience shame—the type of men who might become career criminals or politicians—never voluntarily allow themselves to feel small or degraded. They rarely recalibrate their behavior for the sake of remaining in good standing with others. Instead, they recalibrate to manipulate others or avoid punishment.

At the other end of the spectrum are men who routinely marinate in shame. They live in an ongoing state of feeling degraded, small, and foolish. They "recalibrate" themselves practically into nonexistence. That's why the man trapped in a shame-based relationship usually has the bearing of a small boy. He's trying to stay out of trouble with an overbearing maternal figure. He's distressed. Embarrassed. He seems physically smaller than he should be. He might wear a smile, as shame-faced people often do, but he's taking up as little space as possible.

If this describes you to any degree, I'll hazard a guess that an overzealous propensity toward shame once served you well. It was a survival mechanism to preempt punishment.

A behavioral principle is at play when a man falls into such a miserable pattern. It involves an open secret all couples understand but few will say aloud: We train our significant others the same way we train dogs. We offer ongoing encouragement for behavior we like, and we discourage behavior we dislike. It's called *operant conditioning*, and every Psych 101 class covers it.

Healthy couples rely on reward more than punishment. They express gratitude and affection. They give to each other simply because it feels rewarding to do so.

Unhealthy relationships are more transactional. They rely on punishment and quid pro quo exchanges. These couples shout and criticize. They take passive-aggressive jabs or subject one another to the silent treatment. They withhold affection, and they track little slights and errors to build a case against one another. These are all forms of petty punishment and coercion.

However, take note of an insidious little tactic common in unhealthy couples. Technically, it's a reward rather than a punishment, and that's what makes it so devious. It's called *negative rein-*

forcement. It's difficult to see if you don't know what you're looking for, but it's a tremendously important concept for the shame-prone man to understand.

Negative reinforcement rewards behavior by removing an aversive stimulus. For example, suppose you have a headache. You take an aspirin, and the headache vanishes. The relief you experience negatively reinforces the act of taking aspirin, which increases the likelihood you'll take aspirin next time you have a headache.

Unhealthy couples rely on negative reinforcement. It's the coin of the realm. *I'll stop punishing you if you do what I want.* It usually takes the form of unspoken blackmail:

- *You want me to stop yelling? Then take out the trash.*
- *You want me to stop harassing you at work? Then pay attention to me.*
- *You want me to stop giving you the silent treatment? Then figure out why I'm angry.*

Why is negative reinforcement an important concept in a discussion on dignity? Because shame is uniquely aversive to men when it's applied by women. We're vulnerable to their shaming tactics because women are important to us. Remember: shame is designed to protect relationships. Most men don't like to be on bad terms with women, so their disapproval is the headache we want to eliminate. Some of us will jump through any hoop to find the "aspirin."

In my clinical experience, it's clear that shame is a weapon wielded to devastating effect by unhealthy women. Consider nagging, shaming messages such as these:

- "What kind of man spends that much time with his friends?"
- "No man I know would let people walk all over him like that."
- "A real man would earn more money."

The subtext to messages like these is, "Shame on you. You're a disappointment." The shame-driven man will try to eliminate the feeling of shame by doing what's implicitly asked. He wants that sweet negative reinforcement. This is what manipulative and abusive relationships look like.

If conditions are right, shame disconnects from a man's behavior and attaches to his very existence. Rather than simply causing him to reevaluate his behavior, it leads him to think of himself as worthless and undignified. His shame is ever-present and ripe for the picking by anyone willing to exploit it.

These men, prone to shame and self-loathing, tend to find women who can deliver it with stunning efficiency. They get lost in a cycle of negative reinforcement, always trying to eliminate shame that is so ever-present and overwhelming they can't see it clearly. These men might experience fleeting moments of relief when others aren't displeased, but soon enough, it's back to business as usual: desperately trying to fend off disapproval.

A streak of that man exists in most of us, or at least those of us who care about our standing in the community. An insidious trap lies within. We can fall into a cycle of trying to preempt disapproval by stifling and limiting our behavior to only that which we believe others will accept without punishing us. Making ourselves small and unobtrusive earns us sweet negative reinforcement: if we do nothing that displeases others, then we won't experience their disapproval.

Let's give this pattern a name: compulsive self-policing.

Compulsive Self-Policing

As we dive into this soul-crushing, shame-based behavior, recall these three aspects of the subterranean emotional mind:

- Rewards of varying frequency and intensity—the slot-machine effect—are powerful motivators.
- Negative reinforcement is a reward by way of removing an aversive or painful stimulus.

- Shame is an emotional experience that causes us to slow down and recalibrate our behavior.

When these three behavioral principles collide, they create ideal conditions for *compulsive self-policing*. Men in shame-based relationships monitor themselves endlessly in the hopes of preempting the disapproval of their women. They rarely realize they're doing it.

Self-policing isn't about being polite or reasonably accommodating, though we may tell ourselves that's what we're doing. It is instead an anxious compulsion to avoid disapproval, often because disapproval has led to unreasonable reactions in the past, such as abuse or hysterical meltdowns. Pervasive shame can make us submissive in hopes we can avoid re-experiencing such punishment.

In my profession, "compulsion" refers to anxious behaviors like hoarding, checking locks, or chasing down sex with strangers. Those kinds of anxious compulsions relieve tension in the moment, but they cause distress in the long run. The person who compulsively checks locks, for example, goes through a cycle of mounting tension. *Did I check the lock? I'm certain I did. Did I? I don't want to check it again but … argh! I have to check it!*

Checking the lock relieves tension, but only temporarily. The mind can immediately descend back into doubt. In the worst cases, it just won't let go no matter how many times you check the damned lock. (Recovery usually involves counterintuitively learning not to care when the mind perseverates.)

That type of compulsion is coercion from within. It's the emotional mind saying, *This awful feeling will go away if you simply do as I say: check the lock.* It's self-propelled, self-contained negative reinforcement. All the while, freedom withers. Every moment spent checking and re-checking locks is a moment of life stolen by anxiety.

The man who compulsively self-polices in relationships has learned—in a manner similar to the man who compulsively checks locks—that it's less painful to suppress his own normal behavior than to let women punish him.

For example, this man might want to have a drink with his buddies after work, but he stifles the desire in order to avoid disapproval from his wife or girlfriend. She doesn't need to shame him into compliance because he shames and silences himself. He's like the man who compulsively checks locks in that he gets a moment of short-term relief from anxiety by sacrificing a little piece of his freedom.

How do men end up so emasculated? Usually by some combination of predisposition and having been neutered by a thousand cuts. That's what happened to Marcus, our next case study.

Marcus and Jamie

Marcus had been a dedicated jiu jitsu student for several years when he started dating Jamie. Unfortunately, she wasn't supportive. She quickly became jealous of his training schedule. That was the beginning of his descent into shame-based self-policing.

It started innocently enough, or so it seemed at the time. Marcus trained three evenings per week, after which Jamie always sent him text messages such as "I miss you" or "When can you call me?" In retrospect, Marcus realized her texts seemed more needy than flirtatious. The messages weren't about her affection for him. They were about how she suffered in his absence.

Soon enough, he sacrificed a class every couple of weeks because she had scheduled an activity like dinner with friends or movie tickets. *No big deal,* he thought. *People make compromises in relationships.*

Still, he felt conflicted. He noticed she wasn't asking for his time. She was confiscating it, and she pouted if he resisted. This didn't feel like compromise. It felt like emotional blackmail. He dismissed the concern by telling himself, *No big deal. She just wants to be with me.*

Despite his niggling doubts, they moved in together. (I'll forgo my usual rant about reckless entanglement so we can stick to the point of this case study.) That's when she turned the screws, urging him to skip classes to spend more time with her. She said things like:

- "What kind of couple are we if we don't spend our evenings together?"
- "It's time for you to get into boyfriend mode."
- "I don't know why we live together if you're not committed to this relationship."

Her messages shamed him, as if to say, "A real man would make me feel secure."

Marcus succumbed to the manipulation. He reduced his training to two evenings per week, and it came at a cost. His classmates razzed him for missing class, and he noticed they were learning more than he was. This was his first double-bind with Jamie: he could endure her shaming, or he could sacrifice his training.

A quick aside. Double-binds are contradictory demands, such as:

- *Be spontaneous, but not like that.*
- *Don't do it because I asked; do it because you want to.*
- *Make more money, but spend more time with me.*

There is no winning response to a double-bind; there is only the lesser of punishments. Marcus reckoned the least painful option was to spend increasing amounts of time with Jamie and away from his training. Though it was his choice, he resented her for it.

Some readers might think, *Who cares if she's angry? He should stand up for himself!* Doing so is easy for some men. For Marcus, it was difficult for a couple of reasons.

First, Marcus was agreeable by disposition. He simply didn't like conflict. Second, his mother and sisters had taught him that angry women can be vindictive and punitive. He had developed an organizing principle concerning women with whom he had close relationships:

> *Women are volatile and easily enraged. It is my responsibility to keep them calm.*

He had fallen into the cycle of compulsive self-policing. He tried to avoid punishment by tamping down his desires. Of course, that approach has a built-in problem: the more he sacrificed for Jamie, the more she wanted. Thanks to her insecurity, Jamie had an insatiable need for demonstrations of commitment. Today's grand gesture of commitment became tomorrow's baseline expectation.

Marcus had to devote increasing effort to avoiding her displeasure, which meant sacrificing increasing amounts of his own needs and desires. He felt as though she were constantly scrutinizing and testing his devotion. Soon enough, he ran every personal decision through this filter: *If I do this thing, will it upset Jamie?*

When their relationship began, Jamie policed him with small demands and expressions of disappointment. She subtly shamed him into compliance. Within a few months, Marcus policed himself—and she was no happier than before.

❄ ❄ ❄

Shame has a place in interpersonal relationships ... a small place. It gets a bad rap, as if we need to eliminate it entirely. That's only true in its most pernicious form, where our identity and relationships revolve around the sense that we are fundamentally flawed. That kind of pervasive shame belongs on the trash heap. However, justified shame helps us recalibrate before we permanently damage important relationships. It's difficult to earn trust and connection without an internal governor, and that's where the capacity for shame comes in handy.

One group of researchers examined the mental architecture by which people compute each other's social value, as well as their own. The research suggests we use private, recalibrative emotions to predict how our behavior affects our standing. Experiences like pride and shame help us determine whether we're worth keeping around, and we adjust accordingly because they give us a sense of how others perceive us.[40]

Pride feels wonderful. It makes us stand tall and look people in the eye. It's an internal barometer that says others value us at

---

40 Sznycer, D., D. Xygalatas, S. Alama, et al. 2018. "Invariances in the Architecture of Pride Across Small-Scale Societies." *PNAS Proceedings of the National Academy of Sciences of the United States of America* 115: 8322-8327.

the moment. As a result, we expand our behavior and take up space. We act with confidence when we can honestly tell ourselves, *I slayed the beast today. Everyone knows my value.*

Shame feels awful. Shame says, *Sit down, shut up, and figure out what you're doing wrong before you make things worse.* According to the researchers, displaying shame is essentially an admission of guilt and a request for forgiveness.

In our relationships with women (this is me talking, not the researchers), this predictive system can go terribly awry in men. If a man who is motivated by approval (as many of us are) meets a woman who relies on shaming others to get her needs met (as some women do), then he is at risk of sacrificing his values to avoid her disapproval. He can burn his purpose at the altar of her consent, even at the expense of his reputation in the larger community.

That's exactly what Marcus did. He neglected himself and his purpose. He sacrificed important, collegial relationships. He was so busy avoiding shame that he deprived himself of pride. His jiu jitsu classmates noticed, and their ribbing was *their* way of trying to shame him back into being the self-possessed man they once knew. It's heartbreaking to be disappointed by a friend or colleague who has pledged his allegiance to a shame-based romantic relationship. Imagine this written on your tombstone: "He accomplished nothing of value because he spent his life trying to avoid the disapproval of women."

Not good. The cherry on top? Men who fall into this trap lose the respect of the women to whom they're catering. Those women can see how their men have sacrificed their value to society. They can see their beaten spirits and diminished effectiveness more clearly than the men can, and the women don't respect it one bit. Why should they?

Men don't sign up for that relationship dynamic because it looks fun. We can usually trace it to childhood, when every important aspect of a boy's life was in the hands of an unreasonable authority figure. Such was the case for Marcus. Decades later, he was still catering to the emotional whims of a controlling woman—a woman he himself placed in a position of authority.

She probably didn't even want that authority and craved a man with a backbone. Pervasive shame and self-policing deprived both of their desires. Pervasive shame is a sneaky bastard that operates beneath the surface and beyond our awareness, but we might as well be wearing shackles for its limiting effects on us.

Marcus was susceptible to Jamie's manipulation because it felt familiar. Jamie had difficulty regulating feelings like fear and anger, but she was sophisticated at controlling others so that she wouldn't have to encounter the intensity of her own emotions. Marcus learned to navigate that treatment long before he met Jamie.

Their respective emotional challenges were part of their affinity for each other, though they didn't realize it. She found someone she could manage more easily than she could manage her emotions, and he found a controlling woman who fit his organizing principle. He didn't enjoy the dynamic, but perhaps some part of him enjoyed knowing how to operate within it. This is what happens when a relationship is governed by interlocking sets of counterproductive emotional logic.

As always, the first step toward overcoming the machinations of emotional logic is not to silence the emotional mind but simply to heed the impulse when it's useful—shame, in this case—and disregard it when it's misplaced. After all, shame has a place within healthy, high-functioning relationships.

For example, maybe a guy forgets he had plans with his girlfriend, or he went too far with a joke, or he inadvertently insulted her mother. These little one-off mistakes cause hurt feelings. That's when well-adjusted people experience a pang of shame: *I screwed up. I better slow down and adjust my heading.*

Here's the piece that's missing for so many men: When he takes responsibility and makes a corrective plan, *that should be the end of the matter*. A mature, healthy woman doesn't dwell and punish. She forgives and moves on, never to bring it up again unless her man forces her to by repeating the careless behavior. She doesn't weaponize shame, use it as a bartering chip, or add it to her ever-growing grudge.

Shame will dissipate when the relationship is back in order, provided the man in question has a healthy relationship with shame. The apology says, *I understand how I hurt you. It wasn't my intent. I will take specific measures to ensure it doesn't happen again.*

Forgiveness says, *I also value our relationship. I will disregard what happened because I believe you didn't intend to hurt me.*[41]

This is how shame functions in a healthy relationship. It shows up only when needed. Because so many men experience shame as a bludgeon, it needs to be spelled out: *shame is meant to be a transient experience that repairs the relationship.*

Our safeguard against being manipulated by shame—our path to dignity—is in keeping pride and shame closely tied to the pursuit of values and purpose rather than to the approval of any single person. Had Marcus kept his eyes on his purpose, he could have avoided those first distasteful concessions to Jamie's demands. He could have protected himself from the endless pursuit of negative reinforcement, which is like a beaten dog trying to predict and avoid his master's displeasure.

What my father's generation called "pussy-whipped" is more precisely understood as a pattern of doing what women want in order to avoid the anxiety that accompanies their disapproval. Self-policing isn't necessarily the realm of soft-willed, spineless men. Even the most capable and resourceful men are susceptible if their personalities and relationship training created the predisposition. Countless leaders of men are cowed into self-policing at home. Imagine how much more effective they could be if their romantic commitments were assets rather than liabilities.

A healthy woman wants you to succeed. She's happy when you're happy. Your commitments outside the relationship don't in-

41 See, for example, Rosenstock, S., and C. O'Connor. 2018. "When It's Good to Feel Bad: An Evolutionary Model of Guilt and Apology." *Frontiers in Robotics and AI* 5: 1-14. The authors wrote that guilt leads to three classes of behavior. "First, the anticipation of guilt prevents social transgression. … Second, the experience of guilt leads to a suite of reparative behaviors including apology, gift giving, acceptance of punishment, and self-punishment. … Lastly, expression of guilt leads to decreased punishing behaviors, and forgiveness, by group members."

timidate this woman, nor does she compete with your obligations. She understands that having a central place in your world means allowing your world to exist.

What Women Cannot Teach Men

Here's the paradox of self-policing: a man can't earn a woman's admiration by seeking it any more than a woman can earn a man's respect by demanding it. Men who are desperate for women's approval are handing their women the problem of defining their masculinity. They're saying, "Tell me how to be a man." What woman admires such a deficiency of self-determination?

Still, I'll wager that most of us (including me) have fallen into the self-policing trap, often by an upbringing that taught us female disapproval is dangerous. However, healthy women don't want the burden of telling us how to be useful or interesting. That's our job.

Besides, women aren't skilled at telling us how to be men of purpose. For example, the years preceding this book saw many feminist admonitions for men to be less competitive. Yet, any man who obeys that command places himself at a disadvantage in life. We can choose not to compete with the world, but the world will compete with us. It doesn't care if we sit on the sidelines.

That misguided feminist message appeared prominently in a set of mental health treatment guidelines for working with boys and men, written by the American Psychological Association (APA). They wrote:

> "... traditional masculinity—marked by stoicism, competitiveness, dominance and aggression—is, on the whole, harmful."[42]

The mission statement from the APA group responsible for the guidelines said it "acknowledges its historical debt to feminist-in-

42 Pappas, S. 2019. "APA Issues First-Ever Guidelines for Practice with Men and Boys." *Monitor on Psychology* 50: 35-38.

spired scholarship on gender." They removed that acknowledgment from their website after receiving public pushback against their guidelines.

But true to their redacted acknowledgment, the authors of the guidelines proposed a new feminist-based recipe for masculinity, and they encouraged other mental health workers to evangelize their message in the clinic. Their message was clear: Men should be *less* stoic, *less* competitive, *less* dominant, and *less* aggressive—in other words, softer and more feminine. (Perhaps they modeled the new masculine ideal after themselves.)

The authors didn't seem to understand the upside of traditionally masculine traits, such as being stoic enough to remain composed in an emergency; competitive enough to possess clarity about goals and ambitions; dominant enough to be independent-minded and purpose-driven in the face of opposition; aggressive enough to strive for self-improvement. People who only see the downside to masculine traits can't teach us how to be men. They can't teach us how to walk with dignity.

Early family experience isn't the only influence on our relationships. This type of cultural messaging also seeps into our relationship patterns. On that front, I'd say men's biggest challenge is to resist the drumbeat of messages from people whose apparent goals amount to emasculation. Across cultures, healthy women prize men who possess the qualities that certain cultural and political factions disdain, and that makes me wonder if those factions really have men's best interests at heart.[43]

Men who mold themselves to the ever-shifting desires of others set themselves up for spectacularly unsatisfying relationships. It's the unapologetically purposeful man who is likeliest to succeed in life and in romance. He doesn't surrender his mission to the shifting winds of culture or to the disapproval of people who have no interest in his success.

---

43 Buss, D. M. 1989. "Sex differences in human mate preferences: Evolutionary hypotheses tested in 37 cultures." *Behavioral and Brain Sciences* 12: 1-49.

Consider the leader who must take a position unpopular among his subordinates, like reallocating funds or sending people on an unpopular assignment. He may not like it himself, but if he recognizes how the decision fits into a larger purpose, then shame becomes irrelevant. Values are the compass; purpose is the guide. *These* are the qualities women find attractive. That includes the willingness to make unpopular (but values-driven) decisions.

It's most men's nature to serve those around us. The ancient injunction that we produce more than we consume is, in my estimation, our glorious burden and the source of our joy. The benefits of unapologetically pursuing our purpose are innumerable, beginning with the sense of dignity a purposeful man feels in his bones.

There's a downside: it's easy for the dutiful man to sacrifice his own agenda in the service of approval-seeking. Bad actors can manipulate our drive to bring comfort by saying, "You want to make us happy? You want us to stop complaining? Be small, be quiet, and be domesticated." The skilled gatekeeper disregards those voices.

In so many cases, women who train their men to self-police do so because they have difficulty regulating their own emotional reactions. The reasoning is something like *If I can get you to stop upsetting me, then I won't have to feel the intensity and pain of my own emotions.* The man who signs on to that agenda creates a relationship in which his reason for being is simply to reduce the amount of griping he must endure. He chases negative reinforcement, prioritizing approval over purpose.

I believe men must mostly ignore feminine critiques of masculinity in order to reach our potential. The moment men allow women to dictate how we pursue our purpose is the moment we become precisely what repulses them. That doesn't mean we ignore their needs and desires. It simply means our purpose belongs to us, and it is not to be molded by negative reinforcement in shame-based relationships, nor is it to be influenced by cultural forces with questionable motives. Ironically, conscientious men who have the best intentions toward women and society seem to be the most vulnerable to such weaponized shame.

Why Men Choose Shame over Dignity

If a man's romantic relationships have the power to help him walk with dignity or the power to reduce him to a self-loathing ball of pervasive shame, why on earth would any man choose the latter?

The answer lies in the fact that the emotional mind is concerned foremost with not dying. It's happy if we get through the day without being eaten by a bear or hit by a bus. One of its favorite survival strategies is avoidance. It's the supercharged power tool for remaining not-dead, and it has much to do with pervasive shame.

It's a good survival strategy to avoid activities like swimming with sharks, parking on train tracks, handling venomous spiders, wandering into traffic, dancing on rooftops, taunting lions, and strolling past jet intakes ... There's no end of hazards to avoid in the world. That's why avoidance is one of our strongest instincts, passed down to us by ancestors who mastered the skill.

But what happens when the thing we're trying to avoid comes from within? You can walk away from a rattlesnake, but you can't simply walk away from an internal experience like the anxiety triggered by female disapproval. There's no "anxiety" switch we can simply turn off.

This is where a normal human being can veer into the avoidance trap we discussed in the chapter on composure. Emotional logic would have us routinely trade long-term discomfort for short-term relief. The alcoholic who drowns his thoughts and feelings is happy tonight, but tomorrow morning brings a new level of pain. That's the same basic dilemma of the man who trades his long-term dignity for momentary relief from shame.

In my clinical experience, breaking this type of pattern begins with giving the emotional mind a bit of grace. Some psychologists use the word "maladaptive" to describe self-destructive patterns. That suggests bad wiring. I find it more useful to assume such patterns come from old survival strategies that have outlived their usefulness. Good wiring; bad timing.

Shame is a tremendously aversive feeling. We want it to disappear. For some of us, the emotional mind insists we remain in the good graces of others, even if it's to our own detriment. That part of our mind operates on context more than specifics. Our more primitive structures don't know what time it is, but they know when a situation feels familiar.

Suppose a man grew up with a mother who used shame to control him. She didn't respond to normal childhood mischief and mistakes with compassionate corrections and genuine forgiveness. Instead, she treated him as if he were broken and contemptible. When he made a normal, honest mistake, she told him a good little boy would never act like him. There was no path to redemption for that boy, so he learned to avoid disapproval by being still and silent in her presence.

Why should that man's adult mind respond any differently to any woman who shows displeasure? Emotional logic operates on context less than on specifics, and the context is: *disapproving woman*. That's close enough for the emotional mind, so it sounds the alarm: *Sit down! Shut up! Get small!* It has its own nonverbal way of conveying that message.

Those parts of the brain we associate with emotional logic, like the limbic system, are nonverbal systems. Nevertheless, their messages are clear. When we're frightened, we know it. When we're disgusted, it's no secret. Hunger, joy, or rage? Those feelings are easy to identify.

However, feelings and motivations can be more nebulous when the emotional mind is acting out old organizing principles. If relationships have gone poorly, we're left with a vague cloud of emotion that feels like we're damaged or that trusting women is dangerous. That's when we're likely to overgeneralize with thoughts like *I will never succeed with women* or *Women hate guys like me*.

The mind that was sufficiently mistreated is snake-bit. It forevermore assumes danger lurks behind every bush. Old experiences can be an ever-present, overgeneralized, nonspecific dark cloud. The result? A vague feeling of dread, anger, sadness, or anxiety whenever we approach that old familiar relationship context. For many men, physical sensation is the first sign of an old principle taking control: tightness in the chest, fists clenched in defensive anger, a powerful urge to escape or to shut down. That's the language of an emotional mind struggling to avoid another painful experience.

We have already seen how organizing principles can be self-fulfilling. Rationally, we can wrap our intellect around the cause and effect of our earliest relationships, but the emotional mind doesn't think in those terms. It simply gets stuck in its pattern unless we intervene and give ourselves new experiences.

When we put words to those old, counterproductive organizing principles, we create options we didn't know we had. We can disobey the well-intentioned mandates of emotional logic but only when we know what we're up against. Without words, the emotional mind has free rein. We are likely to repeat that which we don't understand about ourselves.

Shame is so potent and so easily manipulated that I believe every man should take a hard look at his earliest lessons about shame to avoid reenacting destructive relationship patterns. The most ingrained lessons are those we learn early with the people on whom we depended for survival. If the adults in your childhood handled shame well, then great. Check that box and move on.

If they handled it poorly, then why not bring that history into the open? You can finally face the enemy when it's no longer hiding in the shadows. Shame shows up in the smallest of ways. The boy whose mother degraded him becomes the man who hesitates to hold the door for a stranger for fear of what his girlfriend might think. It's the mind's recalibrative system twisted against the self by a painful upbringing.

Most parents did the best they could, and most suffer from the fact that parenting is a tricky business. Those who handle shame skillfully make sure their kids have a way to succeed. They offer a path to redemption. If a child is struggling, a skillful parent figures out why and creates conditions for success. These parents focus on incentives and rewards rather than on punishment. They keep the home calm and peaceful. They guide the child in age-appropriate tasks, like keeping up with homework and learning how to navigate the social landscape.

Unskilled parents focus on disincentive and punishment. They dwell on failures. Whether from a lack of know-how or a more malevolent motive, they hope expressing anger or disappointment will motivate the child to improve. Here again, we see negative reinforcement: *I'll stop scolding you if you do what I want.* Their children often feel irredeemable and incompetent. They will freeze in the presence of any task that might earn disapproval.

In my clinical experience, mothers and fathers handle shame differently, and they leave us with different lessons about ourselves.

Good-enough mothers dispense this type of message: "You're perfect just as you are, sweetie." Too much of that hobbles a kid with entitlement, but every child needs some amount of that positive feminine messaging in order to possess basic self-regard.

Good-enough fathers provide a different, complementary experience: structure and warmth. Fathers roughhouse with their kids. They teach boundaries, risk management, and emotional regulation. Skilled fathers also provide this kind of message: "That was good, champ, but I think you can do better." This teaches children they have agency in the world, and they can handle setbacks and responsibility.

The healthy mother offers healing and nurturing, while the unhealthy mother offers injury and discouragement. The healthy father offers structure and challenge, while the unhealthy father brings chaos, along with the insult of low expectations or the demoralizing effect of impossible demands.

It probably goes without saying, but these messages aren't gender-bound. Good fathers also provide unconditional love, and good mothers also offer challenges. What matters is that a child experiences warmth, challenge, growth, and a consistent path to success and redemption.

Self-esteem also has a place in this discussion. Some people take that term to mean feeling good about ourselves in a way that is untethered from our performance. However, the famous behavioral psychologist B. F. Skinner gave self-esteem a more meaningful definition. He considered it the inverse of anxiety.

When we're anxious, we don't know what to do or we don't trust that our responses will have an effect. The man with self-esteem, however, can always find his bearing. He's not obsessed with feeling good about himself. He is consistently competent and accurately self-assessing.

The feminine and masculine influences in our early development shape our sense of shame and dignity, along with our self-esteem, in that classic sense of the term. These are powerful background forces in our relationship choices. When our earliest models were healthy, then shame and dignity are mere tools to improve our wisdom and choices. If they were unhealthy, then a guy might need to redefine his relationship to shame. (A good place to start is with a specific, detailed inventory of how others have manipulated him with shame.)

Men who are driven by shame often underestimate their value, so they commit themselves to low-value relationships. These men are eager to please and therefore deserving of women who won't take advantage. Instead, they choose women suffering from entitlement and abiding dissatisfaction. That drives these men further toward compulsive self-policing.

Their shame-based organizing principles (which we'll discuss shortly) don't allow them to recognize the possibility of healthier relationships. Those principles prime them, as always, to the familiar. They lead them to tolerate shaming behaviors like these:

- **Shifting the responsibility for managing emotions.** Rather than speaking directly about her sadness or anger, this woman criticizes her man's fundamental nature with statements like "Did you really need to say it that way?" or "Only someone with serious problems would act like that." These are ad hominem attacks. She is manipulating him into changing his behavior rather than expressing her pain or disappointment like a fully functioning adult.
- **Forcing him to play the guessing game.** Instead of explaining her needs or desires simply and clearly, she as-

serts that her man has failed before he has even tried. She uses statements like "If you cared about me, you would have known what I needed" or "Why are you so unfeeling?" This puts him in the position of having to guess why she's upset at present and to proactively guard against her disapproval in the future.

- **Emasculation.** Some women go directly for our masculinity with statements like "A real man would ..." rather than clearly stating their desires, expectations, or disappointments. This shaming tactic relies on subtle manipulations like "I guess I just expected more from you." They can also involve comparisons to other men showcased (for the moment) as the masculine ideal—for example, "I wish you were more like your brother."
- **Character assault.** "You always do that," is a common shaming tactic that shifts responsibility for a dispute entirely onto the target. The subtext is clear: *You hurt me because you are unthinking or unskilled. I bear no responsibility for the conflict.*
- **The silent treatment.** This shaming tactic involves withdrawing communication and affection. It's akin to saying, "Go stand in the corner and think about what you've done." Plenty of men put up with it because they simply haven't experienced mature conflict resolution.
- **Nagging and badgering.** This is a relentless, implicit *shame on you*. The target is always on the defensive, always striving for negative reinforcement. He alone bears the burden of improving the relationship. If he accepts that arrangement, he'll jump through hoops to get her off his back.
- **Exploiting regret and apologies.** In shame-based relationships, bad actors exploit apologies for points. A few examples: directly refusing an apology, responding with the silent treatment, dodging responsibility for her contribution to the problem, or continuing to punish after accepting an apology.

- **Blame-shifting.** Some women are adept at mistreating their men then playing the victim. It's the "I wouldn't have mistreated you if you hadn't hurt me" argument. Mature adults do not approach their relationships from a stance of righteous victimhood.
- **Emotional sucker punches.** A particularly nasty shaming tactic is to demand that we disclose our feelings then deliver a sucker punch by telling us to man up, stop feeling that way, or stop being dramatic. It's the emotional equivalent of Lucy pulling the ball away when Charlie Brown tries to kick it. This behavior has absolutely no place in healthy relationships.

The common theme in these tactics? They all imply that we alone bear the responsibility for repairing the relationship. These shaming tactics put us back on our heels. If a man operates under the sort of organizing principle that makes him vulnerable to shaming tactics, then his mind will do what minds do: Run toward the burning barn of the familiar. That involves doing whatever is necessary—however undignified—to eliminate the feeling of shame.

Pathways to Shame

What makes men vulnerable to shame-based relationships? Time to get into the specifics. Let's look at a sampling of organizing principles. If any of them feel familiar or elicit a gut reaction, I hope you'll pause and give it a more accurate description. As always, we will follow this section with strategies for getting past these relationship patterns.

I have to take whatever attention I can get.

Unhealthy, shaming parents are hypersensitive to imperfection in their children, and they are overly critical of mistakes and shortcomings. As his parents judge and criticize, this child develops the belief that he's broken and that no amount of effort will earn approval. If he succeeds at a thing, the parents move the goalpost and deny him the victory.

Imagine (and some of you won't have to try very hard) growing up in an environment where warmth and acceptance are conditional based mostly on how a child makes the parents feel about themselves. If the kid does well in school, the parents get a break from their own self-doubt. If the boy does poorly at an activity—sports are a common example—the parents experience turmoil that they can only exorcise by shaming the child into better performance next time.

This boy is likely to become a man who believes he is only as good as he can make others feel about themselves. He can only catch brief glimpses of acceptance. Nor does he believe he's worthy of a healthy relationship with a woman who treats him well. That's simply not yet in his vocabulary. He thinks he has hit the jackpot if people merely tolerate him. Being demeaned doesn't feel like an insult; it simply feels normal.

I have to be what others want me to be.

Imagine a different child who grew up in a different home. This kid's parents created a high-conflict atmosphere where he often had to witness loud arguments over trivial topics that masked deeper issues. They screamed at each other about potato salad or the TV remote instead of calmly negotiating their needs and expectations.

Different kids will react in different ways to that type of war zone. Some will act out by fighting or failing classes. (Teachers and other authority figures might overlook his difficulties and dismiss him as having "behavioral problems.") Other children will try to avoid trouble by being the good kid. This child reckons the best way to avoid conflict is to mold himself to the expectations of others. (This boy's difficulties are also overlooked because he doesn't draw attention to himself.)

His parents may never have attempted to heap shame on him. Still, whenever there were problems, he figured it was because he failed to keep the peace. It's simply how a child's mind works. That boy is likely to become a man who ruminates over every mistake.

It takes effort for him to learn that people can be unhappy and it's not a reflection on him. Even if his rational side understands that, his emotional logic can still operate on the principle that he must make others comfortable at all costs.

I have never been worthy of a healthy relationship.

This man has never possessed a realistic appraisal of his own value. There are many paths to this organizing principle, and they typically involve messages of inadequacy that go back to a man's earliest days.

Maybe this man got off to a poor start at school, and his teachers were uncaring or critical rather than encouraging. Maybe his parents were distant or preoccupied, and they didn't notice his struggles. Whatever the case, this boy was adrift and left to sort out childhood and adolescence on his own. He didn't know he should have had more support, especially when he struggled, so he placed blame on the only person he could control: himself. He concluded early in life that he was inept and inadequate.

That pattern has a nasty way of propelling itself indefinitely, partly because others detect his lack of confidence. They assume he's incompetent because that's how he views himself, so that's what he projects. (People usually believe what we project about ourselves.)

This man falls into a pattern of looking and feeling like a failure, even though he has never really explored his full capabilities. Unless he lucks into finding people who believe in him, he will surround himself with friends, bosses, and girlfriends who refuse to be satisfied. He simply clicks with people who see him the way he sees himself: good-natured but inept.

If he isn't careful, he will develop an endless supply of *poor me*, and he might come to rely on sympathy from those occasional cheerleaders in his life. A statement like "I can't believe she doesn't appreciate everything you do for her" is enough of a jackpot to keep him going for more.

At its extreme, this belief can veer into dark territory. This man can become obsessed with winning praise and admiration instead of repairing his broken sense of self. When sympathy and admiration from one person run dry, he finds a new supplier.

This is the narcissistic personality style. It only thrives under a special predisposition and circumstance. One study suggests people with a narcissistic personality style often had parents who thought their children were special and deserved special treatment, while simultaneously being cold and distant.[44]

By demanding special treatment, these parents were outsourcing to other adults the affection they were incapable of offering to their own children. It should be no surprise when this boy becomes a man who outsources to others the approval he cannot find within himself. At the extreme, this man doesn't merely have an external point of reference for his self-worth; he actively cultivates a rotating cadre of ego-attendants to soothe his lack of self-worth.

More ordinarily, he's simply caught on the inadequacy treadmill, never benefiting from realistic self-appraisal or a sense that he can attain a relationship in which he is valued. As a result, he's over-reliant on external approval to regulate his sense of self. He is ripe for manipulation by any unscrupulous soul willing to capitalize on his need for validation.

I'm only as good as her current level of happiness.

This organizing principle has as many paths leading to it as there are men to travel them, but they all have this in common: they believe they are only as good as their most recent attempt to please whomever they have appointed as their external source of validation. Once upon a time, it may have been his mother, whose

---

44 Brummelman, E., S. Thomaes, S. A. Nelemans, B. O. de Castro, G. Overbeek, and B. J. Bushman. 2015. "Origins of Narcissism in Children." *PNAS* 112: 3659-3662. The authors noticed that a narcissistic personality style is acquired, in part, by internalizing parents' beliefs that they are superior to others and entitled to privileges. A more functional self-regard, on the other hand, was predicted by parents' ability to express admiration and appreciation for their children rather than overvaluation.

happiness was the barometer by which he measured *his* happiness. Maybe now it's his girlfriend.

This man doesn't know how to regulate his sense of dignity. No one taught him that skill. When she's unhappy, he gets anxious and he goes to work. If he can please her, then the anxiety will vanish … for now.

It's a trap, of course. Each time he experiences her satisfaction, his pattern of approval-seeking behavior is negatively reinforced. It grows stronger with each repetition. Keeping her happy comes at the expense of his values and purpose. A healthy woman would begrudge him for the burden of being the center of his universe, so he seeks less healthy women who are willing to fill that role.

I'm damaged goods.

This man has been so mistreated that he believes he is meant to be used, abused, and disregarded. He organizes his relationships around the belief that important people will eventually betray or mistreat him, or that those who aren't abusive will see how damaged he is and turn away in revulsion.

Men who view themselves in this way often suffered at the hands of the people responsible for their care. They may have even been co-opted in their own abuse by being forced to lie and protect their abusers.

Such experiences in childhood, adolescence, or even adulthood can lead a man to believe no one would want him if they truly knew him. As a result, his relationships are often fleeting and shallow. These men sometimes rely on compulsive sex with multiple women who soon recede from their lives—or he ousts them from his life if they strive for a deeper connection with him.

Who can blame him? His earliest lessons about intimacy involved betrayal, pain, or even the shame of being physically or sexually abused. His life becomes organized around seeking connections while simultaneously avoiding real intimacy so he won't be "found out" as the damaged person he believes himself to be.

As always, this principle operates beneath verbal awareness until we drag it into the light of day. Sometimes the only sign it exists is a string of short-lived, chaotic relationships.

Therapy is a good place to dismantle this view of oneself. The task involves putting words to the swirl of emotion to create a coherent narrative around the history of senseless abuse, and to open the possibility of meaningful connections with adults who are capable of kindness and loyalty.

This takes hard work because the expectation of betrayal makes relationships terrifying. Even the healthiest relationships involve harmless errors that, to the emotional mind, resemble betrayal and incite the urge to flee. A skilled, male-friendly therapist can help navigate those dicey waters.

I don't trust myself to make sound decisions.

One mark of good parenting is encouraging children to make mistakes while the stakes are low. If a young child spills food, the skilled parent will playfully teach them how to clean it up rather than shaming and scolding the child. If the kid misses a homework assignment, the skilled parent won't become a harsh taskmaster but will empathize over the challenges of deadlines and coach the child on how to work more efficiently. If a teenager oversleeps and misses an obligation, the skilled parent will strategize with him about time management rather than shaming him or becoming his personal alarm clock.

The skilled parent also creates age-appropriate guardrails. They don't allow small children to learn about cleanliness by spilling boiling-hot soup, the grade-schooler to learn about responsibility by missing an entire week of school, or the teenager to learn about money by accumulating credit card debt.

Kids need to experience manageable discomfort, not catastrophes. They need to experience natural contingencies like skinned knees and disappointed teachers, and they need their parents to help them succeed by meeting their errors with warmth and good humor.

The parent who acts as a caring coach rather than an overbearing supervisor helps his kid develop a healthy relationship with mistakes. He's also teaching resilience, tenacity, and the ability to keep honest mistakes emotionally uncoupled from his value as a person.

I'm describing normal, sane parenting because, unfortunately, many men haven't experienced it. The boy who was punished for normal mistakes can become the man who doesn't trust himself. For him, errors aren't recoverable events. They're a source of pervasive shame.

If he's not careful, he can become so frightened of errors that he becomes the know-it-all who can't learn from others. "His cup is full" as a martial arts instructor of mine said about that type of insecure student. Such students couldn't contain new information. It just spilled over the brim.

A different reaction to a man's sense of ineptitude is for him to choose overbearing women who correct small mistakes. He can avoid big mistakes by choosing a woman who scolds him for small deviations. She provides a twisted version of the guardrails he didn't receive as a child. Earlier, we discussed self-policing as shame-based behavior. This man doesn't even trust himself to self-police. He outsources that to an overbearing woman.

If he can't find an overbearing woman, he'll make one by teaching her to resent his mistakes. He will be so needy and apologetic and put so much pressure on her to approve of him that she can only stick around under the unspoken agreement that she will act as his supervisor.

My decisions were never my own.

This is another organizing principle arising from a childhood in which normal mistakes were unacceptable. Overprotectiveness is often the culprit behind this principle.

There's a reason we let kids ride bikes on side streets rather than motorcycles on freeways. Skilled parents let their kids make low-stakes errors. As I discussed earlier, a good dad usually lets his kid pick up a few educational scrapes while staying close enough to protect the child from serious injury.

Imagine the kid at the carnival who insists on eating cotton candy before riding the Scrambler. The wise father will warn against that strategy. "You'll probably get sick," he might say. But rather than getting into a battle of wills, he lets the child experience barfing in public. The kid gets a meaningful lesson about limitations, but he doesn't get hurt.

Fast forward ten years when that child's peers are drinking to excess. If the boy learned his lesson back at the carnival when the stakes were low, then the young man will more easily avoid overindulging when the stakes are high.

Overprotective, overcontrolling parents may care about their children, but they do them no favors by trying to protect them from every germ, every scrape, or every moment of poor judgment. The possessive and cautious feminine needs to be balanced by the adventurous and trusting masculine. Without that balance, a boy can have difficulty learning to assess risk with accuracy. The man who views himself this way will likely seek women who fill that protective, maternal role.

Healthy women have no desire for such a mommy-son relationship. She may like him, but she won't admire him. She won't see dignity when she looks at him, and she probably won't be enthusiastic about sex. Who can blame her? A maternal relationship is not sexual in nature.

All the while, his sense of purpose suffers. His compass rarely points toward the path dictated by his values. It points toward the path of least error. He's skilled at avoiding mistakes, but an error-free life makes him a less interesting and less dignified man of purpose.

She has sex with me, and that's good enough.

This is probably the most common reason men lose their dignity to substandard relationships. They trade away their most precious commodity—their commitment—for easy access to sex. These men are more selective about the cars they drive than the women they sleep with. They are the opposite of gatekeepers. They are passive, undiscriminating, and hopelessly horny.

Their lack of intentionality causes them to settle for whichever women happen to pursue them. They don't choose their relationships; they let relationships choose them. There are more ways for this to go wrong than there are fleas on a mangy dog. It's rarely the path to dignity. If I'm describing you, please don't buy into the shame. I've been there, too. The upcoming strategies should help.

An Absence of Constraints

These principles share a common theme: many men seek relationships with overbearing women who use shame as a cudgel. No one showed them the productive side of shame. They don't know how to use it simply to retreat, recalibrate, then reenter the social environment with increased wisdom. They learned to be hopeless in the face of pervasive shame, immobilized by the belief that they have no path to redemption.

These men didn't experience enough grace, forgiveness, or good humor in response to errors. They instead experienced humiliation and loathing. Is it any wonder they gravitate toward women who offer the same experience? These women are their burning barn.

The irony is that the man who chooses romantic relationships characterized by shame doesn't enjoy feeling ashamed. He would prefer dignity of the type he sees other men enjoying, but he'll settle instead for the occasional slot-machine jackpot of approval that keeps him coming back for more.

His fundamental misgiving is the fantasy that a romantic relationship can somehow, by itself, generate freedom and dignity. Romantic relationships don't possess that power. They can support dignity, or they can suppress it. They cannot provide it.

They support dignity by fostering purposeful action in pursuit of values. Good relationships have an absence of constraints and punishment, and they never involve compulsive self-policing.

Shame has its place. We all need to recalibrate occasionally. But if you have been signing up for punishing, dignity-crushing, shame-based relationships, then there's no better time to change course. Here are some strategies.

The Road to Dignity

Earlier, I shared one of my favorite psychological terms: agency. Here is another of my favorite deluxe-sounding terms: *behavioral repertoire*. It means the total range of behaviors and responses of which we're capable. For our purposes, let's call it a person's full range of motion in any given situation. Or maybe we should say full but appropriate range of motion. While we *could* greet new acquaintances by licking their foreheads or shrieking like a barn owl, most of us choose not to.

Just as chaotic relationships violate the Composure requirement by depleting agency, shame-based relationships break the Dignity requirement by constraining our behavioral repertoire. The man in a shame-based relationship hesitates to exercise his full range of motion for fear of female disapproval.

This is why dignity is the inverse of shame. The dignified man doesn't compulsively self-police when it's time to act. He knows how to carry himself, and he acts without the constraints of pervasive shame. A man of dignity follows his well-calibrated internal compass rather than following a fickle source of external approval. With experience and wisdom, a man expands and refines his repertoire. Relationships that satisfy the Dignity requirement support that growth.

Here's a common example of relationships that shrink a man's behavioral repertoire: women who refuse to let their men walk away during an argument.

Some might wonder how it's possible for a woman to prevent a man from exiting an argument, but those who have been there know there are plenty of methods. An abusive woman can block a man's exit by physically cornering him, assailing him when he's in a vulnerable position such as showering or driving, threatening him—for example, warning him she will harm herself if he doesn't comply—or simply berating him into submission.

A man's repertoire shrinks when she forces him to remain in place and argue against his will. She's denying him the opportunity to cool off and consider solutions. She constrains him to minimal options: argue, submit, or risk physical escalation by pushing past her. Rather than consulting his behavioral repertoire and searching for an optimal outcome, he settles for the booby prize of placating an irrational woman.

That's just one extreme example of a relationship pattern that diminishes a man's range of motion. A man's behavioral repertoire diminishes any time he self-polices or succumbs to the stultifying force of pervasive shame.

Shame is one of the most challenging feelings a man can unravel within himself. If a pervasive sense of shame seems like a problem in your life, I can't stress enough the value of working with a competent therapist. Whether or not you have a history of pervasive shame, here are a few strategies for establishing relationships that foster dignity and a full range of motion.

Decipher the role of shame in your upbringing.

Take a few hours (better yet, a few weeks or months) and ponder: How was shame used to shape you as a child?

If you're fortunate, the adults in your life used shame appropriately and correctly. They taught you to reconsider your behavior after you acted selfishly or aggressively (which all children do). Then, after recalibrating your behavior, they forgave you and didn't speak of the incident again. When parents and elders help a child recalibrate and resume, then the child learns he made a mistake, not that he has a character flaw.

Unskilled parents do it differently. They shout, lecture, scorn, and humiliate. They scoff at apologies and ignore goodwill gestures. This parent's child has no path to redemption, and so he learns to avoid punishing interactions with his parents by preemptively putting himself on trial—and always finding himself inadequate.

Most men will have experienced some mix of those extremes. The task is to untangle that experience and label the situations and ways in which adults used shame sparingly in the service of mending relationships or used it excessively in the service of reducing behavioral repertoire.

Every man should take the time and effort to recount how his parents, teachers, and other elders used shame either to further their emotional development or to stifle it. If we know when and how shame was used to constrain us in the past, then we possess a roadmap for when and how others might use it to constrain us in the future.

Be mindful of the distinction between courtesy and self-policing.

A guy really can't go wrong following the Golden Rule (do to others as you would have them do to you) and its cousin, the Silver Rule (don't do to others what you wouldn't have them do to you). In my father's bar, basic morality boiled down to this: "If you don't start trouble, there won't be trouble." Courtesy goes a long way. However, I'm unaware of any rule that says a man must always preoccupy himself with the comfort of others and do so to his own detriment.

Too many men believe they are being discourteous, or even cruel, if others express dissatisfaction with their decisions. They therefore become vigilant self-policers. If that's you, you might experiment with this repertoire-maximizing guideline: *If I know I have acted according to my values and my purpose, then it's okay if others feel disappointed. I am responsible for my actions, not their reactions.*

Reject women who disregard the protocols of apology.

In healthy relationships, apologies send a simple message of goodwill and accountability. Also in healthy relationships, apologies are met with forgiveness and forgetting. Apologies and acceptance show the intent to continue caring for each other. This is normal relationship maintenance, and some men didn't experience it when they were boys.

Instead, they saw manipulative, shame-based relationships in which apologies were chattel in a game of one-upmanship. In that kind of relationship, apologies are only intended to stop the flow of punishment.

Apologies are supposed to be an invitation to converse, not an invitation to abuse, manipulate, or mistreat. I believe every man should adopt this policy: any woman who weaponizes guilt, or who violates the protocols of apology and forgiveness, simply does not belong in their life.

As a personal aside, I cringe when I hear of men apologizing to women by giving flowers. An apology should display accountability and a plan for the future. Flowers say instead, "Please don't be mad at me." That's not the stance of a man on an equal footing with his woman. It's the stance of a shame-faced boy. I'm sure we have all done that sort of thing, but save the flowers for celebrations.

Guilt and apologies exist to help us set the situation right and move on. Your apology should never be her excuse to start a rousing game of one-upmanship, shaming, or griping about every bug that ever crawled up her butt. Women who reject the universal protocols of apology and forgiveness are unprepared for healthy, mature relationships.

Finally—and this needs to be said because some men haven't experienced the healthy give-and-take of apologies—please don't waste time in a relationship in which she refuses to apologize for her mistakes. If she can transgress against her man with impunity, then her man is her punching bag.

Seek feedback from friends and family, and listen to it.

Friends and family may have our best interests at heart, but they are often hesitant to express concerns about our choices in women. Even when they disapprove, they might only offer tepid endorsements like "She seems great" or "I'm happy if you're happy." The wise gatekeeper resists the temptation to glide past these understated warning signs. He might respond with something like "It sounds like you're concerned. Tell me more."

Sometimes friends try to warn us with slightly more direct signals like "Is everything okay with you two?" or "So how are things going with her?" These are invitations to a discussion. Sometimes they see problems to which we are blind.

Finally, there's a particular and subtle phrase from friends and family that men should hear as a blaring alert:

> "You don't seem like yourself when she's around."

Many of my clients have received that specific feedback from friends and family. In nearly every case, it meant the men were compulsively self-policing in the presence of their women. Their friends noticed their reduced behavioral repertoires, and they were probably testing the waters with this delicate phrase because they didn't know how their concerns would be received.

Our friends' warnings are easy to ignore, and few people will push when it's clear their warnings aren't welcome. When you hear words that might be a warning, slow down. Be inquisitive. Ask friends and family what they see in your relationship, and be non-defensive—even if you must pretend. They might be wrong, or they might be saving you from a lifetime of misery.

Choose women of clarity.

The man who is prone to pervasive shame must be stringent about choosing women of clarity, which I wrote about in *The Tactical Guide to Women*. They are women who possess these traits:

- **Reliable communication skills.** These women can clearly articulate their thoughts, feelings, and desires, especially during conflict. They don't succumb to primitive reflexes like pouting or shouting.
- **Inquisitiveness.** Inquisitive women don't jump to conclusions about your motivations. They don't assume they are under attack or that they know what you're thinking. Instead, they ask questions. They listen and observe. They can view situations from multiple angles, including and especially your point of view. Openness and curiosity are their default modes.

- **Assertiveness.** Some of the most insidious and destructive communication patterns are nonverbal: shunning, passive-aggressiveness, martyrdom, avoiding difficult topics, and so on. The antithesis to all of them is calm, polite assertiveness. Assertive women are willing and able to ask for what they want. They have no need for nonverbal power struggles. They don't shame or backbite. Their willingness to speak up about wishes, needs, problems, and disappointments makes them a blessing to live with.

Choosing women of clarity matters for all gatekeepers, but the man who is vulnerable to pervasive shame must be particularly attentive to this requirement. His organizing principles can easily nudge him toward women who rely on more primitive tools like weaponized shame.

Get curious about shaming behavior that seems inconsistent with her character.

The point of this book is to examine relationship quality—what we receive in exchange for our commitment—and we can't ignore ourselves as the common denominator in all our relationships. Women who otherwise operate with clarity sometimes turn to nagging, shaming behavior. However, what may look like a change in *her* might reflect a change in her perception of *us*.

Her change in demeanor might be a way of saying she feels insecure in the relationship. Stabs at our dignity—belittling, criticizing, emasculating, and shaming—might be her way of trying to restore a more solid foundation. Shaming behavior may be her attempt to get her man to step up to the plate.

That's not to say we should tolerate it. The best response to that change in demeanor is born out of dignity and confidence. We can start with the same type of inquisitiveness we expect from women. Take the lead. Ask questions. Show her she can be honest with you.

On paper, it sounds easy, but men burdened by pervasive shame sometimes find it difficult to look past what feels like an attack on their honor. They get reactive. To complicate the situation, some men are so laser-focused on finding solutions that they inadvertently end up talking over or at their women instead of leading a calm, productive discussion.

There's an insidious relationship trap here. It works like this: First, a woman becomes anxious or uncertain about the relationship. She tries to repair it by nagging her man into behaving in a way that relieves her tension.

Next, he perceives her attempt to right the relationship as an act of hostility. He responds by reducing his range of motion or by lashing out at her. Either way, his dignity takes a hit, and so does the quality of the relationship.

Finally, she responds to his waning dignity by piling on more shame in an amplified effort to feel happy and secure like she once did. They're caught in a downward spiral, and they don't know what's happening.

Our challenge, as men, is to respond with calm, masculine energy when we don't feel calm. It may feel satisfying to throw our weight around in the heat of the moment or to retreat from the tension by reducing our range of motion, but we're bound to feel smaller after the short-term relief fades, and the relationship is bound to be in worse shape.

Time-outs are one of the simplest and most universally overlooked strategies for calming everyone involved. Couples overlook this option when one or both participants experience an adrenaline-fueled need to settle the argument *right now*, along with the tunnel vision created by the adrenaline. Stepping away to cool off is an option that simply doesn't occur to many couples.

This is where a gatekeeper takes the lead. Time-outs work well when they're negotiated beforehand, during calm discussions. It's a simple recipe: both parties agree to physically separate and pause communication when either side feels a disagreement is devolving into an unproductive conflict.

Stepping away is half the recipe. The other half is agreeing on the terms for resuming the discussion. Some couples prefer a predetermined time limit—say, an hour. That's usually sufficient time for adrenaline to dissipate and rationality to return. Others prefer more dynamic criteria; for example, when each feels they can return with empathy and a willingness to seek solutions.

One important addendum to this strategy: if sitting in silent tension makes her anxious—as it does for many—then it's unkind to make her marinate in that anxiety beyond what's necessary to resume a productive conversation. Forcing her to stew in silence and tension is torment, not leadership.

Walk with dignity, especially when you don't feel like it.

The mind is divided against itself. Nowhere is that more true than in our lessons about shame. The rational mind can grasp history. It can understand *that was then, and this is now*. The emotional mind makes no such distinction. It blurs and overgeneralizes time and experience. *That was then, and this is then.*

We all have days when the emotional mind is in the driver's seat. We're fatigued, or we got chewed out by the boss, or we just feel small for no reason. Those days require extra effort toward self-respecting behaviors like standing tall, dressing well, and speaking clearly. A man doesn't need to feel dignified to carry himself in a way that commands respect. We're allowed to fake it, especially in the service of disobeying emotional logic.

Define your boundaries.

Kingdoms have clearly defined perimeters to protect against destructive influences. They have boundaries. So must the gatekeeper. Some guys talk a good game about their personal boundaries, but they either never learned what real boundaries are or they hope that simply announcing their boundaries will be enough. They shout at the world, "There's a fence here!" when there's nothing but thin air.

What do I mean by boundaries? They are the structural elements of your life. They protect your values and purpose from infringement. For example, suppose your professional values dictate that you work between the hours of 8:00 a.m. and 5:00 p.m. That is not gaming time. It is not sleeping time. Outside of emergencies like car accidents, it certainly is not wife or girlfriend time. Period. That's a boundary.

A different example: Perhaps you grew up in a home where people shouted in anger, and you have decided *no more*. From now on, disagreements will be calm, and dialogue will be intelligible. Anyone who can't play by the rules doesn't get to play at all. That's a boundary.

How do you identify boundary violations? Intuition speaks (a topic I'll discuss further in Book IV). Intuition is more reliable when a man has done the work of defining what he expects from others and what he will not tolerate. Don't worry if you haven't nailed it down yet. Clarity develops over a lifetime. The boundaries of a sixty-year-old man will be more clearly defined than those of a twenty-year-old. Whatever your age, now is a good time to solidify weak boundaries.

Here's a good place to start: What commitments and structures does your purpose require of you? What does your purpose require of those in your inner circle? What do *you* want from those relationships? What behaviors are off limits?

A man can spend a lifetime revisiting and refining his boundaries. Enforcing them might be uncomfortable, and people might complain. That's okay. You'll live through the discomfort, and so will they.

Enforce your boundaries.

One of the simplest strategies for maintaining dignity is to consistently enforce professional and personal boundaries. It's also one of the more challenging strategies for agreeable, conscientious men to enforce. For example, suppose an agreeable and insecure man skips his usual Saturday morning workout to help his girlfriend paint her walls. This makes her happy.

The following Saturday, she plans to buy a couch. She wants her nice, agreeable boyfriend to help her carry it home. He set the precedent by helping her the previous Saturday, so he agrees to skip his workout again.

Then she asks him to spend a Saturday morning driving her on errands while her car is in the shop. Finally, he draws the line, saying, "I'd like to, but I really need to hit the gym this week."

If his girlfriend is of exceptional character, she will be grateful for his help the previous two Saturdays. If not, she will feel neglected and bitter. It's not her fault. He created his predicament by avoiding the discomfort of her disappointment after her first request. Now, he's no longer the man who works out on Saturday mornings. He transformed himself into the man who spends Saturday mornings helping his girlfriend. Now he feels ashamed if he neglects his new role.

If he had been consistent in taking care of himself—if he were *always* at the gym on Saturday morning—then no one would wonder why he was at the gym on Saturday morning. No one would be confused about his boundaries. The dignified gatekeeper leaves no room for confusion about his priorities or his personal requirements. His clarity discourages others from shaming him into prioritizing their needs over his own.

Avoid relationships built on incompatible values.

I knew a married couple who fell into a vicious conflict over values. She came to despise his avocation of rebuilding cars. She loathed the cluttered garage, and she hated every "junker" he brought home to fix. She resented the money he spent on tools and the time he spent with his "children" (her bitter label for his project cars).

Her biting comments, cold shoulder, and passive-aggressive sniping all had a singular intent: to shame him into relinquishing his cherished hobby. She was trying to humiliate him into following her values rather than his own.

When they were dating a decade earlier, she knew he was a gearhead. He didn't hide it. But even then, she showed signs of jealousy. She took no interest in his hobby. She complained about his dirty fingernails and whined when he wanted to rebuild a carburetor rather than watch a movie.

They both knew it was a point of contention before they married. They both knew his hobby was expensive and time-consuming. Yet they proceeded with the relationship, only for contempt to consume them years later. People usually think about red flags as characteristics of the person, not the relationship. (And it's rarely, if ever, suggested we begin our search for red flags in the mirror.) Yet, misaligned values is the red flag no one talks about, and it has a habit of coming to ugly fruition at the worst moments. "This isn't what I wanted out of life" isn't what you want to hear ten years into a marriage.[45]

Romantic commitment can, and should, support a man's values. That thought is a revelation to men who believe they exist only to serve others, or who have never seen a mutually supportive relationship.

You may have noticed that most of these strategies for avoiding shame-based relationships involve prioritizing our own needs, wants, and values. That might be an uncomfortable proposition for any man consumed by pervasive shame. Unfortunately, being a wise and purposeful gatekeeper is not always comfortable. That brings us to our next foundational skill.

---

45 In a study on ignoring red flags, researchers found, "Even when participants encountered one of their own personal dealbreakers [in an attractive partner], a characteristic that they had previously claimed would make them reject someone as a long-term mate, they did not reliably end the relationship. On average, participants encountered four pieces of negative information, including two of their own personal dealbreakers, before they chose to reject the hypothetical partner." They also noted, "Moving a relationship forward often feels effortless, whereas rejecting a romantic partner is difficult." Joel, S., and N. Charlot. 2022. "Dealbreakers or Dealbenders? Capturing the Cumulative Effects of Partner Information on Mate Choice." *Journal of Experimental Social Psychology* 101: 1-16.

Foundational Skill: Act in the Service of Values Before Comfort

Our first foundational skill was about allowing others to experience discomfort. This time, we look at tolerating our own discomfort when others try to shame us into compliance.

Each man's experience with shame is different, but we have this in common: some women are hell-bent on using shame to control us. We can either get small and let that shame permeate our lives, or we can claim our space in the world.

Disobeying shame preserves our full range of motion. That much is easy to see. But for those of us subjected to punitive shame throughout our upbringing, staying small seems safe. Disobeying the dictates of shame feels like breaking rules that once protected us from abandonment or abuse. An old injunction is seared into the emotional logic of any man who experienced shame as a weapon: it's safer to ignore self-interest than to be mistreated by powerful figures.

Disobeying shame can also be disorienting. *If I'm not trying to avoid disapproval*, says emotional logic, *then what the hell am I supposed to do instead?*

I knew a man who faced precisely that dilemma in his midforties. After twenty years, he had finally worked up the resolve to divorce his shaming, abusive wife. Before marriage, he had spent his life with a shaming, abusive mother. His relationships with women consisted mostly of trying to avoid punishment. (A hallmark experience of abuse is the feeling of resentment combined with the act of compliance. He had both in spades.)

Now, in midlife, he had a newfound freedom. For the first time, there was no harpy of a woman scrutinizing his every move. Like so many men before him, he didn't know what to do with himself. He was professionally successful and financially comfortable, and he had two kids who looked up to him, but he had built none of it on his terms. His choices had always been constrained by the aversive control of shame, first from his mother, then from his wife. As much as he despised the mistreatment, shame was his compass. He felt lost without it.

All the options and choices possessed by younger men were suddenly at his disposal. Once he acclimated to his new freedom—a period during which he drank too much and worked too little—he began the long process of exploring career changes, uncovering his preferences and desires, and learning about healthy relationships with women.

He could have easily retreated into his familiar ways. He could have sought the next overbearing woman to control and degrade him. Repeating his pattern would have been simpler than breaking it. It would have been like slipping into a comfortable, old straitjacket.

But instead of repeating the pattern, he rode out the anxiety and uncertainty. It was an arduous journey. He felt lost in the wilderness for more than a year. For the first time, he got to choose his identity and purpose. Since he had never truly asserted his own ambitions in life, he had to familiarize himself with the anxiety-provoking experience of *not* seeking approval from others.

Old patterns of shame may feel familiar, or even comfortable, but the only reward is the occasional pat on the head. Tiny little payouts can compel a man to pull that lever his entire life unless he snaps out of his trance and starts acting in the service of values rather than comfort.

Imagine if Samuel Adams had asked his wife's permission to dump tea into Boston Harbor, or if Neil Armstrong had begged, "May I please go to the moon, dear?" A man can't carve his own path when he's under the yoke of aversive control, but a man who follows his values can achieve greatness—or at least the satisfaction of knowing he tried.

As for the man I knew, a funny thing happened as his values and purpose came into focus. Sure, people still tried to shame him into complying with their desires. That's what he had trained them to do. However, his urge to bend to their manipulations shifted. He now saw their attempts to control him as tests of his devotion to his purpose. He even came to welcome those challenges as opportunities to strengthen his resolve and hone his ability to be agreeably disagreeable. He learned to say "no" from a position of kindness and self-possession.

How did he do it? He recognized the anxiety for what it was: a feeling. He studied it like a bug under glass. Then, when it appeared, he turned his attention toward his values. He let his values dictate his actions, and he allowed his anxiety to run its course.

It was difficult at first, and then it became easy. The anxiety didn't vanish, but he learned not to care about it. He found the ability to disregard his anxiety to be every bit as satisfying as vanquishing it.

Dignity and shame are two sides of the same coin. As his allegiance to shame receded, his dignity increased. He walked, talked, and acted with steady confidence. For the first time in his life, he took up space in the world. Not coincidentally, his relationship options flourished. Healthy women respond well to unapologetic and purposeful men, as do healthy friends, colleagues, and employers.

That man waded through a swamp of anxiety to get to the other side. He told me he could never return to his old ways now that anxiety no longer controlled him. Now his values are his compass.

FLIGHT CHECK

- **Dignity.** When you were a child, how did your parents and other adults correct your behavior? What did they teach you, implicitly or explicitly, about guilt and shame? How has it shaped your behavior around women?
- **Lessons on masculinity.** What have women tried to teach you about being a man? Have their lessons served you well? What have men taught you about masculinity, and how have their lessons served you?
- **Personal boundaries.** Are you clear with yourself about your personal and professional boundaries? If you were to write a guidebook for others titled, "The Rules of My Kingdom," what might it say? How have you historically responded to people who trample on your boundaries?

— BOOK III —

Resilience

Evaluate her relationship to the world • Clarify your obligation to others • Choose commitments that bring resilience rather than frailty • Embrace the challenge of high-functioning relationships

Our first gatekeeping requirement was Composure. A high-quality relationship brings compounding successes born of a stable foundation. It doesn't hobble a man by bringing chaos. Our second requirement was Dignity. A worthy relationship fosters a man's ability to exercise his full range of motion with his head held high. It doesn't imprison him with shame.

Now we turn to Resilience. Any relationship worth committing to strengthens a man's ability to navigate challenges. It bolsters his ability to tackle life's problems; it doesn't *become* the problem he needs to solve. If we are raising the bar for healthy relationships to an uncomfortable height, then good. That's the point. If you stick with me, we will raise it even higher.

So far, we have focused on you and your organizing principles. Here, we'll direct more of our attention to her character. The relationship is only as healthy as its least functional participant. If the women we choose struggle to manage the basics of life, then the relationship will primarily be about compensating for her slippage. You become her crutch rather than her man. Two hearts and minds working together should be stronger than one, not weaker.

It's a truism that relationships take work, but the variety of the work matters. Healthy relationship efforts leave you feeling more focused, capable, energized, and sometimes humbled. Unhealthy efforts leave you drained from fending off pointless conflicts and cleaning up childish emotional messes.

Carlos, our next case study, had precisely that problem. His relationship didn't suffer from unambiguous transgressions like violent conflict or infidelity. Instead, he endured a steady stream of low-grade crises that choked the life out of his values and purpose. It happened so subtly, and he was so predisposed to it, that he barely noticed until the relationship had compromised his ability to function in the world.

Carlos and Melissa

Carlos and Melissa met in their early thirties. They were instantly attracted. Though Carlos wasn't classically handsome, Melissa admired his charisma and energy that motivated his employees and filled his bank account. Carlos prized Melissa's beauty as well as her story of triumph over an adverse childhood.

Melissa's father had apparently started their family on a whim. She said he never seemed invested in fatherhood. Instead, he spent most of his evenings at the local pub. Melissa's mother, starved for affection, eventually went outside the marriage to meet her physical and emotional needs.

For years, her parents maintained the illusion that all was well at home. The lawn was manicured and the lights were on, but there was no happiness behind those doors. That left Melissa worse than alone. To the outside world, she had an intact home with two loving parents, but no one knew her life lacked warmth or structure.

By her early teens, Melissa had found a circle of girlfriends who were masters of short-term relief. They introduced her to marijuana, which she used to relieve her abiding feelings of dissatisfaction. They also introduced her to a different sedative: commiserating.

Together, the girls would get stoned and complain about parents, schoolwork, bosses, boyfriends, and other girls. The girls didn't generate solutions during these complaint sessions. Solutions weren't the goal, and in fairness, solutions were beyond their capabilities. How is one teenage girl to compensate another for an inadequate father? She has little to offer beyond a sympathetic ear and a sarcastic jab at the source of heartache. In Melissa's friend group, complaining was both a means of connection and the painkiller for life's problems.

By her late twenties, Melissa had stopped using pot and she developed a more active approach to her problems. She excelled in her work as a hairdresser, amassing a respectable stable of loyal clients. Still, in her most challenging moments, she did what we're all inclined toward: her most practiced and primitive coping strategy. Though she mostly abstained, complaining remained her drug of choice.

Carlos's upbringing was imperfect in a different and complementary way. His parents were loving and attentive, though he described his father as a passive, "yes, dear" type of man whose most reliable communication skill was listening and nodding. Unlike Melissa, Carlos's challenges were outside the home, among his peers.

From the time Carlos was young, his classmates had teased him for being short, and he was certainly no movie star. During his freshman year of high school, he discovered that his sense of humor helped him connect with girls. Then, following his father's example, he fell into the habit of listening to girls complain. He became the handkerchief that absorbed their tears and anger. It left him unfulfilled, since there was no room for his needs or desires in the relationships, but at least he got to enjoy their company along with occasional tepid physical affection.

Melissa complained in order to feel intimacy; Carlos listened for the same reason. You can guess where the relationship was headed. They were destined to bring out each other's worst habits.

This kind of misalignment is easy to overlook. Carlos tolerated her moments of melancholy because her more visible assets were well in order. Plus, a person's vulnerabilities have a funny way of looking like strengths at the beginning of a relationship.

For example, early on, when Melissa would complain about her upbringing, Carlos only heard what he wanted: the story of a survivor who overcame hardship. He didn't recognize her words as a bid for affection. He didn't notice that her complaining (and his listening) was reliably followed by sex.

When their infatuation faded, what remained was the pattern that had taken hold early in their relationship. She was regressing to her whiny teenage coping style, and he regressed to his desperate teenage pandering. That type of pattern holds no genuine closeness, only the illusion of intimacy. Melissa got to pretend she had an ally; Carlos got to pretend he was a hero. They were the perfect example of the white knight and the damsel in distress: impotent rescuer meets hopeless project. Their world revolved around her problems.

The relationship broke his concentration at work. It interfered with his workouts at the gym. It infringed on his friendships with other men. It weakened him physically, mentally, and spiritually.

Still, it was tolerable. With Melissa, there were no drunken outbursts at Thanksgiving dinner. No mortifying display at his workplace. No soap-opera drama, abuse, or aversive control of constant shaming. Their relationship offered no single event a person could point to and shout, "*This!* Stay away from *this*!" Just the constant, slow drip of misery draining his vitality like a succubus.

As a teenager, Melissa had stumbled upon avoidant strategies such as pot use and impotent complaining with friends. It's understandable. No child should have to wonder why her parents are inattentive.

Pot and commiserating didn't bring happiness, but they helped her forget about being unhappy. Pot turned off her questioning mind. Complaining about unreliable parents and lackluster teachers helped her create a less distressing explanation for her pain than the story your average emotional mind will devise, which is: *Maybe people disappoint me because I am unlovable.*

To her credit, she overcame those avoidant strategies, but she didn't do the hard work of identifying her own relationship patterns. She never asked herself why she clicked so well with people who shouldered her complaints. Such lack of insight is a path to relapse.

When Melissa met Carlos, it was the perfect opportunity to descend into her old avoidant strategies. His sympathy and reassurance were like a hit of her old drug. It felt great at first, as relapse always does. But soon enough, she found herself in the throes of that old cloud of self-doubt: *Maybe I am unlovable.*

At least, that's what I imagine happened. As for Carlos, I don't need to guess. I know his story: The more she complained, the more useful he felt. Before he knew it, he was on full-time girlfriend duty. He had long operated under the invisible organizing principle that *People only tolerate me if I entertain or soothe them.*

Anxiety is contagious. Carlos didn't just listen to Melissa's angst, he absorbed it. When she was upset at a coworker, he got angry on her behalf. If she woke up on the wrong side of the bed, he also fell into a sour mood. Carlos illustrated the principle that an unhealthy relationship will sink to the level of its most troubled participant.

Carlos and Melissa were both good people, but the relationship made Carlos frail against the challenges of the world. It preoccupied his mind, controlled his mood, and drained his energy. In no way could he meet his potential in that condition. The relationship didn't help Melissa, either. Like all relationships, theirs was a mutual creation. And like any other natural disaster, it was perfectly unique.

Carlos's motivation for staying in such a soul-sucking relationship was partly selfish … maybe more than partly. He got to *look* like the hero, but in reality, he unwittingly encouraged Melissa to be distressed in his presence. Once he uncovered that motivation,

Carlos vowed never again to act on it. The harder a man works in a relationship built on frailty, the worse he functions in his own life and the more he encourages her to continue suffering.

Her Relationship to the World

You might recall from the discussion on Composure that men are quicker to declare their devotion than women, and we're prone to do so before we understand what that commitment will bring into our lives. A man can become so infatuated with a woman that he convinces himself she's "the one" before he has any sense of how a relationship with this "one" might affect his life. Carlos's relationship diminished his resilience.

Resilience is the ability to withstand and recover from unexpected problems. It involves qualities like flexibility, resourcefulness, and toughness. In his book *The Survivor Personality*, famed researcher Al Siebert said resilience involves such traits as playful curiosity, flexibility, creativity, and the wisdom to embrace the fact that life is unfair.

He also noted that those who thrive during hardship possess the talent of finding opportunity in misfortune. He wrote, "I've learned that the best indicator someone has a survivor personality is when they talk about their worst experience and then add, 'It was one of the best things that ever happened to me.'"[46]

Evidence exists that resilience has a genetic basis, but it is at least partly learned. That means we have some amount of choice involved in how we manage stressful life events. Choosing a woman who lacks resilience means that in one way or another, you will have to compensate for her shortfalls.[47]

---

46 Siebert, Al. 2010. *The Survivor Personality: Why Some People Are Stronger, Smarter, and More Skillful at Handling Life's Difficulties … and How You Can Be, Too.* Toronto: Penguin Group. It's important to note the context of that quote. By "worst experience," Siebert was referring to life events such as getting laid off, not tragedies involving the suffering of others.

47 Amstadter, A., J. M. Myers, and K. S. Kendler. 2014. "Psychiatric Resilience: Longitudinal Twin Study." *The British Journal of Psychiatry* 205: 275-280.

Suppose, for example, a man's wife loses her job unjustly. A period of distress will likely follow, but resilient people don't remain distressed indefinitely. They transition into problem-solving mode. If she lacks resilience or the desire to be resilient, she will have a hard time making that shift. She may even become immobilized and helpless, retreating to the bedroom all day or to the bottle all night.

Now, not only must her husband face the original problem alone—her loss of income, for starters—but he must also do the work of holding her together. That's a downward spiral. The less she rises to the occasion, the more he must compensate.

So how can you judge a woman's resilience in the absence of major problems? We can tell a lot by watching how she handles minor problems and disappointments, like lost packages, fender benders, or rude cashiers. An inability or unwillingness to handle minor problems with grace and humor doesn't bode well for life's larger challenges.

Resilience is about her relationship to the world. It's about whether she can accept it as it is, with all its unfairness and pain, and whether she can respond in a thoughtful and effective way when the wheels come off. In my years of working with hundreds of couples, I have noticed three traits that damage a couple's resilience, each having to do with her relationship to the world:

- Ingratitude
- Entitlement
- Victim-based ideology

There's marginal utility in dwelling on red flags. Goals are easier to achieve when we focus primarily on what we want rather than what we hope to avoid. Still, these three red flags are worth examining because we so easily overlook them. Let's shine a light on them and, more importantly, their positive inverse qualities.

Ingratitude

Gratitude shows up in little ways, such as expressing kindness, finding joy in small moments, and appreciating the fact that life is too short to be petty and indignant. The person who lives with gratitude can easily find meaning in unpleasant experiences. It's a joy to be around women who possess this quality.

Gratitude is one of the recalibrating emotional systems we touched on previously. It's like shame but with a positive valence. Specifically, it's part of reciprocal altruism, which builds trust between people and greases the wheels of healthy relationships. Gratitude draws our attention to the efforts of others and reminds us we're lucky to have them around, so we better treat them right.

One group of researchers put a sterile explanation behind it: gratitude encourages mutual exchange of benefits. As transactional as that might sound, it's no minor consideration in romance. The alternative to a give-and-take relationship is one-sidedness.[48]

Gratitude usually requires effort in close relationships. Those same researchers found we are more likely to express gratitude with strangers than with kin. We expect kin to confer benefits, so gratitude with them can seem unnecessary or even forced. Mutual altruism is the arrangement; gratitude is assumed and overlooked.

Too much of that assumption hurts many couples. In my experience, successful couples express gratitude to *prevent* feelings of entitlement and presumption. If she is perceptive enough to notice that she benefits from your presence in her life, then the relationship won't be a one-way street in which she depletes your energy.

Gracious women are notable for their ability to remain happily connected with others. This adds directly to her resilience by maintaining connections that help her weather the storm. Here's another telltale sign: gracious women are simply a joy to be around. Invest in women who realize they are blessed to be alive; avoid those who believe the world is blessed by their existence.

Entitlement

Entitlement is ingratitude's big ugly sister. It's much more than failing to appreciate what's good and fortunate. It's an expectation

---

48 McCullough, M. E., M. B. Kimeldorf, and A. D. Cohen. 2008. "An Adaptation for Altruism? The Social Causes, Social Efforts, and Social Evolution of Gratitude." *Current Directions in Psychological Science* 17: 281-285.

that what's good and fortunate *must* flow toward her. She expects the world (including you, if you're the unlucky man in her life) to scatter rose petals in her path. If you don't, then she's disappointed, at best, and enraged, at worst.

She is the girlfriend who makes her man uncomfortable about the dismissive way she treats others. That look the waiter just gave the poor sap sitting across from her? It was pity. As bad as she is treating him, he's thankful he isn't in her boyfriend's shoes.

She is the wife who relegates her husband's possessions to the "man cave" in the basement while she decorates the main floor with pillows and scented candles.

She is the daughter, sister, or mother who scolds her family with criticism and disapproval until they learn to put her preferences ahead of their own. The family must anticipate her needs if there is to be peace.

A dark, childlike psychology underlies entitlement. It's the belief that rights belong to her, while responsibility belongs to others. She feels entitled to get her way, and she believes you are responsible for seeing to it. Believe it or not, this can feel good (at first) to the man who prides himself on chivalry and generosity. Unfortunately, she's bound to be disappointed in him, and before long, he'll realize even "chivalry" no longer feels good.

One group of researchers looked at the effects of narcissism on relationships, focusing on three aspects: entitlement (expectation of special treatment), grandiosity (unrealistic sense of superiority), and vulnerability (the tendency to feel hurt).

Of the three factors, entitlement was associated with "the greatest interest in alternative romantic relationship partners" along with "a greater perceived availability of alternative partners."[49]

One must always interpret such studies with caution. Samples and effect sizes are small, and a multitude of other variables are at play. It's also important to note that all narcissistic people may

---

49 Balzen, K. M., D. A. Knoch, K. A. Millward, C. A. Corretti, and R. A. Ackerman. 2022. "Narcissistic Traits and Romantic Relationship Outcomes: A Short Daily Diary Investigation." *Journal of Research in Personality* 96: 1-5.

feel entitled, but everyone who feels entitled is not necessarily narcissistic.

Still, the study passes the smell test. Someone who feels entitled to the time and effort of others would want to escape any relationship in which they sense resistance to their need for exceptional treatment.

So what's the opposite of entitlement? Personal responsibility. Rather than feeling entitled to your attention and effort, a responsible woman makes herself worthy of a place in your life. In short, she is thoughtful and kindhearted. Yes, these women exist, and you are allowed to choose them.

Victim-Based Ideology

One personal behavior—a choice, really—entirely subverts resilience in a relationship, and it is completely voluntary. It's the woman's decision to surrender to the seductive embrace of a victim-based ideology; the current iteration of feminism is at the top of the list.

I need to define feminism because two people can describe themselves as feminists and intend nearly opposite meanings. In my experience, most people who call themselves feminists believe that men and women should have equal opportunities and responsibilities and that both should receive equal respect. By that cheerful definition, I am a feminist.

However, that is not what the current iteration of feminism preaches. This ideology stems from a postmodern worldview that sees all human interactions through the lens of power structures. It's a zero-sum worldview in which men's happiness must come at the expense of women. Doctrinaire feminists believe they are victims of a patriarchal conspiracy to oppress them. They view men as adversaries rather than allies.

To be fair, it's possible that the most militant feminists have had few positive experiences with men. If that's true, it's a shame. Nevertheless, just as it is our responsibility as men to clean up our malfunctioning relationships with women, equality assigns the same responsibility to them.

Feminism offers an escape from that responsibility by promoting a comforting, pre-packaged set of beliefs that men block women's path to happiness or success. Women who are injured or angry—and those who don't want to think too hard—can simply incorporate feminism's ready-made complaints into their view of themselves. (Unfortunately, ideologies exist that give men similar rationalizations for pinning unhappiness on women.)

Those who don't follow cultural trends may not realize how vindictive feminist ideology can be. Consider a widely publicized 2018 *Washington Post* editorial titled "Why Can't We Hate Men?" written by a gender studies professor at Northeastern University in Boston. She argued that men are routinely violent and oppressive to women, and she found no redeeming qualities in men. She made the case that men should surrender all positions of power. Her conclusion:

> "We [women] have every right to hate you [men]. You have done us wrong."[50]

The author is by any reasonable estimate one of the most privileged and fortunate people in history. She doesn't face hunger or the elements. She is protected from predators, criminals, and cavities. Her comfort is due mostly to the efforts of men—from the men who collect her garbage to the men who built the throne upon which she perches at least twice daily. Yet her position toward those men is one of open contempt.

Her viewpoint isn't unique among feminist activists and academics. Any gender studies textbook reveals the feminist worldview, which includes these unhappy beliefs:

- **Life is a zero-sum game.** If a man has a good day, there must be a woman somewhere who suffers for it.
- **Patriarchal oppression is endemic.** Men designed

50 Walters, S. D. "Why Can't We Hate Men?" *Washington Post*, June 8, 2018. Downloaded on August 28, 2018, from https://www.washingtonpost.com/opinions/why-cant-we-hate-men/2018/06/08/f1a3a8e0-6451-11e8-a69c-b944de66d9e7_story.html.

all institutions to oppress women, from education to the criminal justice system to marriage.

- **Privilege defines all outcomes.** Any unequal outcome between men and women is due to injustice rather than effort, luck, or individual choice. The male CEO or neurosurgeon didn't attain his position through hard work and long hours. He ascended through patriarchal privilege.
- **Masculinity is built on violence and oppression.** Men owe women an eternal debt for the alleged injustices of our ancestors. Doctrinaire feminists ignore the fact that life has been difficult for both genders. Men have always faced hardships, such as being sent to war or to the bottom of mines, or simply being relegated to the reproductive discard pile. Women certainly haven't cornered the market on existential suffering, but feminists may have cornered the market on complaining about it.[51]

This mindset represents a broken relationship to the world. Imagine a professor telling a classroom full of men, "Failure and unhappiness will never be your fault. Women cause it. Women are your constant opposition." Unfortunately, many young people, at some point in their development, are exposed to precisely that level of animosity toward men.

Women who adopt an ideology of victimhood have no place in your inner circle. If she sees men as her oppressors, she will inevitably see *you* as her oppressor. I have witnessed it many times in my clinic. Feminist ideology invades romantic relationships like a cancer.

Even in the simplest disagreements with a feminist wife or girlfriend, you will be on unequal footing. The ideology teaches its adherents to evaluate all interactions through the lens of institutional power structures, of which you are the beneficiary and she is the

---

51 See, for example, Shaw, S. M., and J. Lee, editors. 2012. *Women's Voices, Feminist Visions: Classic and Contemporary Readings*. New York: McGraw-Hill.

oppressed. Righteousness is her birthright, and you're the unlucky punching bag.

Feminism also supplies pre-made rationalizations to be unkind, such as: "If a woman mistreats a man, it's because the man deserves it." One of my first clinical supervisors was a dogmatic feminist, and she expressed that sentiment after learning that a female client had assaulted her husband. My supervisor took it on faith that the woman had acted in self-defense and that the man's injuries were long overdue.

Later details revealed the woman clearly had *not* acted in self-defense. She was the aggressor, and she had a history of violence. My feminist supervisor was undeterred. She insisted the man was dishonest and manipulative. It's possible she was correct, but she was incapable of entertaining the possibility that she had misjudged the situation. Imagine that trait in a significant other. It's pure misery.

This poisonous ideology has no place in romantic commitments. Not only is a feminist wife or girlfriend primed to evade responsibility for her behavior, but feminism encourages women to practice the wrong skills. The time any woman spends rehearsing her ideological narrative is time she could have spent learning how to coexist with other human beings. Every moment she ruminates over the patriarchy's mistreatment of her is a moment she ignores her own behavior toward others.

The anger in a dogmatic feminist's heart, along with her distaste for personal responsibility, will inevitably find its way into her relationships. It's unavoidable, and it's possible that her feminist ideology is merely a container for preexisting anger. So why would any thinking man pursue a feminist ideologue?

The first and most obvious reason is naivety. Most of us don't view ourselves as victims of massive conspiracies, nor do we view the opposite sex as the enemy. Lack of exposure to such profound animosity makes it difficult for us to recognize it in others, especially when we want to believe the best about an otherwise attractive woman.

A second trap involves dismissing dogmatic feminists as merely angry. This is especially dangerous for the man tempted to rescue women from pain. If she's attractive, and if (in his fantasy) she's merely hurt and angry, then maybe he can treat her well enough to convince her there are good men.

That reasoning contains a fatal flaw. Feminist ideology doesn't allow her to acknowledge good fortune or kind treatment. Doing so would undermine her understanding of the world and her place in it. Until a feminist relinquishes her desire to feel oppressed, she must reject kindness from men.

The ideological feminist believes she suffers from bad luck and poor treatment. Facts are irrelevant. If you date her, you might receive a "good guy" pass during the infatuation phase. But soon enough, you become the embodiment of all the reasons she is unhappy and unfulfilled. If she honestly believes she is the victim of a patriarchal conspiracy, then she is bound to conclude that her most intimate male relationship is the most dangerous relationship—unless, of course, that man is utterly submissive.

Even then, when normal conflict inevitably arises in the relationship, she will see that conflict not through the lens of compassion and inquisitiveness but through her well-rehearsed lens of power structures and oppression.

Do you need one more reason to avoid doctrinaire feminists? There's this: ideologues of any stripe lack humility and openness to alternate viewpoints. Because every ideology has a preordained answer to every question, there's no need to learn anything. Nor is there a willingness to be wrong. That is not the path to resilience.

In my estimation, feminist ideologues, with all their rage and contempt, are not to be engaged with or debated on the dating front. They are to be disregarded. Wish them well, and move on.

In that spirit of turning to brighter topics, how can a man identify high-functioning women deserving of a place in his world? Here is a brief review of an important section from *The Tactical Guide to Women*.

The Bright Triad

When I started my clinical practice years ago, I began asking men to think about who taught them how to choose romantic relationships. Was it their father? An uncle? A trusted mentor?

Almost without exception, the answer was, "No one."

Most of us are left to our own devices regarding the high-stakes game of romantic commitment, and much of the advice we encounter involves red flags to avoid in women. Yet, knowing what to avoid is an incomplete strategy. A man can memorize a list of fifty red flags, only to meet the woman who blindsides him with number fifty-one. That's why we also need to know what to seek in women. "The Bright Triad" is a set of qualities I observed during a decade of clinical work. I based it on the idea that success in relationships requires basic competencies.

That is not an original notion. When I was training to become a psychologist, we were required to complete competency exams in the third year of our doctoral program. The purpose was to determine whether we were "minimally competent" to do clinical work.

Passing the exam meant we still had much to learn before we could be called psychologists. However, we were no longer complete novices. We could at least boast, "I'm minimally competent!" Failing our competency exams meant we couldn't progress on the path until we corrected our shortcomings.

This is how I recommend thinking about the Bright Triad. If she possesses these qualities, then perhaps she is minimally competent to take part in a romantic relationship. This section briefly summarizes chapters four, five, and six from *The Tactical Guide to Women* on the topics of clarity, maturity, and stability.

Clarity

Clarity refers to her level of openness and intentionality in matters ranging from sex to resolving disagreements. Whatever she's trying to accomplish, the woman of clarity does so with honesty and transparency.

The alternative to clarity is repetitive conflict characterized by poorly understood complaints and ill-defined goals. According to one group of researchers, ongoing conflict is among the top three reasons for divorce (along with a lack of commitment and infidelity).[52]

The researchers found that 65 percent of men and 74 percent of women blame their former spouses for their divorce, saying their spouses should have worked harder to save their marriages. (Only 31.6 percent of men and 33.3 percent of women said they, personally, should have worked harder to save the marriage.) Most relationships fall apart because people argue poorly and evade responsibility. Even when relationships *should* end, they too often end with poorly managed conflict and far too many attorney's fees.

However, if each of you can identify and communicate your intentions, then your conversations won't leave you feeling bewildered, frustrated, or outmaneuvered. There are three qualities related to clarity that I have noticed in women who handle themselves well in relationships.

The first is *reliable communication skills*. Anyone can communicate well when skies are blue and everyone is happy. The real test comes when the chips are down—when she's feeling fatigued, angry, or cornered. That's when people can turn toward their most primitive defenses, such as retreating, attacking, or being passive-aggressive. A woman of clarity communicates well, especially during stressful moments.

The second is *inquisitiveness*. Perhaps you have seen this pattern: The high-conflict couple who talk over each other—loud and fast—hoping the other side will shut up and listen for once. On the nineties sitcom *Seinfeld*, George Costanza's parents were a parody of these couples, suddenly and unpredictably screaming at each other to assert dominance.

---

52 Scott, S. B., G. K. Rhoades, S. M. Stanley, E. S. Allen, and H. J. Markman. 2013. "Reasons for Divorce and Recollections of Premarital Intervention: Implications for Improving Relationship Education." *Couple and Family Psychology* 2: 131-145.

It works poorly in real life. The louder each side talks, the less the other side hears. The behavior is a form of what psychologists call functional fixedness: a mental block against trying a new strategy when the existing one continues to fail. The high-conflict couple keeps pushing the "talk louder" button despite its counterproductive effect.

The inquisitive couple avoids that trap. They look beyond their feelings and impulses during a disagreement because they are more invested in understanding and repairing the problem than in being right. Even if they lose their cool, they always come back to earth.

The inquisitive woman is so accustomed to thinking from different points of view that she expects and tolerates differences of opinion. Yes, these women exist. You can hear them saying things like "Tell me what's on your mind" or "I want to understand what you're feeling." Foolish men reject these queries because it makes them feel squeamish. Wise men embrace them. Resilient couples don't squander energy on repetitive conflicts. They get curious and find answers.

The third is *assertiveness*. Many women were taught to put the interests of others above their own. For some men, it feels great to have an overly accommodating woman. However, there is a dangerous possibility that her habit of deferring gratification for your benefit will lead to resentment when she notices her own needs are unmet.

More than a few male clients of mine felt blindsided when their wives or girlfriends suddenly expressed anger because they felt neglected or mistreated. Most of these men, in retrospect, realized they had overlooked subtle signals of discontent.

Some women find self-denial easy, and some men find it easy to tolerate in their women. These people tend to find each other, and it's a recipe for slow-cooked disaster. If she is overly accommodating, it's up to us to let her know—patiently and as many times as necessary—that we want to know what will bring her success and happiness.

A healthy dose of inquisitiveness on our part goes a long way toward preventing resentment from her. Ideally, she is assertive enough to advocate directly for her desires so you don't have to grope for the truth. If not, she must develop the skill if she is to have a place in your life. Anything less is a ticking bomb.

Maturity

Healthy relationships require the ability to navigate difficulty and crisis like a grownup. Unfortunately, emotional maturity can be difficult to assess in the beginning of a relationship when stress is low, good vibes are high, and everyone is on their best behavior. Immaturity, however, is a bit easier to spot. It can show up during ordinary stressors, like small conflicts with friends and family or bad days at work. That's where primitive reactions show up: fighting, fleeing, or freezing.

Humans rely on those three basic defenses like any other animal. We're just more sophisticated about them. Fighting includes behaviors like blaming, dominating, manipulating, or passive-aggressiveness. Fleeing includes avoidant strategies like substance abuse, overeating, overworking, or retreating into fantasy. Freezing includes such delights as helplessness, whining, dependence, or avoiding tough conversations.

None of these behaviors belongs within the walls of your kingdom—allowing for the occasional bad day, of course. I'm of the opinion that good people deserve grace when they deviate from baseline, just as I hope for grace when I deviate from mine.

The emotionally mature woman can tolerate being angry, sad, distressed, or frustrated without losing her composure. Here are five must-have building blocks:

1. **Insight.** This is the ability to apprehend the nature of our own minds. We're aware of our blind spots, biases, and emotional quirks, like the need to be right or the tendency to evade responsibility. Insight is insurance against petty arguments urged on by the emotional mind. The mind can't sneak up on us if we understand what it's up to.
2. **Emotional nuance.** *Splitting* is a psychological term for the inability to hold contradictory thoughts and feelings

about others. The person who splits either idealizes another person or vilifies him, sometimes in quick succession.

Emotional nuance is a term I use to describe the opposite condition. She's able to say, "I care about you, *and* I'm hurt right now." She understands everyone is a mixed bag of strengths and weaknesses, charms and vexations. If she lacks emotional nuance, be prepared for a roller coaster relationship. You'll be an angel one minute and a devil the next.

3. **Coping skills.** A couple in which both parties possess reliable skills for managing conflict and difficulties will fare much better than a couple in which only one functions well during a crisis. If you're the only one who can keep your wits, your attention will be divided between the problem at hand and the woman who is falling apart.

   Consider two aspects of coping. One is *problem-focused coping*. This involves gathering information, devising a plan, and taking action. The other is *emotion-focused coping*, which involves gathering social support, gaining perspective, and avoiding wishful thinking or wallowing.

   Psychologist Richard Lazarus wrote that effective coping requires attention to both aspects. According to Lazarus, effective problem-solving involves making a plan and sticking to it, despite setbacks and discouragement, and being willing to change strategies if the solution fails. The effective problem-solver simultaneously exercises emotional skills like seeking social support and practicing a positive reappraisal of the situation.[53]

4. **Internalization.** Have you ever met a woman who complains about every former boss, landlord, or

53 Lazarus, R. S. 1993. "Coping Theory and Research: Past, Present, and Future." *Psychosomatic Medicine* 55: 234-247.

boyfriend? Her demands for sympathy are exhausting, as are her endless stories of persecution. She is always the victim. One of the greatest qualities in a significant other is the ability to internalize responsibility. Rather than asking how other people can change to suit her, she asks herself how to function well with others.

All good qualities can go too far. Some women absorb too much personal responsibility and marinate in angst over jointly created problems as if she alone bears responsibility for solving them. As we've touched on elsewhere, this is a recipe for resentment.

5. **Self-Maintenance.** I posed this question in the *Tactical Guide*: "Which comes first, self-neglect or the problems associated with it?" In other words, is a person depressed because they drink too much, or do they drink too much because they're depressed? Are they out of shape because they avoid exercise, or do they avoid exercise because they're out of shape?

   If there is an answer, it doesn't matter to the person devoted to self-maintenance. That person doesn't need to *feel* like going to the gym, for example. They just go. If a woman neglects herself physically, spiritually, or emotionally, then she's a liability in her romantic relationships because whatever reduces her resilience also reduces her partner's. The human body and mind are like any other complex machine. Without maintenance, they break down at the worst moments.

Stability

Garden-variety mental health problems such as anxiety, depression, and substance abuse are major obstacles to resilience. So, too, are counterproductive compulsions like gambling, shopping, losing oneself in social media, or even "healthy" compulsions like obsessively exercising or dieting. Then there are the more acute conditions like schizophrenia or bipolar disorder, as well as burdensome problems like borderline, narcissistic, and antisocial personality styles. And, of course, other obstacles include more subtle problems like unresolved emotional injuries that color a person's every relationship.

Any source of mental or emotional instability has the potential to wreck lives, including the lives of family and significant others. Just ask anyone who grew up with an alcoholic parent, or ask the husband of a woman who spent their way into a mountain of debt. It's imperative for any conscientious gatekeeper to screen for mental stability, though my definition might not be what you expect.

I don't expect anyone to have a complete absence of problems. In fact, someone who has faced no challenges presents the problem of being untested, which makes their coping style an unknown element. Instead, I view mental stability as the willingness to face problems and solve them. The stable woman doesn't ignore her difficulties. She doesn't self-sabotage or derail every attempt at a solution with her crisis du jour. Instead, she is honest with herself about her problem and its solution.

She seeks the help she needs, and she does the hard work of maintaining a healthy, high-functioning baseline. She is also wise enough to monitor herself for signs of relapse. If that happens, as it often does when making changes, she learns from relapse and tackles the problem again. Stability doesn't mean she never experiences problems. It means she takes responsibility for her problems, and she approaches them head-on.

❊ ❊ ❊

Too few men are accustomed to the phrase, "What's in it for me?" They approach romantic commitments with all the standards a starving raccoon brings to its culinary choices. They tolerate poor treatment, low character, or incompatible values. They don't know they're allowed to have standards, which puts them at risk for wasting their commitment on women who lack minimal relationship competence.

Yet relationship standards are no trifling matter. Romantic choices affect every area of a man's life, including our lifespans—literally. A 2021 study from Israel followed 8,945 men over the course of three decades. The researchers found that "dissatisfaction with married life was related to increased long-term risk of stroke and all-cause mortality." The deleterious effect of an unhappy marriage is on par with smoking or a sedentary lifestyle.[54]

Not only are you allowed to have standards, but you owe it to yourself. The Bright Triad is a basic framework for testing relationship competence.

The Check-Engine Light

As we approach our next set of organizing principles, I have a new challenge for you: Identify the warning signs that a counterproductive organizing principle is operating in the background. It's often difficult to detect. Sometimes the only evidence is an emotional charge that is vague and easily ignored.

Our emotional reactions can be like the inscrutable "check-engine" light on a car's dashboard. It tells us there's a problem, but it doesn't tell us what's wrong. That check-engine light doesn't mean it's time to panic. It just means it's time to investigate.

So what is a grown man's equivalent of a check-engine light? It could be many internal experiences: that pit-in-the-stomach feeling when a text message arrives. The 3:00 a.m. angst fest. Irritability. The vague impulse to escape. Headaches, rumination, and distraction. Any deviation from our physical or mental baseline might be the mind trying to communicate important information. Or it might not. (I hope that clears things up! Don't worry, I'll be revisiting the topic.)

For now, the challenge is to start identifying your signs. Then, when they show up, make sure you slow down and start asking questions. So many men respond to niggling little doubts by ignor-

54 Lev-ari, S., Y. Gepner, and U. Goldbourt. 2021. "Dissatisfaction with Married Life in Men Is Related to Increased Stroke and All-Cause Mortality." *Journal of Clinical Medicine* 10: 1729.

ing them and charging forward, which they wouldn't do if they suspected a problem with their car.

On a closely related note, many men who are drawn to relationships that weaken them share a particular quality: They have difficulty knowing where their problems end and her problems begin. That confusion often comes from too many occasions in the man's childhood when he had to fulfill the role of problem-solver and peacekeeper with his parents. It's no surprise that man seeks relationships in which he compensates for other people's frailty. The mind prizes familiar patterns.

However, if that man listens closely to his inner sense, he may catch a whisper of the thought *This isn't working*. The mind turns on the check-engine light. Hopefully, he's willing to see it. It's in those vague, dimly lit moments—for example, when the borders between our problems and the problems of others are unclear—that the mind often tries to tell us something is wrong. Maybe that *something* is an outdated organizing principle. Let's look at this chapter's sampling.

Pathways to Frailty

You know what creates the kind of relationship that boosts a man's resilience? Two high-functioning people working as a team. Unfortunately, choosing high-functioning women is a challenge for men whose most important women in their earlier life experiences functioned poorly.

Here are a few organizing principles that lead men to relationships that bring frailty rather than resilience. As always, I hope you will slow down and put words to any that catch your attention.

Other people's problems are my problems.

Sometimes parents are too addicted, depressed, distracted, or otherwise unreliable to properly execute their parental duties. They don't dependably support their children, so the children learn to support the parents emotionally and sometimes even in more material ways—like cooking for themselves or caring for siblings. It's easy to imagine how that manner of upbringing creates a man who has difficulty distinguishing between problems he's responsible for solving and problems that belong to other people.

We can find other paths to this organizing principle, such as falling into a pattern of rescuing others in order to overcome a low opinion of oneself. Whatever the origin, this man seeks fragile women with plenty of problems to keep him busy. He adopts their problems as if they were his own. He is confused about where his problems end and others' problems begin.

I'm supposed to be the hero.

This man thrives on admiration. Playing the hero doesn't merely calm him; it's his identity. He sacrifices his self-interest, his time, his money, and his future for praise and prestige.

It's not necessarily shallow or false praise he's after. People may genuinely admire his self-sacrifice because they don't see the tradeoff he makes. The values and purpose he sacrifices are invisible to his admirers.

He is also purchasing loyalty with his chivalry: *I will make myself indispensable so people can't afford to leave me.* Being abandoned or neglected in previous relationships may contribute to this manner of securing allegiance.

This man's relationships are not built on meaningful, mutually beneficial connection. They're built on mutual dependence. Women depend on him for care; he depends on them for admiration and purpose.

I cannot abandon others.

Countless men are seduced by alluring, affectionate women who turn out to be burdens. They operate under the false belief that they are not allowed to say "enough" and walk away. Once a woman has latched onto him, this man feels duty-bound to endure the relationship, no matter how much it depletes his resilience. To his mind, leaving would be an unthinkable act of betrayal rather than an act of self-preservation. Some combination of disposition and experience made this man conscientious beyond reason. It prevents him from leaving even the most draining of relationships.

Her problems are easier to fix than my own.

The mind has an amazing ability to avoid unpleasant realities. It uses blunt tools like booze, hookers, gambling, and pot, as well as more admirable-looking ways like rescuing damsels in distress. If a man is trying to avoid the thought that he is failing at life, at least he can succeed at saving a struggling woman. As long as he focuses on her problems, he can avoid his own. Her frailty is his life preserver.

This man can even become so lost in her problems that he neglects his own moral compass—like the man who deserts his coworkers to focus instead on his girlfriend's daily crisis, or the man who abandons his children to devote himself instead to a new woman in need of rescue.

This man cares more about his woman's problems than she does. He uses her problems as an escape from his responsibilities.

I feel secure when she is indebted to me.

Sometimes women manipulate men into rescuing them, like a cuckolded animal tricked into feeding his competitor's offspring. But sometimes it's the rescuer who does the manipulating. The man operating under this principle encourages financial, emotional, or other manners of dependence on him.

This organizing principle says, *If they don't need me, they will abandon me*. It accompanies the belief that mutually beneficial relationships don't exist. That's why this man experiences a twinge of ambivalence, or even hostility, when he sees his woman succeeding on her own. Anything that reduces her dependence threatens his security.

At the darker end of the spectrum, men who operate under this type of principle can become exceptionally controlling. They gravitate toward people who struggle with the basics of life. They can even undermine people who succeed on their own, doing so to maintain a place of prominence in others' lives.

She will crumble if I leave.

At one time, this man found it thrilling to be needed by a woman, so he embedded her into his life. Now he sees her more as a parasite than a partner. They each buy the story that her life will crumble if he leaves.

Shame has written itself across his mind. If he doesn't want to feel guilty—and men usually telegraph this clearly through obsequious efforts to please and rescue—then she knows how to gain his compliance. This man has lost the plot. He has forgotten that she survived before he came along, and he doesn't realize that she will survive after he's gone. He believes her frailty is genuine, and he makes it his problem to solve.

Sometimes emotionally immature women throw tantrums to avoid what they see as abandonment. They may turn violent or threaten self-harm. The wise gatekeeper lets the authorities handle those problems. It is not your job to tolerate threats or to be her therapist. Threatening a man with violence or self-harm if he leaves is abusive. Men consumed by pervasive shame are especially vulnerable to that dynamic.

A high-functioning woman could never trust me.

Sometimes men choose poorly functioning women simply because they lack experience with high-functioning women. We have an epidemic of men and women who desire healthy relationships but are unsure what qualities to search for because they have never seen such a relationship. Instead of stability, their families created a river of low-rent drama and domestic disputes.

The man from this background knows healthy relationships exist. He's heard the rumors, but he has never seen one up close. He overlooks high-functioning women because his mind says he doesn't belong in their world, nor do they belong in his. It's likely he believes relationships necessarily reduce a man's resilience because he has never experienced an alternative. To him, romantic relationships have always resembled a burden, not a blessing.

A high-functioning woman will see how broken I am.

This man believes he is damaged goods. Maybe he comes from an abusive home or a home in which he endured consistent rejection, shaming, or double-binds. Children often make sense of such experiences by assuming they somehow deserve mistreatment.

It's a self-concept that forms early in a boy's mind. He carries it into adulthood, where it takes on a new twist: *anyone who gets to know me will see how broken I am*. As a result, high-functioning women are off limits.

By gravitating toward women who struggle with emotional regulation or with handling day-to-day disappointments, his sense of brokenness recedes into the background. It seems counterintuitive, but difficult relationships calm him.

Like any other organizing principle, this one is self-perpetuating. By choosing women who function poorly, he handicaps his own resilience, which reinforces the belief that he's broken. He also sees himself taking part in low-quality relationships, which further confirms his belief that he deserves nothing better.

Women are my useful oppressors.

This man is conflicted. He wants meaningful connection with women, but experience has taught him they only bring pain. He may have had a maternal figure who degraded or abused him. Or perhaps he had a good-enough mother, but other important women mistreated him, like teachers, classmates, or girlfriends. Perhaps he learned to fear women through the vicarious pain of important men in his life—his browbeaten father or his divorced uncle.

Whatever his origin story, this man has a chip on his shoulder. He's angry, and the anger protects him. It prevents him from letting women close enough to hurt him financially, emotionally, or physically.

By choosing women who are emotionally frail and underperforming, he keeps the upper hand. He finds these women annoying, but at least they are powerless. As a bonus of sorts, their chaos and disorder give him fuel for a soothing combination of anger and condescension toward the opposite sex. He may fear women, but he always gets to look down on them.

Women are his useful oppressors. He can blame women for his pain without scrutinizing his role in perpetuating it. He can use women for company and pleasure, while preventing any real emotional connection. This organizing principle reduces a man to the equivalent of a doctrinaire feminist: he resents the opposite sex while simultaneously obsessing over them. Underneath his resentment is the fear of injury and the pain of isolation.

Junk-Food Relationships

It's vital to acknowledge the upside of any poorly functioning relationship pattern because the upside is what maintains the pattern. One can find advantages to choosing emotionally frail women. At the top of the list: giving them a central position in our lives lets us feel useful and productive.

Conversely, there's a downside to choosing high-functioning women: they require men capable of thriving in high-functioning relationships. Some men decide—however unintentionally—that it's easier to tolerate noxious relationships with chaotic women than to do the hard work of putting themselves in order.

It's unlikely any man who has read this far suffers badly from that condition, though I suspect most of us have indulged in it at some point in our lives. Some temptation is always waiting to weaken us: junk food to damage our bodies, social media to weaken our minds, and chaotic relationships to provide relief from self-scrutiny.

Just as sugar and salt can trick our minds into believing we have eaten substantial food, relationships with emotionally frail women can convince our minds we are engaged in a worthwhile activity. That's what happened to a man named Lee, until he recognized and eliminated the pattern.

Lee was a successful engineer with two patents to his name, the respect of his colleagues, and an impressive salary. He was also a compulsive, pathological rescuer, and it almost cost him his life. It's no mystery how he ended up there.

His parents' relationship was a match made in hell. He described his father as a "spineless alcoholic" who abandoned Lee and his siblings when they were young children. That left Lee, the oldest, to protect himself and his siblings from a neglectful, unpredictable mother.

For example, Lee recalled her throwing a kettle of boiling water at the kitchen wall one warm summer morning. She was angry at Lee's young sister for interfering with her romantic life. The mother had brought home a strange man the previous evening. He left when one of Lee's sisters became sick in the middle of the night, requiring their mother's attention.

The boiling water splashed through the corner of the kitchen where Lee and his sisters were eating dry cereal for breakfast. He remembered the milk had gone sour. No one was injured, but such was the volatility of his upbringing. After their mother had thrown the kettle, Lee ushered his sisters out of the house and escorted them to a nearby park. He knew their mother would regain her composure by the time they returned, and she would not discuss it any further.

Lee was rescuing his sisters even before he reached adolescence. Among other interventions, he sometimes kept their mother calm by intercepting bad news, such as subpar report cards. It's no wonder Lee developed organizing principles leading him to chaotic relationships with emotionally frail women. He understood how to operate in that realm. He felt worthwhile when he was serving and rescuing.

A second motivation for choosing low-functioning women was a vague sense that he was unworthy of high-functioning women. He didn't want them to see how broken he was, so he avoided meaningful connection with them.

He ended up engaged to a troubled woman named Janice, and it was then—as the wedding preparations were unfolding—that he realized she had latched onto him before he knew how unstable she was. Her behavior resembled that of his mother so many years before: chaotic and sometimes violent. Still, he felt honor-bound to marry her. His primary job as a husband, he figured, was to keep her calm. He was living his childhood all over again.

Over the years, Lee developed a double life. He excelled at work thanks to his intellect and his ability to remain calm in a crisis. At home, he was browbeaten and defeated.

Eventually, Janice wore him down with her various tantrums and crises. The relationship also tormented him with its utter lack of joy and sex. Lee gained weight and aged before his time. Still, he always put her back together when she fell to pieces. That is, until he could no longer do it. When he finally pushed for divorce, Janice became enraged.

For months on end, she threatened, berated, tried to turn his sisters against him, and even harassed him at work. There, Lee had always been the reliable one. Whatever the problem, he simply pushed through. But even he had his limit. The relationship whittled away at his job performance and his work relationships.

Lee contemplated suicide more than once during the lengthy divorce process, but his story has a happy ending. Although the divorce had been costly and brutal, Lee felt like a new man when the dust settled. He'd had enough of abusive, chaotic women. Lee wanted more out of life than the empty achievement of calming enraged females. He had done it for so long he didn't know how to replace the pattern, but he resolved to learn.

Lee got to work. He started to read self-help books and joined a men's group. He entered therapy, where he dissected his relationship patterns and designed his ideal future. He resolved to associate with only healthy, high-functioning women.

His first step was simply to avoid women who showed the same moodiness and lack of fortitude with which he was so familiar. He forced himself to steer clear of female friends, coworkers, and acquaintances who would have once drawn him in with their tales of woe, and he prohibited himself from dating any woman whose frailty felt comfortable and familiar.

The shift was uncomfortable, but he forced himself to interact with healthier women. At first, he had difficulty connecting with them, even in a platonic context. The familiar interface of frailty and misfortune was missing. He had to discover new ways to connect.

It didn't take him long to find his footing with healthier women. He discovered that his interpersonal skills weren't as lacking as he had assumed. His years of managing crises had given him more depth and insight than he had given himself credit for.

Over the next couple of years, Lee pieced together a roadmap for healthy relationships. He learned that he could find good, mature women—a reality his mind struggled mightily to reject at first. He cataloged his own worth as a man and as a romantic partner, and he unearthed the organizing principles that would have kept him stuck in a cycle of junk-food relationships for the rest of his life.

Lee's old beliefs and principles didn't vanish, but they faded, and he learned to ignore them. He compared those old principles to a small scar he earned during one of his mother's fits of rage decades earlier. That scar on the back of his hand would always remind him of his origins, but he could choose to view it dispassionately.

The Road to Resilience

Most of us expect the treatment we have always received. If others don't give it to us, we find ways to recreate it. Choosing different relationships is the way out, even if they seem out of reach. As gatekeepers, the responsibility to broaden our horizons falls entirely on us. Here are the strategies that helped Lee, and countless others in his position, to find relationships that stoke resilience rather than frailty.

Embrace rejection.

Many of the organizing principles that threaten resilience involve an abiding need to be needed. It's the most natural desire in the world for humans, but it comes with an equally natural unwillingness to experience rejection. A man like Lee can fall into frailty-inducing commitment, in part because he believes healthier women will reject him or, more accurately, that he doesn't belong in their world at all and they will turn him away.

When a woman rejects a man, his rational response would be: *Good. She didn't belong in my life. I wish her well.* Rationality says, "I have endless opportunities. Move on to the next." However, disobeying organizing principles isn't so simple. The mind protests with anxiety about loneliness and abandonment. It's difficult to summon the rational response when the emotional response feels overwhelming. For reasons that are as old as humanity, being rejected by women carries a sting like no other. It hurts all the way down to our DNA.

However, as Lee discovered, even that level of anxiety loses power when we stare it down. The more we walk ourselves through the experience, the less power it has. With enough practice, we can even learn to laugh it off.

If a man chooses to face his anxiety over female rejection, it's useful to remind himself why he's doing so. In Lee's case, it was for the sake of his purpose and for the new relationship possibilities that might open up. He faced his anxiety in the service of his values. That's a winning recipe.

Be a reliable presence rather than a knight in shining armor.

A healthy woman will need occasional help, as we all do. It may involve nothing more than listening and hand-holding. In healthy relationships, there is rarely a need to step in, take over, and control the situation. The wise gatekeeper saves that level of intervention for genuine emergencies, like a physical injury or her being stranded on the side of the road.

Merely being present can feel painfully inactive to a compulsive rescuer. Doing nothing feels like more work than charging in like the cavalry. Remaining non-reactive—that is, not rescuing troubled women—is difficult for many men, but we can do it when we resolve to ride out our own anxiety about her discomfort.

The theme of this book is: Raise your standards. Transcend old patterns. We're better off, and we can better serve our purpose, when we surround ourselves with resilient people. For men who feel they're only valuable when they're being used, the task is to learn how to be present for high-functioning women rather than being a crisis counselor for low-functioning women. That means learning to tolerate the anxiety of *not* rescuing when there's no actual emergency.

Invest in resilient people.

Endless people, projects, and institutions threaten to consume every ounce of our energy if we let them. The resilient man guards his time and resources. Just as the resilient man has clearly defined personal values, he also possesses clear guidelines about the conditions under which he serves others.

He requires women to function like adults in order to have a place in his life. He realizes the folly of being more invested in solving her problems than she is, and he understands the futility of trying to manage her emotions for her. He is also willing to receive kindness and accept help when he is in need.

An economic element is present here. Just as money is a store of value, healthy relationships are a store of strength. When we reserve our romantic efforts for women of the Bright Triad, then not only can they lean on us in times of need, but we can also lean on them.

Choose relationships of mutual benefit.

This should be the most obvious point in the section, but it is the most elusive to many men: Healthy relationships are two-way streets. Pathological rescuers, on the other hand, view themselves as a resource to be used up. Their mantra: from *him* according to his ability, to *her* according to her need.

Men like Lee, at the beginning of this section, are taught by their families of origin that the safest role with women is that of rescuer. It gives them a sense of control to overcome the fact that relationships with women have always felt perilous. Yet, pathological rescuers usually have a measure of contempt for the women they serve because frail women are a pain in the ass. When Lee began spending time with high-functioning women, he noticed that his disdain for women in general receded.

Maintain the margin.

Men beyond their twenties face a particular challenge in the dating scene: many of the women have children, debt, ex-husbands, and other complications. Becoming romantically attached means adding their complications to their partners' lives.

This is not necessarily bad, but every budget, including a man's relationship budget, should include enough margin to absorb the effects of added complexity. Relationships with preexisting complications are expensive to a man's purpose, though they can also be rewarding if there is enough spiritual and material margin to absorb the costs.

Investigate her values and beliefs.

Most men like to get laid, to point out the ridiculously obvious, and we will overlook a multitude of deficiencies to make it happen. Easy access to intercourse is a prime reason men tolerate miserable relationships, but the failure to investigate her character in advance is another dangerous form of unprotected sex.

Curiosity is a highly underrated skill in vetting relationships. I hear tales of hours-long dates in which the prospect asks no meaningful questions. I suppose some people are so motivated to be interesting that they forget to be interested. Others have simply never learned basic conversational skills.

When vetting relationships, ask questions. Be inquisitive. There's no need to interrogate her like an agent in a Soviet gulag, but there is a vital need to exchange information about values and beliefs. If you struggle with these skills (men of purpose often do), then you might make use of classic works like Dale Carnegie's *How to Win Friends and Influence People*. The most basic responsibility of the gatekeeper is to study the nature of any applicant to his inner circle. That means asking questions, even if the answers might rule out an otherwise attractive applicant.

Penetrate her inner circle.

One way to study how she will conduct herself in your inner circle is to study how she conducts herself in her own inner circle. Make an apples-to-apples comparison.

I knew a man who, in a rush of passion and desperation, moved a woman into his house after knowing her for just two months. As infatuation wore off, he noticed she had enduring anxiety that gave rise to hoarding behavior. He also learned that her dependence on pot far exceeded the casual use she had led him to believe was the case.

She was a good person, but she neglected her mental health. She was frail. He could have known this, and so much more, had he slowed down and become acquainted with her friends and family, where a person's true characteristics reveal themselves. He might have noticed her friends and family obliquely referring to her high-strung nature, or the lapses and misfires that accompany heavy pot use.

He could not see her relationship patterns, both good and bad, in a vacuum. They're only visible within actual relationships, and any romantic prospect should have personal relationships that are rich sources of information about a potential future with her. (The absence of relationships can be equally telling.) Dispassionate observation lights the way.

Beware the glimmer of resilience in an ocean of helplessness.

A well-known phenomenon in psychotherapy is called "flight into health." It refers to a remission of psychological symptoms to avoid an unpleasant event or discussion.

For example, a person with a costly and dangerous substance abuse problem might suddenly discover religion rather than face the harsh necessity of inpatient treatment. Mind-blowing insights appear with astounding reliability when people are looking down the barrel of overdue consequences.

To onlookers—and to naïve therapists—this looks like a miraculous recovery. *All is well! Huzzah!* In reality, relapse is almost certain because the underlying conditions remain unchanged and ready to reassert themselves.

Troubled couples also take flights into health. They convince themselves that a vacation or having a child or reaching some mystical insight will prevent an impending crisis, such as breaking up. But if they don't tackle whatever pattern created their misery, these flights into health only temporarily mask the problem.

To the well-intentioned man whose resilience is being drained by a frail woman, these flights into health can seem like a godsend. *All is well! Huzzah!* In reality, she may pull herself together only long enough to avoid losing the relationship.

This is another example of the insidious slot-machine effect. A flight into health feels like a jackpot, but it's just a temporary win among a baseline string of losses. The wise gatekeeper attends to that baseline, not to the exception to it. Those who play the slots will lose everything if they play long enough.

Foundational Skill: Embrace the Challenge of High-Functioning Relationships

Men do well in life when we choose resilient women with compatible values and robust characters, but healthy relationships aren't cost-free. The price is that we, ourselves, must be high-functioning men—not just in the world but in our romantic relationships. Here are a few strategies for the lifelong endeavor of pursuing relationship excellence.

Embrace the discomfort of violating outdated organizing principles.

Today's malfunctioning organizing principle is yesterday's survival skill. That's why breaking old patterns is anxiety-provoking.

Even when we're on dry land, removing the life preserver feels risky. To make the task even more challenging, we're bound to get scraped up and disappointed when we try to establish new relationship patterns. That can prompt a swift reaction from the emotional mind: *What was I thinking? I knew I shouldn't have tried that!*

Comfort is the enemy when it keeps us mired in patterns that have outlived their usefulness. Growth usually involves heartache. Luckily, heartache isn't deadly.

Be uncompromising about self-maintenance.

Self-respecting habits like standing tall, dressing well, and speaking clearly can be tough to maintain. Yet these habits and practices send a potent message to ourselves and the world that we are formidable men deserving of respect.

To the pathological rescuer, prioritizing his own needs is uncomfortable. He doesn't believe he deserves the same consideration he gives others. He might not believe he's worthy of basic care and maintenance such as good sleep and quality food.

Yet, self-maintenance isn't optional for men of purpose. A well-functioning machine requires regular care. Getting started begins with small habits such as how we eat, exercise, dress, and sleep. One of the simplest steps a man can take toward self-respect, besides high-quality food, is to upgrade his wardrobe and begin dressing like the man he wants to be. In the US, it takes minimal effort to dress better than most other men, and it makes a tremendous difference in how we carry ourselves and how others perceive us.

We can hardly demand high-functioning women if we ourselves are struggling with the basics. If the idea of uncompromising self-maintenance is uncomfortable, then I have good news: once you prioritize the basics of self-maintenance, you will soon wonder how you ever lived any other way.

Continually improve communication skills.

Learning to communicate clearly is a lifelong endeavor. We can refine it well into old age even as other capacities decline. The ability to communicate improves every area of life, especially our closest relationships.

So how does a man learn to use words effectively? The same way you build any other muscle: by using it. This means by reading, writing, and speaking. If you are weak in this area, I can't overemphasize its importance.

I write from experience. As a young man, I had difficulty expressing my thoughts, and it was damn-near impossible to express my feelings. With women in particular, my communication skills were a mess. If I had a desire, I didn't know how to ask for it. If there was a problem, I couldn't describe it. When girlfriends asked me perfectly reasonable questions about my emotions or motivations, I would sit slack-jawed, wanting to speak, but feeling as if some gremlin was throttling my vocal cords.

I didn't know how to arrange my ideas and discuss important topics. I could barely decipher my own emotional logic. None of those skills had been part of my upbringing. My communication deficit opened the door to chaos and distraction.

No, it was worse than that. It *ensured* chaos and distraction. It made me frail.

I got to work. I read, even when I didn't understand the content. I studied the techniques of persuasive speakers, even when I couldn't emulate them. I spent my hard-earned money on college courses, and I stuck with it even after I flunked out my first semester. Now, decades later, I'm reasonably effective at expressing myself, and I'm still working to improve. Learning how to use words has made me immeasurably more resilient.

Where learning to communicate is concerned, each of us has precisely the same amount of work to do. Whatever our current ability, we can each claw our way to the next level. The more clearly we communicate, the greater our options in life. As a bonus, reliable verbal skills allow us to detect and defend against those who use words as weapons or tools for manipulation.

Focus on relationship patterns more than relationship incidents.

In my many years as a psychologist, I have noticed that resilient couples focus on patterns within their relationships. They discuss their communication, their underlying motives, and their desires. They work to understand the themes that drive their behaviors and interactions.

Low-resilience couples, on the other hand, argue about events. Yesterday they bickered about paint color. Today it's the dog. Tomorrow it will be the bills. They don't understand that they're having the same argument repeatedly because they can't see the theme.

Maybe one of them feels disrespected, or the other feels unloved. Maybe they're fighting for opposing sets of values, or one of them is trying to shame the other into silent obedience. Whatever the pattern might be, it eludes them, and their constant bickering eats away at their resilience.

It can take years to learn how to focus on patterns rather than events, especially for those who don't possess the skill. The ability to look beyond specific grievances when emotions are high is a skill unto itself. There's no quick and easy way to fill this toolbox. The most reliable means are insight-oriented therapy (see the next strategy) and books that focus on relationship patterns. Even self-help books that don't automatically appeal to us can get our minds thinking about the patterns we unwittingly enact.

This is another area where the wise gatekeeper takes the lead. Become a great communicator who can think and speak about patterns, and watch your relationships improve and your resilience bloom.

Consider insight-oriented therapy.

This book contains at least one inherent problem: no matter how well I describe relationship patterns I have encountered, I cannot capture the nuance of *your* patterns and organizing principles. This is where hiring a consultant to help you decipher yourself can save years of effort. A skilled therapist is interested in discovering a shared understanding of how you operate.

So, what might you expect in therapy? At the end of the first meeting, you should have a clear goal—for example, to understand why you repeatedly fall into the same type of relationships—as well as a tentative plan for reaching that goal.

If therapy is going well in subsequent meetings, you will find yourself thinking, *Of course! That's why I approach relationships this way. It makes perfect sense!* You'll understand why, as one of my former professors put it, you tend to react to what was rather than what is.[55]

Eventually, you'll understand when and why your mind is divided against itself. You'll be able to give yourself a bit of grace, and you'll become more flexible around the parts of your mind that are unlikely to change.

You might even see the humor in the workings of your mind. When you've reached that level, chances are good that your old organizing principles are no longer driving the bus. They'll still be present; they just won't be in charge. Is there any better ingredient for resilience?

---

55 Shedler, J. 2006. *That Was Then, This Is Now: Psychoanalytic Psychotherapy For the Rest of Us.* Retrieved from http://jonathanshedler.com/writings/. This paper is a jargon-free example of the way skilled clinicians think about the work of therapy. It's therefore a useful illustration of the type of mindset to seek in a therapist.

FLIGHT CHECK

- **Female character.** Think back on the women you have dated, married, or found attractive. Would you describe them as women of the Bright Triad? What patterns can you identify in their collective character and personalities? Would you say they were on good terms with life and with other people?
- **Fortitude.** Would an impartial observer say you are drawn to women who need rescuing? How does it feel when you fail to anticipate or repair women's problems?
- **Worthiness.** What does the emotional side of your mind say about your worthiness of high-functioning women and relationships? What does your rational side say? How have you handled rejection from women? How have you handled being the one to reject them?

– BOOK IV –

Joy

The "happy wife, happy life" problem • Create and protect the joyful condition • Respect intuition

No matter what you're trying to accomplish in life, someone or something will try to stand in your way. Your relationship should not be one of them. It should be a soft place to land in a world filled with hard edges. If you're not happier with her than without, then why should she be in your life?

Here, we focus on creating what I call the joyful condition, which is not a state of constant bliss. The joyful condition is much more nourishing than that. It exists within the relationship you look forward to coming home to. It exists with a woman of outstanding character and shared values who offers kindness, benevolence, acceptance, and a good laugh now and then.

Unfortunately, too few men have seen real-life models of the joyful condition. Instead, they have seen their fathers, brothers, friends, and colleagues suffer through burdensome, unhappy relationships. They have witnessed men who joke about "the old ball and chain," men who hide money from their wives for a moment of unsupervised fun or who hide booze in the garage for a quick escape from their miserable marriages, men who work extra hours to avoid going home, or men who develop frantic social lives to avoid the solitary company of their women. For those unfortunate souls, the world with all its hard edges is a softer place than their own living rooms.

These men all have a commonality: they're *tired.* Tired of the conflict, the double-binds, the anxiety, the depression, and the prickly moodiness that permeates their homes. Our next case study offers insight into how such a state of affairs can overtake a man's life.

Tony and Cynthia

Tony was a joyful man in a soul-crushing relationship. Optimistic and upbeat, he enjoyed his work. There, he could solve any problem. Unfortunately, that tenacity didn't work at home. Try as he might, he just couldn't make the home-front tolerable. He didn't dislike his wife; he was fond of her as a person, but he despised their relationship.

It was fun at first. Even ten years into the marriage, when I met Tony, he continued to catch glimpses of the way things used to be. That's why he still liked her. Long ago, they enjoyed volleyball during the day and raucous parties at night. They had similar desires for physical activity and social lives, which is usually a good predictor of relationship satisfaction.

After a year of dating, with plenty of fun and sex, they moved in together. They had wanted to cohabit sooner, but they waited until their first anniversary, as if that were a meaningful demarcation that improved their chances of success.

It didn't. Their situation changed for the worse almost immediately.

Suddenly, Cynthia felt the weight of the relationship. Sharing her space had always been difficult for her. It wasn't selfishness, precisely. Her retreating and protective nature was an old survival mechanism that developed after her father disappeared when she was four years old and her self-absorbed mother retreated into short-lived romances.

As a result of that disruption, young Cynthia spent much of her time at her uncle's house, where she had three cousins who usually excluded her from their adventures. Feeling ignored and rejected both at home and abroad, her bedroom became the one space to which she could retreat. That's where she enjoyed some measure of control. Understandably, she became protective of that space. She bristled when friends and family invaded it, and that made her appear remote and selfish.

Now, as an adult, she had a powerful compulsion to control every aspect of her living situation, from her finances to the arrangement of the decorative pillows on her bed. She had never come to terms with her turbulent childhood, and so the girl who once appeared remote and selfish to other children now seemed anxious and controlling to other adults.

That pattern asserted itself when she moved in with Tony. She was especially territorial about finances. She even partitioned part of their pantry to contain her private stash of food, which was off limits to him. That is not the stuff of healthy relationships.

She was similarly controlling about sex. When Tony initiated, she usually had an excuse not to engage. The lack of sex was a departure from their pre-cohabiting days. Cynthia initiated consistently while they were dating, which thrilled Tony. Now he saw a different side of her: sex, like money, would be managed on her terms.

Being an agreeable, optimistic man, he accommodated. He wanted her to be happy. Unfortunately, what made her happiest was his continual acquiescence. Stated more accurately, his acquiescence staved off her disapproval. (Once again, we see the power of negative reinforcement. Tony tried to reduce the amount of punishment from Cynthia by being agreeable.)

At his workplace, his agreeable nature was an asset. Clients adored him, and he made good money. He couldn't understand why the same strategy failed at home. He couldn't see that his desire to serve was a perfect, pathological fit for Cynthia's need to control. The more control he ceded, the more she wanted and the less satisfied she was. (Not that resisting would have necessarily given him a different result.) Within a few years, she was consistently unhappy. In time, her unhappiness grew into moments of open hostility toward him.

By the time I met Tony, he was overweight, sexless, addicted to weed, and utterly depressed. Consumed by shame, he called himself pussy-whipped with the resigned smile of someone who is avoiding tears. He had even contemplated suicide during moments when death seemed like the least painful option. His marriage had become his second job, and no amount of work would turn the tide of joylessness and gloom that permeated the house he had paid for.

I should also mention this: He was the sole provider. Early in the marriage, he took a major misstep in his endless journey to stave off her unhappiness. He agreed she could quit her job while he worked extra hours to support their lifestyle. She kept herself busy with travel, shopping, tennis, and yoga. Unlike Tony, Cynthia was a picture of physical health.

He wanted to divorce, but he concluded leaving would be more painful than staying. He knew Cynthia would seek an extortionate divorce settlement, and she would succeed since family courts in his area were sympathetic to women who had been outside the workforce for many years.

Tony felt completely stuck. In a word, he was exhausted.

"Happy Wife, Happy Life"

When I last heard from Tony, he and Cynthia had reached an agreement of sorts. She granted him a bit more leeway to assert himself, but only within bounds. He wore a slightly longer leash, and he was slightly less unhappy.

It only took one joyless relationship to turn happy, optimistic Tony into a depressed shell of his former self. Before we dissect the tactical errors that created his miserable relationship, let's acknowledge what Tony did right.

First, he didn't rush headlong into an obvious disaster. The relationship started off joyfully. He thought he was bringing someone pleasant into his life.

Second, he was doing what had been effective elsewhere. His accommodating nature had served him well at work, with his family, and with his previous girlfriends. Unfortunately, as the relationship with Cynthia deteriorated, he fell into the trap of trying harder. He was so busy being optimistic and dutiful that he didn't recognize the counterproductive results of his efforts.

As to his errors, Tony's first major blunder was cohabiting and marrying too quickly. My general guideline for marriage is to conduct no less than one year of vetting after the infatuation fades, and to only share a home as part of a larger plan to build a life together.

The decline of idealization is the most reliable sign of a waning infatuation. That's when couples begin to see each other as three-dimensional. The little quirks that were once adorable lose their charm. If all goes well, a more mature and measured attachment overtakes infatuation. Whatever timeline a man chooses, prudence requires a long period of observation in which to experience plenty of real-life trials. Proper vetting requires shared adversity of some kind.

The infatuation phase is dangerous because both parties want to focus on the best aspects of the relationship (like sex) and ignore the worst (like troubling personality traits). Infatuation is a terrible state of mind from which to make life-altering decisions.

Tony and Cynthia convinced themselves that one year was sufficient to assess the relationship. Clearly, they were still infatuated at the end of that year. He would have otherwise detected the utter joylessness he would receive in exchange for his devotion.

Tony's next tactical error was buying into the hackneyed, deceptive, misery-inducing platitude "happy wife, happy life." Of course, we want our women to be happy, but this saying contains a specific and remarkably unhealthy insinuation. It assumes the wife—and only the wife—should never be unhappy or uncomfortable. That assumption puts both parties at the mercy of her emotions. That's a rotten deal for a man to make with himself, and it's a condescending way to treat her. She's not an infant. She must be capable of surviving discomfort and managing her emotions if she is to have a place in the world of any wise gatekeeper.

Unfortunately, beaten-down men like Tony use the phrase "happy wife, happy life" to mean, "Maybe she'll stay off my back if I make enough concessions." He turned Cynthia into a prison guard, and her own history of neglect and insecurity predisposed her to the role.

Tony and Cynthia were co-conspirators in their own misery. Because they both believed she should never experience unhappiness or discomfort, they were both fearful and intolerant of disappointment. For Tony, that translated into walking on eggshells and attempting to eliminate her discomfort at any cost to himself.

I can't think of a faster way to create an utterly joyless relationship. Trying to avoid discomfort in a world full of sharp edges is like trying not to think of monkeys … at the zoo … on Simian Appreciation Night. The harder you work, the worse it gets.

So how do men fall into the happy-wife-happy-life trap? In Tony's case, it started early and started small. He noticed Cynthia would pout when things didn't go her way. He found (in retrospect) that her pouting made him anxious, and the real purpose of relieving her dissatisfaction was to eliminate his anxiety.

For example, he recalled long ago shopping with her for a new refrigerator. He wanted to buy one with the same dimensions as their previous refrigerator. She wanted a larger unit that would require him to detach and move a cabinet to make it fit.

Right there in the middle of the store, Cynthia pouted and Tony got anxious. To relieve his anxiety, he quickly relented and promised to move the cabinet despite how busy he was. She hugged him, and his anxiety vanished. *Happy wife, happy life* became his mantra.

Over time, Cynthia's pouting grew into nagging and hostility. She no longer expressed gratitude when he bent to her will and instead showed signs of entitlement and dissatisfaction. No amount of "happy wife, happy life" could make her happy.

To minimize her hostility, Tony became the consummate self-policer. Like any other man living in that self-imposed prison, he stopped being impulsive. He wasn't excited unless he was supposed to be; never happy unless she wanted him to be. He was never horny, angry, or opinionated without monitoring for signs of disapproval.

To a man in that position, every act is purposeful and every word and facial expression carefully chosen. He only experiences real joy when he steals a moment away from her, though the feeling more closely resembles relief than happiness. His life is void of unguarded moments.

This type of relationship is utterly pathological. Tony didn't have a partner and teammate. He didn't have a wife. He had a taskmaster and an opponent, and he arrived at that position one minor concession at a time.

Sex was one of the first activities to disappear when the cycle of joylessness consumed their relationship. Sex mattered a great deal to Tony, and being deprived by an increasingly frigid wife made him immensely unhappy. He also felt she sold him a bill of goods. Where was the passionate woman he used to know? He consoled himself by complaining about "the old ball and chain" to any man who would listen.

Cynthia wasn't happy, either. She didn't have a husband. She had a beaten-down dog who smiled to her face but resented her behind her back. No healthy woman wants an obedient doormat for a husband, or to hear a disengaged "yes, dear" to her every question. That's a lonely marriage.

The problem with chasing happiness is its proximity to the pathological avoidance of discomfort. "Happy wife, happy life" is a recipe for neurotic safety-seeking. Chasing values and purpose, however, is a pretty good bet. Even when happiness is elusive, a guy can take a step in the direction of his values. Cognitive psychologist Steven Pinker wrote,

"... the study of happiness often sounds like a sermon for traditional values. The numbers show that it is not the rich, privileged, robust, or good-looking who are happy; it is those who have spouses, friends, religion, and challenging, meaningful work."[56]

High-functioning relationships don't revolve around the desperate avoidance of discomfort any more than do high-functioning individuals. By obsessively eliminating discomfort, Tony was drowning in a swamp of his own making, and Cynthia was supplying the alligators. High-functioning relationships are joyful. It may be their most distinguishing characteristic. These couples enjoy humor, affection, gratitude, sex, conversation, and above all, mutual support of values and purpose.

Men of purpose must jealously guard the joyful condition against all usurpers. The gatekeeper isn't merely selective about women. He is also selective about the men in his life, and he surrounds himself with examples of health, maturity, and success.

Beware of Men Who Normalize Misery

Men like Tony are a danger to themselves and others. Sure, we can blame Cynthia for being a miserable dragon. But it was Tony who not only allowed her misery to overtake him but who also tried to spread his contagious condition to other men.

How? By telling his bitter jokes about "the old ball and chain" and by suggesting to other men that it's normal to submit to "the boss." He spread his misery at parties through his sly, passive-aggressive jabs at his wife and his marriage; by the way he hid from her at work; and by his liberal use of that insipid phrase "happy wife, happy life."

Tony, despite being a great guy with a generous soul, was a normalizer of misery. He sent the message to friends, family, and coworkers that his wretched relationship was the normal state of affairs between men and women.

---

56 Pinker, S. 1997. *How the Mind Works*. New York: W.W. Horton and Company.

His brand of misery is contagious. On a closely related topic, a 2013 study found that a couple is 75 percent more likely to divorce if a close friend or family member divorces. They're 33 percent more likely if a friend of a friend gets divorced.[57]

Divorce flows across social ties. The authors of the study wrote:

> "Attending to the health of one's friends' marriages may serve to support and enhance the durability of one's own relationship … divorce should be understood as a collective phenomenon that extends beyond those directly affected."

While not directly describing Tony's situation, the study underscores the point that our relationships are healthier when we surround ourselves with other healthy relationships. At the very least, we certainly won't be worse off for it. Unfortunately, people in healthy relationships rarely advertise their happiness. They don't boast about their contentment the way men like Tony boast about their misery. That's why we're more familiar with unhappy relationships. Men like Tony spread their hard-luck sermons like it's an assignment from God.

I have noticed two ways in which men justify and normalize their joyless relationships. The first is what we might call the Covert Normalizer. This man believes women are dangerous, but he won't say it directly. He simply speaks of his unhappy arrangement as if it's normal, and he mocks any man who claims to have a joyful relationship. "She's good to you? Yeah, right, just give it time, buddy! Ha ha!" This man needs everyone else to feel beaten down like he does. His affable, joking manner can draw men into the same trap that claimed him.

Recall that one of Tony's first "happy wife, happy life" incidents occurred while shopping for a refrigerator. He succumbed to Cynthia's pouting rather than insisting on a more mature exchange.

57 McDermott, R., J. Fowler, and N. Christakis. 2013. "Breaking Up Is Hard to Do, Unless Everyone Else Is Doing It Too: Social Network Effects on Divorce in a Longitudinal Sample." *Social Forces* 92: 491-519.

Now imagine a young coworker listening to him describe the incident and complain about his wife's behavior, then finding himself in a similar situation in his own budding relationship. Such minor incidents are where the virulence of negative attitudes flow across social ties.

That young man, persuaded by Tony's story and attitude, could easily slide into the same miserable pattern—especially if he likes and respects Tony. I have yet to see a man break social convention by publicly disagreeing with his type of anti-happiness propaganda.

Imagine Tony recounting his refrigerator incident to an audience in the break room at work, and a bystander chiming in: "You know, Tony, miserable relationships haven't been my experience at all. Have you considered couples therapy?"

Sadly, there's a good chance that man would be mocked. Some men assume that any man who speaks well of his relationship is obeying a woman who instructed him to do so. I suppose people enjoy singing the blues together, and they don't appreciate a ray of sunshine mid-tune.

The second type of normalizer I have seen in the wild is what I call the Overt Normalizer. This is the man who believes women are duplicitous and menacing, and he won't stop shouting it from the rooftops. These men are the walking wounded who have suffered at the hands of women. They are fixated on their injuries, and they are on a mission to save other men from the same fate.

Because intimacy requires a willingness to get hurt, and because these men have relinquished that willingness, they create dead-end relationships that are shallow and cynical. They recreate relationships bound to fail, and they broadcast their tales of woe like a town crier.

People are mostly neurotic creatures capable of joy, not joyful creatures capable of neuroticism. That's why neurotic warnings are easy to digest, and hopeful messages are tempting to dismiss. Still, Covert and Overt Normalizers aren't always wrong. Romance is risky. It's up to each of us to find the utility of their messages, to leave the rest behind, and to surround ourselves with examples of success.

Pursue Joyful Women

Neuroticism, one of the highly studied big-five personality traits, is the tendency toward negative emotions like sadness or anxiety. We each have our baseline level of neuroticism. Whether it's high, low, or somewhere in between, it usually remains stable throughout life. Momentary experiences can shift our mood temporarily, but we return to baseline.

Psychologists call that *hedonic adaptation*. It serves a purpose. Adhering to a baseline emotional state keeps us from becoming complacent and unfocused when life gets comfortable or from becoming distraught and immobilized when times get tough. Remaining steady as conditions change helps people adapt to a variety of situations, from paradise to prison camps. Our brains will even recalibrate and adapt to recreational drugs such that we need increasing amounts to achieve the same high.[58]

Some women are fortunate enough to have a cheerful baseline emotional state. Experiences like gratitude, amusement, and pleasure are effortless. These women are a joy to be around. (I should know. I married one.)

For women who are higher in neuroticism—and most women are higher in trait neuroticism than men—experiences like anger, disappointment, fear, and anxiety arrive more easily. However, this woman can contribute equally to the joyful condition if she chooses habits that keep her from succumbing to constant dissatisfaction.

The wise woman avoids a steady diet of complaints and contrived grievances on social media. She doesn't participate in a League of Broken Women, either online or in real life, who encourage each other's worst attitudes. She takes care of herself physically and mentally, and she has a spiritual or religious prac-

---

58 Brickman, T., and D. T. Campbell. 1971. "Hedonic Relativism and Planning the Good Society." In *Adaptation Level Theory: A Symposium*, edited by M. H. Apley. New York: Academic Press. 287-302.

tice that reminds her to be grateful. If she goes to therapy, she uses it to increase her insight and accountability rather than wallowing in misery with a therapist of the "poor you" variety. She might even read upbeat self-help books to practice optimism and gratitude.

This woman has an inner circle of high-functioning people who respect the opposite sex and enjoy healthy relationships, and she's not a servant to her emotions because she lets values guide her decisions.

During the infatuation stage, giddy enchantment can mask high neuroticism. Infatuation blinded Tony, and he was still under the influence when he married Cynthia. Had he waited longer, he might have detected Cynthia's habit of retreating into misery whenever she was on the verge of happiness. He might have noticed that her hedonic set point was hovering between "glum" and "tragic" and she instituted none of the measures I listed earlier for maintaining a positive mindset.

So much of our attitude toward romantic relationships boils down to who we surround ourselves with. Deliberately associating with people who enjoy healthy relationships is a potent way to cultivate the joyful condition.

Cultivating the Joyful Condition

In the early, cruel days of psychiatry, agitated patients were sometimes "calmed" by sadistic means. One such treatment was to induce vertigo by strapping patients into chairs and spinning them. Another was locking patients into crib-like cages. Patients would usually emerge from these treatments quite compliant, probably because they wanted the torment to end. (The patients must have understood negative reinforcement, but I'm not sure the psychiatrists did.)

Yet another cruel intervention involved wrapping patients in wet blankets for hours at a time. That was the origin of the term "wet blanket" to describe someone who is a killjoy. Physicians reportedly thought the treatment relieved symptoms. It's likelier that confining patients in heavy, cold, restrictive blankets defeated them by slowly draining their strength.

A wet-blanket relationship has the same effect. Over a long enough timeline, a person in this situation will become weary and spiritless. So why doesn't every man choose the joyful condition? Why are there so many Tonys in the world? The answer lies partly in the mind's tendency toward pessimism.

Focusing on the negative is the human default. We are predisposed to see imperfections, even as we remind ourselves to look on the bright side. Here's a thought experiment: Imagine you are standing before a beautiful stained glass window, an elegant work of art. Now imagine that the corner of this window is missing a piece of glass. You see bright, sterile daylight where there should be a vibrant fragment of color.

As you stand before this masterpiece, where do you suppose your mind will dwell? It will want to perseverate on the missing fragment. That's by design. Our minds are supposed to be somewhat neurotic so we're aware of the dangers of the world. Pessimism is a speedy heuristic based on the reality that false positives (mistakenly assuming a safe situation is dangerous) are more sensible than false negatives (mistakenly assuming a dangerous situation is safe). Better to assume the rustling in the bushes is a bear and not a bunny.[59]

The downside to this survival mechanism is that it's harder to enjoy imperfect stained-glass windows. Our minds evolved to latch onto anomalies and assume the worst, even when we would prefer to see the best. Once again, the mind is divided against itself. This time, the desire for optimism is pitted against the need for vigilance.

There's an optimal level of pessimism. It appears to be what researchers have called *defensive pessimism*, in which a person explores

---

59 See, for example, Haselton, M. G., D. Nettle, and D. R. Murray. 2016. "The Evolution of Cognitive Bias." In *The Handbook of Evolutionary Psychology*, edited by David M. Buss. Hoboken, NJ: John Wiley & Sons.

and acknowledges what might go wrong without being immobilized by emotional horror stories.

What does this have to do with vetting relationships? We align with people who share our worldview, even (especially) if that worldview is painful, so a strong propensity toward pessimism predisposes a man to the Misery Normalizers of the world with their messages of hopelessness and despair.

I'm not suggesting this is a character flaw. It's useful to spot trouble before trouble spots us. That's why I don't believe in trying to eliminate pessimism. Even if I wanted to, I don't know how. However, with insight into our own predisposition, we can be flexible when our minds fixate on the missing piece of glass—or the most miserable voices on the internet.

Most of us have a natural predisposition toward neuroticism, anxiety, and pessimism; some of us are just more high-strung than others. In addition, some of us come from families in which the joyful condition was thwarted by the misery of our parents or by garden-variety mental illness, substance abuse, neglect, poverty, or unreasonable or unpredictable punishment … families have endless methods of stifling happiness.

Those of us born into such families can end up believing joy is unsafe. Happiness can evoke dread if it's been consistently paired with punishment. When that's the case, we respond to happiness as we would respond to a rustling in the bushes: we expect the worst.

But we don't have to remain in joyless relationships any more than we must remain in jobs, neighborhoods, or friendships that bring us down. We can replace jobs that make us miserable, find homes that better suit us, and develop friendships that improve our lives. Likewise, the wise gatekeeper doesn't waste time in soul-sucking relationships.

I met a man named Jim, who was both an outstanding gatekeeper and highly skilled at romantic commitment. I met him at a point in his life when everything seemed to be going wrong. He was losing contracts at work. His mother fell ill. Even his dog died. It was like he was living in a sad country song.

In addition to his own problems, his new wife was having difficulties at work and with her teenage son from a previous marriage. On top of these struggles, Jim worried that his falling income would diminish him in her eyes. Sometimes the problems just pile on.

However, these two never lost the joyful condition throughout their difficulties. After they had navigated those troubled waters together, Jim and I took an inventory of the strategies that saved them:

- They held no expectation that she must be comfortable at all times. No "happy wife, happy life" nonsense. Jim had married a mature woman who accepted the fact that life is unfair.
- They each took care of themselves. They watched their diet and avoided alcohol. They exercised and protected their sleep.
- They attended to their sex life, even when they didn't feel like it. (Funny how people can get in the mood for sex once they start.)
- They based their decisions on shared goals and values, not on their wildly fluctuating emotions.
- They fought the urge to naval-gaze and feel pitiful. They capitalized on ordinary distractions like watching movies. They didn't avoid their pain, but they deliberately took breaks from it.
- They maintained good social support. She avoided membership in the League of Broken Women, and he avoided men who dwell on stories of misery. They both minimized exposure to news and social media outrage.
- They approached their individual problems as a team, and they invested in each other's success and well-being. They displayed no backbiting or undermining.

Jim didn't marry a wet blanket who would have compounded his problems. He married a woman of the Bright Triad. They maintained the joyful condition, not through obsession with comfort or avoidance of pain but through values-driven action. (It helped that their values were aligned. As I said, he was a skilled gatekeeper.) Their relationship became that much stronger after they survived the tsunami of problems together.

A common vulnerability emerges in a wet-blanket relationship involving two positive personality traits—agreeableness and conscientiousness. You might expect those traits to ensure happiness, but they can undermine it.

I'm sure we all knew a kid with *agreeableness* traits who was a target for bullies. Many of us *were* that kid. Sometimes we were bullied because we were highly agreeable and predisposed to avoid conflict and unlikely to fight back. The highly agreeable child hopes to stay out of trouble, and he fantasizes that others also want to avoid problems. But bullies love agreeable people because they're the last to defend their boundaries and the last to fight back.

Then there is the trait of *conscientiousness*. This child strives to excel at school, to keep his locker orderly, and to complete his homework ahead of time. His conscientiousness is a magnet for bullies who tear others down because they don't know how to build themselves up.

Fast forward a couple of decades, and it's these two positive qualities in combination—agreeableness and conscientiousness—that can predispose good men to joyless, punishing romantic relationships. Their agreeable nature makes them ripe for the "happy wife, happy life" trap, and their conscientiousness means they don't easily tire of unreasonable tasks and demands.

These guys are like border collies. They're happy, they live to serve, and they have stamina. This combination of traits works great in healthy relationships with mature, good-natured women, but it's a tremendous liability with women who, like schoolyard bullies, dominate and mistreat others.[60]

---

60 See also Pumphrey, C. 2022. *Insight Is 20/20: How to Trust Yourself to Protect Yourself from Narcissistic Abuse & Toxic Relationships*. New Degree Press. The author makes a similar point, contending that the combination of agreeableness and conscientiousness makes women vulnerable to abusive relationships.

These positive personality traits can set the conditions for joylessness. Just like the young target of a schoolyard bully, a grown man finds himself in a relationship he's unprepared to handle. He didn't ask for it; he didn't encourage it—but there he is. From that point on, unless he intentionally chooses a different path, miserable relationships can become his norm.

Pathways to Fatigue

The agreeable, conscientious man must guard the joyful condition as if his future depends on it. So does every man who was taught, either implicitly or explicitly, that joy is off limits. Copious statistics cover divorce, alcohol abuse, infidelity, and mental illness, but I'm not aware of a statistic that captures what so many men have experienced: utter joylessness among the adults who raised them during their upbringing and the price those men pay later in life.

Here are seven organizing principles that can lead men to exhausting, joyless relationships. As always, we'll follow this sampling with strategies for creating the joyful condition, and I encourage you to slow down and put your own words to any principles that resonate with you.

I'm prone to negative emotions, and I choose similar women.

Here's an old question in psychological research: Do people with depression or other mood problems tend to marry each other? We have good evidence that they do. For example, a 2001 meta-analysis found evidence of it in seventeen of twenty-three studies.[61]

---

61 Mathews, C. A., and V. I. Reus. 2001. "Assortative Mating in the Affective Disorders: A Systematic Review and Meta-Analysis." *Comprehensive Psychiatry* 42: 257-262. The researchers found that men with bipolar disorder were almost four times as likely as those without to have a spouse with an affective disorder.

A different study from 2018 noticed that Americans with bipolar disorder are three times likelier than Europeans to marry someone who struggles with depression or alcoholism. This study also discussed the heritability of psychiatric problems, stating, "Risk of major psychiatric difficulties in the offspring of mood disorder patients … in the US is not trivial."[62]

It appears that people prone to negative emotion tend to find each other. The reason and mechanism are unclear. A 2022 study suggests it's not based on directly observable traits associated with depression but on an indirect assessment of secondary traits. The authors didn't specify what types of traits might be at play, but it's easy to imagine that we simply jibe well with people who have a demeanor like our own.[63]

In vetting relationships, self-knowledge contains tremendous value. Do you tend toward anxiety or depression? Do you find pessimism impedes you more than it serves you? Even a simple tendency toward negativity is worth monitoring. Research suggests it's a stable characteristic that may emerge as early as six months, but a neurotic streak doesn't have to rule your future.[64]

Every man, but especially men who tend toward neuroticism or mood problems, owes it to himself to seek the company of positive women and to adopt a practice of monitoring negativity from within.

---

62 Post, R. M., L. L. Altshuler, R. Kupka, S. L. McElroy, M. A. Frye, M. Rowe, H. Grunze, T. Suppes, P. E. Keck Jr., and W. A. Nolen. 2018. "More Assortative Mating in US Compared to European Parents and Spouses of Patients with Bipolar Disorder: Implications for Psychiatric Illness in the Offspring." *European Archives of Psychiatry and Clinical Neuroscience* 270: 237-245.

63 Torvik F. A., E. M. Eilertsen, L. J. Hannigan, R. Cheesman, L. J. Howe, P. Magnus, T. Reichborn-Kjennerud, O. A. Andreassen, P. R. Njølstad, A. Havdahl, and E. Ystrom. 2022. "Modeling Assortative Mating and Genetic Similarities Between Partners, Siblings, and In-Laws." *Nature Communications* 13: 1108.

64 Norris, C. J. 2019. "The Negativity Bias, Revisited: Evidence from Neuroscience Measures and an Individual Differences Approach." *Social Neuroscience* 16: 68-82.

Relationships are supposed to be difficult.

Some men have simply never seen a joyful relationship that flowed easily and naturally. Instead, they witnessed their unfortunate fathers, uncles, and brothers for whom romantic commitments were one of life's unpleasant obligations. These boys heard men say such things as:

- "We stay together for the kids." (Meaning they would divorce if not for the kids.)
- "When it's good, it's great." (And when it's bad, it's terrible.)
- "A man honors his commitments." (Might as well hold a sign saying, "I don't want to be here.")

In such an environment, it's only natural to draw the conclusion: *If a relationship is fun, then I must be doing it wrong.*

Sometimes this organizing principle involves more than a tolerance for joyless relationships. It's a commitment to the notion that romantic relationships lack meaning if they aren't *burdensome*. Men operating under this principle endure the complaints, the tension, and the interminable 3 a.m. gripe fests because doing so seems like an obligation. For them, romantic connection is synonymous with struggle.

For some men, a bit of masochism may be at play in the form of the belief that suffering is a virtue. Some people believe—or were actively taught—that it's moral to be in more pain than the next person. They seek it out without realizing they're invested in suffering. Often, people with this approach to morality simply feel depressed, and they don't know why.

I have heard the phrase "When it's good, it's great" more times than I can count. Only men in unhealthy relationships use that phrase, and they're generally describing women who turn cruel or abusive at regular intervals, despite being "good" most of the time. Their relationships are like cars that are perfectly dependable except when they occasionally throw a rod.

In my estimation, this phrase is often a display of ambivalence about leaving the relationship. These men know they are being mistreated, but they cannot or will not tear themselves away. Even if they want to, they may be entangled with property, children, or other commitments. Since they can't leave, they use the good times to justify the bad.

Whatever the motive at play, these men are so invested in suffering that they never consider the economics of the situation. They don't ponder how they could better allocate their commitment, as if it never occurred to them that a relationship can be an asset rather than a liability.

Such men are often masters of compartmentalization. They have learned how to put relationship misery out of their minds. As one man told me, a low-quality relationship is tolerable if the rest of your life is enjoyable. He saw his marriage as entirely separate from his work and social life rather than as an integral part of his existence.

I don't know how to seek joy because I was punished for success.

Some families have a distinctly joyless atmosphere. No happiness or success goes unpunished. Their motto: "We are the noble sufferers. Let others succeed in our place." Here are a few examples of how parents and other adults undercut joyful moments in a boy's life.

- **Neglecting to celebrate success**. One of the first jobs of any parent is to encourage behavior that will help their children succeed in the world. That doesn't mean everyone gets a trophy for showing up—empty praise also undercuts success by cheapening genuine effort—but it means celebrating success. Some men experienced far too little praise to develop an accurate view of themselves.
- **Shifting the goalpost**. This child achieves the expected goal, only to be told he could have done better. When children hold up their end of the bargain and adults don't, it sends a powerful message: *You can't win*. Parents

who send that message prime their sons to play out the same dynamic in their adult relationships.

- **Actively punishing success**. There are mothers and fathers who treat their children poorly after a victory. Consider the mother who chooses the moment after her son throws the winning touchdown to lecture him about his grades, or the father who is suddenly cold toward his daughter when she earns straight A's. Maybe this mother has a narcissistic streak and can't tolerate sharing the spotlight with her son. Maybe the father avoids his daughter because he is ashamed of his own failures. This child learns to associate success with punishment.
- **Low hedonic adaptation within the family system**. For some families, unhappiness is a way of life. When one person succeeds or expresses happiness, the others drag him back to their miserable baseline, but it may be more out of habit than malevolence. They are crabs in a bucket. Family systems usually resist disruption, even if the disruption is positive. That's just how social systems work.

I was taught to serve women, so I gravitate toward women who demand service.

The man with this organizing principle lives to feel needed. He's usually kindhearted, and he has a soft spot for a good cause. He was conditioned to serve women without affection, gratitude, or compensation. Like a draft horse, he works without bitterness or complaint. As long as he's pulling that load, he knows where he belongs. That's the payoff. His emotional logic says it's better to be overworked and underappreciated than to be emotionally adrift.

As you might imagine (or as you might have experienced), this man fits with a demanding, ungrateful woman like a lock and key. He gets endless demands to help him feel needed, and she gets someone who will tolerate her subpar life skills.

It's my job to prop up children of misfortune.

The man operating under this principle feels lost without the yoke of a joyless relationship. He may have been the kid forced to compensate for his immature parents, or the awkward high school student who enjoyed an ease of acceptance from his most troubled classmates.

Whatever path brought him to this principle, he is a sucker for women who lead with their stories of misfortune. This man is not interested in resilient survivors. His place is at the side of a woman who constantly stumbles. The payoff is straightforward. In exchange for his time and effort, he experiences a kind of purpose and competence.

Of course, this type of relationship is the fast lane to misery. What starts off feeling wonderful—the princess and her champion—ends up in a twisted cycle of self-imposed adversity. She must feel dissatisfied with life to keep him engaged, and he must face her dissatisfaction as a challenge to conquer.

Dissatisfaction and joylessness aren't mere byproducts of this man's organizing principle. His relationships depend on them to maintain his sense of self.

I don't deserve joy.

Organizing principles are usually more visible in our external behavior than in our internal thoughts. Nowhere is that more true than in what psychologists refer to as masochistic or self-defeating personalities. Think of the guy who just can't get out of his own way. He works a job he hates, marries a woman he resents, and snatches defeat from the jaws of victory at any opportunity. He quits his job when he's on the verge of a promotion, or he buys his neighbor's lemon of a car instead of the dependable alternative down the street.

Self-defeating personalities are vexing since every animal with a central nervous system seeks to maximize comfort and minimize pain. Yet people exist who denounce pleasure and devote themselves to joyless burdens. *Why*?

Part of it, as we've seen elsewhere, is an adaptive tendency run amok. A good mother, for example, at times renounces her own needs and comforts in order to care for her infant. It's human nature to sacrifice joy and comfort for a larger cause.

However, the man who believes he doesn't deserve joy isn't doing so for a greater cause. Self-abnegation is simply part of his personality. Nancy McWilliams, a renowned clinical psychologist and professor, described the emotional experience of the person with this personality style:

> "The affective world of the masochistic person is similar to that of the depressive, with a critical addendum. Conscious sadness and deep unconscious guilt feelings are common, but in addition, most masochistic people can easily feel anger, resentment, and even indignation on their own behalf. … many masochistic people see themselves as suffering, but unfairly; as victimized or just ill-starred, cursed through no fault of their own."[65]

This man may not think, *How can I suffer today?* but he will undoubtedly suffer and resent the world for it. Some men choose women who help them fulfill that role by providing a consistent supply of misadventures or mistreatment.

Pessimism about relationships is safer than optimism.

Earlier, we looked at the survival value of defensive pessimism, that tendency to plan against possible negative outcomes. The defensive pessimist has a sense of agency and control, if not directly over the outcome, then at least over his own performance.

Another type of pessimism that interests researchers is *dispositional pessimism*. This pessimist sees no possibility beyond negative outcomes. He doesn't plan or prepare because he has no sense of hope. He may come from a home in which problems simply never got solved. Disagreements were never settled, or even household repairs were done haphazardly with baling wire and duct tape—just enough to hold things together for one more day.

One line of research found dispositional pessimists can improve their outcomes simply by anticipating and planning for possibili-

---

65 McWilliams, N. 2020. *Psychoanalytic Diagnosis, Second Edition*. New York: The Guilford Press.

ties, both good and bad. The mere shift in focus toward open avenues, rather than dead-ends, can eliminate helplessness.[66]

The man who suffers from dispositional pessimism about romantic relationships sometimes follows this emotional logic: if he doesn't expect much from women and relationships, then he has a good reason to keep romantic connections at bay. Throttling his own happiness, for example, by choosing women who make him miserable, is a strategy, not an error. This man believes avoiding joy today will reduce his pain tomorrow.

❄ ❄ ❄

You may have noticed how many of these principles involve the belief that commitment only brings misery. Even for men who don't dwell in utter hopelessness, far too many enter relationships under the grave misapprehension that the joyful condition is optional. It isn't. It's an absolute necessity. Let's look at strategies to make sure the necessity of joy doesn't fall off your radar.

The Road to Joy

There are men who will risk their lives for duty or fun but who cannot tolerate tension with women. Such was the case for one Army Ranger whose work was full of joy and purpose but who feared tension at home. This man, who would happily operate on a deadly battlefield, would avoid his own home if he thought his wife was unhappy with him. He would work extra hours or find reasons to run trivial errands to delay facing her.

However, the danger didn't come from her. She was direct and sometimes forceful when she had a complaint, but she was never unreasonable. She was a skilled listener, and she was always willing to meet him halfway.

---

66 del Valle, C. H. C., and P. M. Mateos. 2008. "Dispositional Pessimism, Defensive Pessimism and Optimism: The Effect of Induced Mood on Prefactual and Counterfactual Thinking and Performance." *Cognition and Emotion* 22: 1-13.

So why did he hide from her? As we've seen elsewhere, he wasn't avoiding her so much as his own anxiety. He fell into the age-old anxiety trap of creating the condition he was trying to prevent. His attempts to avoid tension created tension. She brought the joyful condition; she was a woman of the Bright Triad. He was the source of their problem.

His withdrawal at the first sign of tension usually left her feeling hurt and angry. She wanted a husband, not an absentee roommate. Nor did she enjoy being deprived of necessary conversations. She knew he couldn't relax if tension lingered between them, so she suppressed her dissatisfaction. Our Ranger was unwittingly forcing her to manage his anxiety by avoiding uncomfortable topics. She was certain to become resentful about that.

Luckily for both, a fellow Ranger noticed his behavior and encouraged him to repair his relationship. The friend's sage advice sounded like "Get your shit together at home." Thanks to that intervention, our soldier realized he couldn't continue hiding from his anxiety.

He started putting words to his anxiety about women—he had never done that before—and he started allowing his values to dictate his actions. For example, when he felt like avoiding home, he did the opposite: he forced himself to converse with his wife. His attempts were awkward at first, but she was thrilled at his effort, and it got easier with practice.

A large piece of his anxiety was the belief that women *can't* be happy, *won't* be happy, and any attempt to make them happy only makes them less happy. That had been his experience with women. To his credit, he chose a woman who had a positive demeanor. She wanted the joyful condition. The only obstacle in his way was his own anxiety. It didn't vanish when he faced it, but it lost its power over him.

By facing his anxiety and examining his patterns, our Ranger transformed his relationship into what they both wanted: a soft place to land. His story matters because it illustrates the point that building the joyful condition isn't merely a matter of selecting a joyful woman. It requires identifying the forces within us that draw us to plodding, joyless relationships. Often, there's a bit of anxiety associated with relinquishing the safety of pessimism and old patterns.

If you're up for the challenge, here are ten strategies for building a relationship you will look forward to at the end of a hard day.

Embrace productive conflict.

For some men, conflict in an intimate relationship is loathsome because their families of origin handled it so poorly. They grew up in houses where people fought dirty.

For other men, conflict isn't necessarily a dirty word, but it is an unknown quantity. For example, I knew a man who worried his marriage was ending the first time he and his wife had a serious disagreement. He had never seen his own parents argue. Understandably, the appearance of this strange and unsettling dynamic alarmed him.

He didn't realize that conflict can be a positive force in a relationship. It's an opportunity for teamwork and problem-solving. That's not just a specious platitude. I once watched a couple disagree about how to respond to their toddler, who was within a hair's breadth of a major tantrum. This happened in a crowded restaurant during a family gathering. Talk about pressure. Not only are tantrums a miserable and embarrassing experience for new parents, but there was also the looming specter of family judgment (and worse, unwanted advice offered during a crisis).

"Let's distract her," said the father. He wanted to remove the daughter from her chair and go for a walk.

"That will just set her off," said the mother. She wanted to feed their daughter immediately.

"There's nothing on the table she wants," said the dad.

They were each worried that the other's intervention would trigger a public tantrum. Conditions were perfect for a meltdown between the parents. Each could have felt criticized and undermined by the other. Some parents would snipe at each other, but not this couple. After a brief and efficient negotiation, they decided to employ distraction—the walk—as the best option.

"Come on, Emmy, let's say hello to the flowers outside!" the dad said excitedly. They toddled off together, hand in hand, and that was that. No hurt feelings between the parents, no resentment, no tantrum. Just good teamwork. They succeeded with their daughter, and as a bonus, they helped her develop the critical skill of managing emotion.

When people think about conflict between couples, they often think about the big triggers: substance abuse, infidelity, intrusive in-laws, or money problems. However, it's often in the accumulation of brief moments where relationships succeed or fail. The couple in the restaurant succeeded, and there's a good chance their small victory was part of a larger pattern. The joyful condition requires facing those small moments head-on with a trustworthy teammate.

Be impeccably honest.

This is a corollary to embracing productive conflict. The joyful condition is well served when we bring unpleasant realities into the light of day rather than hiding them in a dark corner.

You'll notice I didn't suggest being *perfectly* honest. *Impeccable honesty* implies virtuousness, whereas *perfect honesty* implies a disregard for her feelings and well-being. Some people boast about their "brutal honesty," in which they speak any "truth" that comes to mind, regardless of effect. Imagine the man who points out a physical imperfection in his wife, then protests, "I'm just being honest" when she's hurt. As a supervisor of mine once speculated, one must wonder if brutality, rather than honesty, is the goal.

At the other extreme is nice-guy honesty. This is the man who won't tell his wife he hates her tuna casserole and instead says, "You did a really great job on dinner." It's not a lie, technically, but it is dishonest and detrimental to the joyful condition, if only because he will spend his life choking down repulsive casserole.

In my opinion—others believe differently—impeccable honesty is honesty that is both necessary and kind. That doesn't rule out giving bad news. It just means being thoughtful about how we present the truth.

As I write this, it all seems pedantic. These are truisms bordering on platitudes. But it's worth discussing because honesty, particularly about emotions, is a tricky skill for men raised to be overly accommodating or stoic.

People in my profession routinely advocate for men to be more emotionally expressive or "vulnerable," apparently unaware or unconcerned that people judge men harshly for being too expressive—and it's difficult to define the line beyond which a man is too expressive.[67]

Consider crying, for example. Men have few allowances for openly crying. We're allowed to shed a tear at funerals, when our dogs die, or at the last scene of *Saving Private Ryan*. Beyond that, people become uncomfortable with men who appear emotionally unrestrained. A man who cries because he didn't get a promotion or because somebody insulted him will certainly suffer from a diminished reputation.

I'm not endorsing this reality as good or bad. I'm simply acknowledging it. Regardless of the time, the culture, or the prevailing social winds, societies expect men to possess a level of stoicism that is poorly defined.

That demand makes sense from society's point of view. If a man can't be trusted to contain his tears, how can he be trusted to contain his rage, his lust, or his lethargy? Yet the man who suppresses his emotions risks a host of problems, like depression, substance abuse, the inability to connect with others, and physical health problems.

We men walk a tightrope regarding emotional honesty. We pay a heavy price for erring too far toward stoicism, and we risk losing prestige if we err too far toward emotional vulnerability.

---

67 See, for example, Di Bianca, M., and J. R. Mahalik. 2022. "A Relational-Cultural Framework for Promoting Healthy Masculinities." *American Psychologist* 77: 321-332. The authors argue that "hegemonic masculine socialization" must be replaced with socialization that leads to "social change efforts at the social, community, and systems levels." Such language suggests the authors are less concerned with male mental health than their personal agenda to shape society.

That tightrope should be less stringent in our homes. The joyful condition doesn't exist if we can't be impeccably honest with our women, especially when we are troubled.

In my clinical experience, most men err on the side of being too stoic and withholding at home. I am prone to it myself. But it's unfair to keep our women in the dark. It forces them to devise their own explanations when they sense our suffering or disappointment.

The most common reason I have heard to explain this pattern of withholding personal expression, aside from men simply not practicing it, is men's fear that admitting to failure or disappointment will diminish them in the eyes of their women.

My humble suggestion: if the person closest to you can't handle that you sometimes face problems, like everyone else, then she probably doesn't deserve your commitment. Healthy women want strong men but not men carved out of stone. How is a woman to connect with an unfeeling machine?

Emotional honesty can be easier if we reassure her when she is not responsible for fixing our problems. We can let her know we have a plan, even if the plan is merely to create a plan. Clarity about which problems belong to *me*, which belong to *you*, and which belong to *us* opens space for a man to communicate without putting his wife or girlfriend in the position of managing his emotions.

Another helpful technique when we're struggling for words but haven't yet found them is to reassure her we're searching for the words and we will include her as soon as we're ready and able to talk. Healthy women find it painful to be shut out when they know we're suffering. The promise to include her as soon as possible eases her burden.

Impeccable honesty is subjective. It's bound to be shaped by each man's individual values. Whatever else impeccable honesty may be, it certainly excludes concealment and avoidance. The joyful condition cannot survive under a veil of secrets, even if they are well intentioned.

Monitor growth in the relationship.

How do you know if conflict serves to improve the relationship? In the same way you know if you're improving at the gym: you monitor the results. Dispassionate observation lights the way.

Relationship growth is less easily quantified than personal records on the bench press, but the relationship should continuously improve in terms of communication, pursuit of values, and avoiding repetitious arguments.

I knew a couple beset by chaos and endless bickering. Between them, they had subjected each other to drunken infidelity, profligate spending, and one physical assault. (She hit him with a flashlight.) As a result, they shared a mutual suspicion of each other that bordered on paranoia. They eventually broke up, thankfully.

They were an almost cartoonish example of what we might call masturbatory quarreling. They never solved problems. The relationship itself became one self-contained, self-perpetuating, irreconcilable equation. The purpose of every argument was merely to keep the relationship from falling apart. No growth survives in that soil. Never mind the relationship supporting a larger purpose in life.

That level of wheel spinning is a good sign that the relationship has lost the plot. Men of purpose cannot afford such affiliations. The effort invested into a relationship should yield results. Most disagreements should lead to smoother communication in future disagreements. Joyful relationships get easier with time and practice, not harder.

Beware of the walking wounded.

A man once approached me at a conference.

"So. You're a head shrinker?" he asked.

"Yeah, I'm a psychologist," I responded.

"You do couples therapy?" he asked in an unfriendly tone.

"Yep," I answered.

He scowled. "Yeah. That shit doesn't work."

Unsurprisingly, he was divorced, he was angry about it, and he wanted me to know he blamed my profession. It also turns out this man was vocal in men's online spaces, spreading uncharitable theories about female behavior. I don't doubt that women mistreated him, but nor do I doubt that he managed his pain by spreading it to others.

Whether it's friends, family, or gurus on social media, men who only see the worst in women will shout it at the masses, just like women who only see the worst in men. These are the walking wounded. They are snake-bit, and their safety-at-all-costs strategy frames the opposite sex as the enemy.

It's an effective but costly approach. Keeping women at arm's length reduces the chances of getting hurt, though it does so at the cost of constant guardedness, loneliness, and feelings of hostility. These men often cloak their messages in humor and feelings of camaraderie. They want you in their Despair Club for Men. Their motto: "Misery loves company."

To complicate matters, they may honestly think they're saving men from the experience they endured, like infidelity or costly divorces. Their words of warning usually contain some truth plus a large measure of overgeneralized fear.

Fear-based emotions are contagious. Consider voodoo death spells, which work by theatrically generating negative expectations within victims. The victims then succumb by manifesting their own voodoo-induced anxiety. Voodoo also requires a community that believes in its power. The walking wounded, whether they intend it, are working their voodoo on anyone who will align with their community and take their message seriously.[68]

It's important to listen to the walking wounded. They have lessons to impart. It is equally important to limit exposure to them. Some men look at women and see only narcissism, daddy issues, unrestrained hypergamy, brattiness, and the horrors of family court. These men are not at peace with women. In their world, the joyful condition is a laughable fantasy.

---

68 Benedetti, F. 2013. "Responding to Nocebos Through Observation: Social Contagion of Negative Emotions." Pain 154: 1165. See also: Cannon, W. B. 1942. "Voodoo Death." *American Anthropologist* 44: 169-181.

Take their warnings to heart, but don't forget about the quieter side of reality. While those who only see the worst in women are shouting their message to anyone who will listen, those who are on good terms with women are quietly enjoying their relationships. It costs the walking wounded nothing if they persuade you to resent women, but if they succeed, it might cost you more than you know.

As a couple, pursue meaning before happiness.

I knew a couple that devoted their lives and their relationship to sensual delights. They drank expensive wine, took extravagant vacations, dined in fancy restaurants, and attended the trendiest parties.

A problem was lurking: they could barely tolerate each other outside these fleeting indulgences. They distracted themselves with extravagant fun, but they certainly were not living the joyful condition. As evolutionary psychologist Donald Campbell warned, "The direct pursuit of happiness is a recipe for an unhappy life." This couple was evidence of that.[69]

In a well-constructed study on happiness, researchers found that genetics account for between 44 percent and 52 percent of the stable portion of a person's subjective well-being—their hedonic set point. Factors like socioeconomic status account for a smaller slice. Our moods may shrink and swell like the ocean in response to good news or bad, but our baseline happiness is more like the Rock of Gibraltar.[70]

Those of us who tend more toward angst or depression, rather than a happy-go-lucky demeanor, need to put special effort toward avoiding instant gratification. A relationship can and should be a fun place, but it's wise to approach purpose and satisfaction as a

---

69 Pinker, S. 1997. *How the Mind Works*. New York: W.W. Horton and Company.

70 Lykken, D., and A. Tellegen. 1996. "Happiness Is a Stochastic Phenomenon." *Psychological Science* 7: 186-189. The authors wrote, "Based on the retest of smaller samples of twins after intervals of 4, 5 and 10 years, we estimate that the heritability of the stable component of subjective well-being approaches 80%."

team. Avoid chasing the ever-receding target of immediate gratification. A man is well served by taking the lead on this front.

Flatly reject women who embrace a victim-based ideology.

We discussed ideological feminism as a threat to the resilience requirement. There's not much to add here, but the point is worth underscoring because it is so central to the joyful condition: if she views men as her oppressors, then she will eventually view *you* as her oppressor. Save your commitment for those who value your masculine virtues.

Identify and eliminate counterproductive self-policing.

Self-policing, which we focused on in the chapter on Dignity, is one of the oldest ideas in clinical psychology, though it's usually presented in slightly different terms. For example, in the 1960s, the brilliant psychologist David Shapiro described what he and others at the time called the obsessive-compulsive personality style.

The term today suggests someone who compulsively checks locks or avoids germs, or in sloppier usage, someone who is simply fastidious. However, Shapiro used the term to describe a more pervasive and nuanced way of navigating the world. He described a personality dominated by rules and structure. This person agonizes over decisions and puts a great deal of effort toward doing things correctly, sometimes at the expense of actually doing them.

An important feature of this person is that he thinks of himself not in terms of what he wants in life but in terms of the roles he fills. Shapiro wrote:

> "Once his role is established in his mind, it becomes a general directive for behavior, one that is often capable of including even the details of facial expressions, ways of speaking, and the like."

And what drives the man with this personality style? He has an abiding sense of obligation to the roles he believes he inhabits. Here's Dr. Shapiro again:

> "The obsessive-compulsive person functions like his own overseer issuing commands, directives, reminders, warnings, and admonitions concerning not only what is to be done and what is not to be done, but also what is to be wanted, felt, and even thought. This is the meaning of the single most characteristic thought-content of obsessive-compulsive people: 'I should.'"[71]

This man is primed for *happy-wife-happy-life* relationships. A demanding or domineering woman allows him to fulfill the subservient role he longs for, an uncompromising framework in which to operate, and an endless supply of obligations.

I'm spending time on this obscure psychological concept for a reason. In my experience, most conscientious men have a streak of this tendency. It may be a little, or it may be a lot, but any of us can get lost in our roles and obligations and forget about ourselves. This is a path to joyless relationships.

The first step, as always, is to notice it's happening. We can watch for thoughts and language like *I should* or *I'll try to.* We might remain on alert for decision-making that satisfies role requirements when it would more appropriately satisfy personal needs and desires.

Personal desires are a foreign concept to some men, but they start to familiarize themselves with it by asking *What do I want to do?* And *What might happen if I don't do what I'm "supposed" to do?* Some men don't know the answer because they have never considered the question. If this concept is completely foreign, try a small experiment. Replace questions like *What should I eat for dinner?* with *What do I WANT to eat for dinner?* Even that can be a struggle at first. Believe it or not, the answers lie within. Outside of eating the last endangered white rhinoceros, there are no wrong answers. Your desires are dictated by your desires.

You know my stance by now. There's little advantage in battling the emotional mind. Better to let it exist while we explore options

71 Shapiro, D. 1999. *Neurotic Styles*. Basic Books.

that emotional logic cannot see. For those with an obsessive devotion to role and obligation, the joyful condition is anxiety-provoking because of its absence of constraints. Fortunately, the conscientious man has spent a lifetime practicing self-discipline, so he already possesses the skills and demeanor to work through that discomfort.

Respond to bids for connection.

Here's one surefire way any man can destroy the joyful condition in his relationship: ignore her subtle attempts to connect. These can be her attempts at small talk, cracking a joke (even if it isn't funny), making simple requests, physical touch, invitations to share an activity, and talking about her day … endless examples abound of what Dr. John Gottman calls "bids for connection." In a 2018 paper, he wrote:

> "While heart-to-heart conversations create moments of closeness, a more pervasive sense of emotional connection is found in nuanced day-to-day interactions that may not seem particularly significant or even noticeable at the time."[72]

Small bids are easy to overlook because they're subtle and because purposeful men are often preoccupied with their mission. Gottman found that responding positively to these small interactions is a reliable predictor of relationship satisfaction. Don't be the chump who destroys the joyful condition by overlooking subtle attempts to connect.

Choose someone who is pleasant to come home to.

Imagine coming home to your wife or girlfriend after a hard day. Which of these alternatives is most appealing?

- Option one: an upbeat woman who is happy to see you.

---

72 Navarra, R. J., and J. M. Gottman. 2018. "Bids and Turning Toward in Gottman Method Couple Therapy." In Lebow, J., A. Chambers, and D. Breunlin (eds.). 2018. *Encyclopedia of Couple and Family Therapy*. New York: Springer.

Sure, she has her bad days, but she takes comfort in your presence.

- Option two: a bitter, critical woman. Sure, she has her good days, but you're just one wrong word away from her rage.

Which do you choose? The question seems silly because the answer is so obvious. Yet we have all met men who seem to choose option two. I'm hoping any man who has read this far will never again make that mistake. A necessary corollary to this strategy is to *be* someone who is pleasant to come home to.

Observe your behavior in her presence.

How would you respond if friends and family said you have changed for the worse and they're worried about you? The answer depends on whether they are attempting to encourage you or undermine your success. Sometimes, especially as young men, we outgrow things that no longer serve us, and our friends will try to pull us back into their comfort zone. "You've changed, bro. You don't party with us anymore."

When that's the case, a useful answer is, "Thanks for noticing. It hasn't been easy. Want to hit the gym with me?"

However, when their comments hint that we have moved away from health or values—as is often the case for men in unhealthy relationships—that's when we need to shut up, get curious about what our friends and family are trying to tell us, and reflect.

I know whereof I speak. One of my biggest relationship regrets is that I didn't listen when a good friend told me I had changed for the worse after my then-girlfriend came into my life. He was right, but I didn't want to hear it.

Unfortunately, friends aren't always willing to speak up. A great life skill is the ability to observe our own behavior and to ask tough questions like:

- *Why am I smoking more pot since she came into my life?*
- *I feel like I have to hide my phone from her. What's causing that urge?*

- *Why do I drive so aggressively when she's in the car?*

Bringing explicit awareness to the emotional mind is a topic that deserves its own section. Men can fall into joyless relationships because they disregard their personal check-engine light. That's why this chapter's foundational skill is respecting intuition.

Foundational Skill: Respect Intuition

Picture this situation. A man—we'll call him Jamal, but he could be anyone—is at a gathering with his new girlfriend. He has dated her for a few months. So far, she appears to possess the Bright Triad traits, and her values complement his. At this gathering, a friend who shares Jamal's political views makes a joke at the other side's expense. Jamal laughs, and then the conversation continues in a different direction.

However, from the corner of his eye, he noticed a fleeting look of contempt from his girlfriend. She seemed disappointed to discover his political opinion. Her expression conveyed the briefest flash of rage, and she seemed distant for the rest of the evening.

This was a pivotal moment. It injected doubt into the relationship. So far, her character had been wonderful. The sex was great. Their values seemed compatible … but that look of contempt was alarming.

On the other hand, the contemptuous look was brief—a split second—and the two of them ended up having passionate sex later that night.

This type of incident should raise uncomfortable ambivalence. That flash of contempt might be a warning sign of issues to come. Suppose they get married. Will that brief flash of contempt grow into full-on, abiding bitterness? He could dismiss the look and focus on the fact that her behavior went back to normal soon enough. Why rock the boat over a trivial moment?

Still, the situation nags at Jamal. It's as if one part of his mind wants to scrutinize the situation, but a larger part wants to pretend it never occurred. What should he do about his relationship?

Let's come back to that question. First …

What Is Intuition?

Intuition is not mystical. It's not a spiritual connection to an unseen world, nor is it a uniquely feminine asset. Intuitive hunches, doubts, and cravings result from nonverbal information processing in parts of the brain that operate beneath our explicit awareness. Nothing more. Many of us, for various reasons, cut ourselves off from those hunches and feelings, and that's to our detriment.

Luckily, we can all hone our attentiveness to those subtle messages from within. Respecting intuition is easier if we know how it works, so let's start here: There are at least two types of mental activity. The first is knowledge and information processing of which we are aware. We'll call this *explicit* thinking. The second is knowledge and information processing of which we are unaware. We'll call that *implicit* thinking.

Some might call them *conscious* and *subconscious* thinking. Those terms are more familiar, but they are less precise because consciousness is difficult to define. We can keep it simple and accurate by saying this: there is information we know that we know, and information we don't know that we know.

We have the power to play with that dividing line. We can make implicit knowledge explicit by putting words to it, and we can render explicit knowledge implicit (in a way) by ignoring it.

For example, Jamal has a nascent awareness of his girlfriend's contemptuous look, but he could easily choose to direct his focus away from it. He can relegate his girlfriend's contemptuous look to the mental junk heap while he focuses on more pleasant aspects of their relationship—like sex—and tells himself everything is fine. Essentially, he can forget about the incident the same way a person forgets the combination to a lock: by focusing elsewhere, neglecting to rehearse the information, and letting it fade.

Much to my frustration, I see men do this when vetting relationships. It's not that I want men like Jamal to pick a particular course of action. It's not my place to write a prescription for his life. I simply want men in his position to work with all available and relevant information. That contemptuous look, and the cold shoulder that followed, was entirely relevant to the commitment he was considering, and he would be wise to scrutinize the behavior.

The mind is divided against itself, even in allocating attention. Parts of our minds are always processing information of which we are not explicitly aware. Imagine working at your desk, intently focused on your task, and in the background, a small fly is buzzing around, barely audible.

You may not be *explicitly* aware of the fly because you are focusing your prefrontal cortex on work. But other areas of your brain (like the ascending reticular activating system, if you're interested) are acutely aware of the fly. We're just not explicitly aware that our mind is monitoring the situation.

That kind of information doesn't percolate up into explicit awareness unless those systems monitoring the situation notice an important enough detail to override our attention and hijack explicit awareness. If that little fly whispered your name, your mind would make you instantly, explicitly aware of it.[73]

Intuitive hunches are based on implicit knowledge and thinking. Intuitive hunches and their accompanying physical sensations are indications that the divided mind is wrestling with itself. It's trying to turn implicit information into explicit knowledge we can act upon.

In some ways, the mind is pretty good at handling implicit knowledge. In other ways, it isn't. A 2013 article about intuition, for example, noted that our minds are good at handling implic-

73 Lieberman, M. D. 2000. "Intuition: A Social Cognitive Neuroscience Approach." *Psychological Bulletin* 126: 109-37. This paper reported that implicit and explicit learning are different processes that operate on different neural pathways. The author hypothesized that implicit learning is the basis of intuition.

it problems of physics. We react thoughtlessly and efficiently to physical events. Imagine using your slow-moving rational mind to catch a ball. It would be an uncoordinated mess. Such tasks are best left to the wordless depths of our lightning-quick implicit understanding of the world.[74]

We also need slow-moving rational logic to solve conceptual problems like probability. Our implicit thinking is terrible at that sort of task. The author of the article about intuition gave this example from the work of Amos Tversky and Daniel Kahneman: Imagine you have a six-sided die. It has two green faces and four red ones. Which of these sequences is likeliest to emerge if you roll the die twenty times?

1. RGRRR
2. GRGRRR
3. GRRRR

In the experiments carried out by Tversky and Kahneman, most people intuitively chose option two because the proportion of greens and reds in that sequence matches the proportion on the faces of the die. Our implicit reasoning tells us to go with the most representative option.

That's a mistake. Option one is a smaller subset of option two, so it is statistically likelier to emerge. Here, our implicit reasoning is relying on what Tversky and Kahneman call a representativeness heuristic that can mislead us. Slow-moving explicit reasoning can give a correct answer that feels wrong to our intuitive, implicit thinking.

Here's another example of errors in implicit thinking. In one of their most famous experiments, Tversky and Kahneman asked students to guess the field of study for a hypothetical student, Tom, who they described as orderly, dull, and "occasionally enlivened by somewhat corny puns and by flashes of imagination of the sci-fi type."

74 Strevens, M. 2013. "Your Instinctive Genius." *New Scientist* 220: 28-29.

Over 95 percent of the students intuitively predicted that Tom was more likely to study computer science than other disciplines. This was a reasonable prediction, except at the time, it was unlikely that any particular student was a computer science major. (Less than one chance in three.) There was no reason to believe a student of the humanities, for example, couldn't also fit Tom's description. Statistically, that's the likelier possibility.[75]

However, the same rapid, implicit reasoning that gave us the wrong answer about Tom can give us the right answer in a less abstract situation. If we suddenly find ourselves isolated in a dark alley and we feel the urge to flee, it's because we have learned dark alleys represent danger. We have nothing to lose by heeding that intuitive message, but ignoring it may be costly.

Our intuitive judgments are based on patterns we have experienced. That's why chess players gain intuitive expertise with practice. The more patterns they experience, the more implicit knowledge they develop.[76]

The sentiment that we should always obey our intuition—or that we should disregard it—is questionable advice. Here's a better bit of wisdom: When intuition speaks, slow down, ask questions, and put words to the situation. Maybe your mind is noticing a detail that deserves explicit attention.[77]

I treat my intuition like a trusted advisor who is missing some data. It has the advantage of speed and pattern recognition, but it suffers a couple of disadvantages. Namely, it's insensitive to the quality of information, and it relies on fast, sloppy heuristics.

---

75 Kahneman, D., and A. Tversky. 1973. "On the Psychology of Prediction." *Psychological Review* 80: 237-251.

76 Kahneman, D., and G. Klein. 2009. "Conditions for Intuitive Expertise." *American Psychologist* 6: 515-526.

77 For intuitive hunches regarding performance-based endeavors, you might follow intuition provided 1) you have sufficient experience in the domain to have developed an accurate nonverbal familiarity with its base rates, and 2) you have engaged in a tremendous number of trials for which you received immediate feedback. Otherwise, the better bet is to note your intuition but attend to the facts of the situation.

This foundational vetting skill—respect intuition—isn't complicated. It involves slowing down and asking questions. Was Jamal's new girlfriend showing a troubling signal of things to come? He could only find the answer by acknowledging that the question matters. He was at an opportune moment to employ two of the gatekeeper's primary tools: time is your ally, and dispassionate observation lights the way.

Ignoring a feeling of trepidation is a sucker's bet. We have little to gain by turning our attention away from our feelings, aside from the questionable goal of avoiding discomfort. But the cost of ignoring intuition can be astronomical.

How to Hear Intuition

Jamal might be in trouble if he's especially conscientious because dutiful men are good at forgoing the joyful condition. They're more interested in fulfilling their self-imposed responsibility to spare others from discomfort.

For example, in response to that fleeting look of contempt, Jamal might choose to self-police. From then on, he could avoid mentioning whatever seemed to have irritated his girlfriend. This would set a precedent for the rest of their relationship. She will have the power to remove words and actions from his repertoire with nothing more than a glance from her angry eye. She would have the power to control him with a look. Devastating.

We know where that precedent leads. As one man said of a relationship that had descended into pure resentment, "The hair on the back of my neck stood up whenever she came home." He told me he had been so disconnected from his emotion and his intuition, and such a dutiful husband, that he barely noticed he was suffering until his physical health declined.

We each have slightly different intuitive signals. They can manifest as physical sensations, sleeplessness, dreams, behavior changes, anxiety, depression, or health problems.

Intuitive hunches can be so subtle that they're easy to ignore, or so thunderous that they misdirect us. Such was the case for a man who spent months searching for the nonexistent physical cause of his migraine headaches—the same headaches that disappeared immediately after his divorce.

It doesn't matter how idiosyncratic our emotional signals might be. Our awareness of them is what counts. Some men are exquisitely attuned to the messages from their emotional side; others have yet to identify them. Cultivating that connection isn't complicated, but it requires work. Here are six tips for learning the language of the nonverbal mind:

- **Identify the physical sensations that amount to your emotional check-engine light.** What does it feel like, physically, to have a visceral reaction to a situation? For many men, the first sign is some sort of gut sensation. Others describe tension in the chest or neck. You can also watch for changes in breathing or pulse, though these are more subtle.
- **Expand your emotional vocabulary.** Many men have a limited list of words to describe their emotions. They haven't looked beyond words like "happy," "angry," "hungry," or "horny." Every computer and smartphone has access to a thesaurus. We can search for words that have subtler shades of meaning and avoid meaningless, catch-all words like "frustrated." We can grill ourselves with questions like: *What's a more precise word for this emotion? Is it urging me toward something? Away from something? Are my emotions aligned with my intellect, or am I conflicted? If so, then how?* Words are key to transforming implicit hunches into explicit knowledge.
- **Study your shifts in emotion, like anger that appears out of the blue.** Slow down and ask questions. It's okay to physically remove yourself from a situation and then literally talk to yourself about whatever is happening. (Just tell people you have to go take a piss.) This can be a challenging process with plenty of false starts. Keep at it. Feelings are fast, but logic is slow. Sometimes we don't even know we're bothered until someone else

points it out. Give yourself grace if it takes a while to notice what's happening emotionally.

- **Study your cognitive patterns.** How does your rational mind respond to little tingles of intuition? Do you enter problem-solving mode? Do you ruminate on certain topics rather than attending to your emotions? What about rationalizing, justifying, or inventing explanations? Noticing shifts in cognition can be difficult because, at times, we engage the rational side to avoid the emotional side. Journaling is an excellent way to bring patterns out of the shadows.
- **Meditation.** I can't speak much about this because I have never found meditation to be helpful, but many men have. You can find countless books, websites, and videos to help you use meditation to notice what your mind is up to. It doesn't have to be traditional meditation; movement and exercise can be meditative. For some, rhythmic activities like running or walking can generate great clarity of thought.

It's my hope that any man in Jamal's position will not push past his own emotional reaction but will instead slow down and decipher his implicit thinking. Respecting intuition creates options we might not otherwise notice. If Jamal puts words to his implicit thinking, then all options are on the table except one: ignoring what might be a dangerous warning sign.

Intuition is no trifling matter. One man told me what happened after ignoring his emotional check-engine light: "She lost her temper with me a couple times before we got married. I had a feeling that was a bad sign, but I ignored it. I told myself she was working on it."

Predictably, her anger increased after the wedding. Eventually, he walked on eggshells, hoping to avoid her rage. It was a case of self-policing and negative reinforcement in the extreme.

Stories like that are a dime a dozen. Don't do it to yourself. Don't talk yourself out of those intuitive messages. I don't know the best course of action for Jamal. I only hope that men like him will consider all the information at their disposal, both explicit and implicit.

FLIGHT CHECK

- **Disposition.** What was it like growing up in your home? Would you describe it as joyful? What childhood lessons did you learn about happiness in relationships? Are you prone to negative emotions like depression or anxiety? If so, what is your practice for managing it?
- **Conflict.** Do you have a history of avoiding conflict in a way that causes conflict to escalate? What did you learn about conflict as a child, particularly conflict between men and women? Do you self-police to avoid disapproval from women?
- **Intuition.** What are the subtle signs that the wordless, subterranean part of your mind is trying to tell you something? What physical sensations, thoughts, emotions, and behaviors make up your emotional check-engine light?

Just One More Thing ...

So far, we have examined four bare-bones relationship requirements for men of purpose. They are composure, dignity, resilience, and joy. We've looked at how they work, why they matter, and the reasons men disregard them.

We need to discuss one more trait of healthy relationships. It involves the word I refused to write until we concluded more important business.

We hear many opinions about this word. We're told it is all we need. It makes the world go 'round. It conquers all, and it completes us. It makes us want to be better men. It is patient. It is kind. It is blind.

That's what we hear.

I will concede that healthy romantic relationships cannot exist without this word. I will even admit that it is one of life's great experiences. However, the grievous error of prioritizing this word over more pragmatic considerations has been the downfall of innumerable men.

In fact, the reckless exultation of this word has harmed so many men I can barely bring myself to type it. But we might as well get it out in the open. Here goes ...

— BOOK V —

Love

Build a masculine frame for love • Choose commitments that bring peace rather than torment • Reduce risk and uncertainty by setting the speed limit

I'll wager nearly every man reading this book has met at least one woman to whom he was attracted against all rationality and common sense. It has certainly happened to me. These women play on our idiosyncratic desires like Liberace's fingers danced over the keys of his rhinestone piano. She's our romantic nemesis, the woman who would steal our heart and drag us through hell if we let her.

Up to this point, we have focused on rational considerations. We have methodically dissected the forces that drag men into destructive relationships. This is where we enter more dangerous territory. Emotions and hormones can compel us to pursue our romantic nemesis against all better judgment.

Hopefully, I have given you an armor of confidence and protection against the nemesis. Boiled down, this book is just one big if-then statement:

> *If* the relationship brings composure, dignity, resilience, and joy, *then* the gatekeeper takes love into consideration.

I hope this blunt approach will rule out each gatekeeper's romantic nemesis so he can reserve his commitment for only healthy relationships with women of admirable character and shared values.

The cravings and urgings we associate with romantic love are the product of a mind shaped by hundreds of thousands of years of pair bonding. Emotional logic doesn't strive for composure, dignity, resilience, or joy. It doesn't care about long-term success and happiness. It simply wants what it wants, even if she is the perfect romantic nemesis.

Let's define romantic love as best we can. Psychologist Michael Karson has boiled it down to a manageable notion. When you love someone,

> "... the other person's happiness and well-being operate as reinforcement for oneself, and injuries to the person are aversive. You know how you are happy for people who get good news but you're also kind of resentful of them? When you are only or almost only happy, that's called love. Romantic love is the same thing plus sex."[78]

I'll take it a step further: If she does not clearly rejoice in your success and commiserate over your setbacks, then you are not experiencing love. It may resemble love, but the most important ingredient is missing: investment. That's what makes mature love a behavior we choose more than a feeling we surrender to. Some men get their emotional wires crossed on the matter. (Women, too.) When we're seeing her through infatuation goggles, it's easy

---

78 Karson, M. 2018. *What Every Therapist Needs to Know*. Boulder, CO: Rowman & Littlefield.

to imagine we're receiving love when we're actually receiving nothing more than tolerance or the willingness to accept gifts and favors.

Researchers write about two kinds of love: companionate and passionate.

Companionate love grows slowly, involving much more than sex. It's strong friendship, attachment, admiration, and a shared vision for the future. It's what comes from building a shared foundation for life and family. Unlike the lust that consumes us at the beginning of a romance, companionate love doesn't sneak up on us. It requires time and intention to nurture.

Passionate love is the kind that can get us into the most trouble. It might be more accurately called lust or infatuation. It's effortless, and it involves excitement, obsession, idealizing, and downplaying each other's shortcomings. It's a wonderful slice of life.

It is, however, a deviation from our brain's normal state. Infatuation reflects a change in serotonin signatures, appearing to last between twelve and eighteen months, though some couples report their infatuation lasts longer. Being infatuated is a bit like being stoned. We don't see the world, or her, as we normally would.[79]

It's during this period of lovestruck intoxication that we're most tempted to entangle ourselves in a love nest from which we may never escape. Worse, the infatuation may be based on a fantasy she can't live up to. The most fulfilling relationships develop into a combination of passionate and companionate love.

That type of love is not a figment of Shakespeare's imagination or an invention of greeting card companies. Passionate, committed relationships are universal throughout the folklore and history of every culture investigated.[80]

There's no reason to assume a man from a thousand years ago—or a hundred thousand—didn't experience the same irresistible draw to particular women. One researcher found good evi-

---

79 Fisher, H. 2016. *Anatomy of Love: A Natural History of Mating, Marriage, and Why We Stray*. New York: W.W. Norton & Company.

80 Jankowiak, W. R., and E. F. Fischer. 1992. "A Cross-Cultural Perspective On Romantic Love." *Ethnology* 31: 149-155.

dence of monogamy and marriage among the first hunter-gatherer migrations out of Africa.[81]

The ubiquity of romantic love might arise from the fact that pair bonding is a successful reproductive strategy for humans. We also enjoy more adventurous alliances like polyamory and serial monogamy, but the reliable mom-and-dad arrangement is most common.

Romantic love is powerful because it solves the problem of getting human parents to commit and invest long enough for their children to thrive on their own. Children are more likely to survive when dad sticks around, and dad is likelier to stick around if he loves the mother. If nature asks, "How can I maximize the survival of a big-brained species whose children are essentially useless for the first decade?" a major piece of the answer is, "Get the parents to feel attached to each other."[82]

Along with all the titillation of romantic love comes some nifty psychological tricks that keep us invested, such as finding other potential mates less interesting than the one in our arms, strategies for guarding our mates, and feelings of jealousy that (when functioning correctly) help us monitor our significant other's level of interest. And if the sex is good, then we're all in, or at least our emotional minds are.

Whatever the cause and explanation for romantic love, you and I must contend with the urge to commit reckless acts of lust.

---

81 Walker, R. S., K. R. Hill, M. V. Flinn, and R. M. Ellsworth. 2011. "Evolutionary History of the Hunter-Gatherer Marriage Practices." *PLoSONE* 6: e19066.

82 Campbell, L., and T. J. Loving. 2016. "Love and Commitment in Romantic Relationships." In *The Handbook of Evolutionary Psychology, Volume 1*, edited by D. M. Buss. Hoboken, NJ: John Wiley & Sons. The authors wrote, "Over evolutionary time, increased infant dependency placed greater burdens on human mothers and increased the value of paternal support in feeding and protecting young. Given that men have a genetic interest in the survival of their offspring, fathers were able to benefit reproductively by forming committed, investing relationships that would have reliably increased the probability of offspring survival."

These minds of ours require supervision. That's why love is the wise gatekeeper's last consideration when vetting relationships.

I hope this sterile discussion is taking some of the shine off love. Our emotional minds are single-variable thinkers in a multivariate world. They fear no consequences of running us off a cliff for love. That's why the rational mind needs to be involved in these decisions.

What's needed isn't cynicism about love but clear-eyed detachment and the willingness to put words to our inner workings. Love is one of the greatest experiences in life if we view it through a mature, masculine frame. Otherwise, we risk losing composure, dignity, resilience, and joy. In the worst cases, men lose their children, their futures, their fortunes, and even their lives.

For men, romantic commitment is no trivial indulgence. It is an investment and a responsibility. Our romantic love is a commitment to give our attention and our resources to a particular woman. That relationship choice may be the furthest-reaching decision of our lives, and she may be the single largest beneficiary of our effort, time, and talent. Why should we carelessly give away our greatest assets? Why should we donate it to the first random woman who lays claim to a position in our lives?

We may not get to choose who we find attractive, but we can absolutely control our decisions. We can walk away from the wrong relationship, knowing that doing so won't kill us, no matter how painful it might feel for the moment and no matter how much the mind frets that there may never be another opportunity.

The right relationship fills a man's sails. The wrong one is a relentless headwind. That much ain't rocket science. The tricky part is to realize the winds don't change because we want them to.

Love Is Not Enough

> "A worthless girl has enslaved me, me whom no enemy ever did." — Epictetus

I'd like to introduce you to two more men: Adam and Ben. Neither man is real; they are composite sketches illustrating two common relationship patterns that destroy men's lives. Both men feel beaten down and miserable, and each is in "love" with his romantic nemesis. What looked and felt like love (to them) more closely resembled cyclical patterns of mistreatment or even abuse. Yet, these men remained invested.

Chances are high that you have met men like them or even walked in their shoes. Most of us have, even if we only walked a short distance. Let's start with Adam and his devotion to a relationship in which composure, dignity, resilience, and joy simply were not on the menu.

Adam's Foolish Love

Adam is the office nice guy; the agreeable peacemaker. He wants to be good at his job and go home to a loving family. He is the behind-the-scenes hero who keeps society running. Just like his father, Adam keeps his head down, pays his taxes, and considers others before he attends to himself.

Adam thought he had struck gold when he met his nemesis. She was gorgeous, and the sex was great. This seemingly perfect woman assured him he was the perfect man. In those intoxicating early days, he didn't realize he was in the first stage of a cycle that would repeat throughout their relationship. He would vacillate between hero and villain, and each iteration would drag him further into chaos and fatigue. Here's how the cycle played out:

1. **Idealization.** At this stage, Adam is on a pedestal. Affection and sex flow freely. They both are on cloud nine and deep in the throes of infatuation. Life is rainbows and unicorns.
2. **Rupture.** Adam's nemesis perceives a minor slight in his actions or tone. Affection suddenly dries up. He feels as if she is looking for reasons to be cold and angry. She says things like "I deserve better than this" when he has done his level best to treat her well. He's confused. He doesn't understand her pain, and he tries to soothe her.

3. **Demonization.** Adam can find no way to calm her. In fact, the more he tries, the angrier she becomes. She lashes out with reckless behavior, like driving home drunk after a night with her girlfriends. (They undoubtedly affirmed her belief he's the bad guy and he mistreats her.) Still, he loves her, and he believes love means being a better boyfriend.
4. **Crisis.** Finally, after days of torment, they engage in a long, arduous argument about their relationship. She says she feels neglected, abandoned, and mistreated. He doesn't understand why. They hash and rehash their history. They revisit previous arguments and grievances against him. At points, he angrily defends himself, but eventually she wears him down. He promises to try harder, though he's not entirely sure what that means. Eventually, her anger recedes. Feelings of affection wash over them again. She melts into his arms.
5. **Resolution**. Although he doesn't understand what happened, she feels rescued and understood. Adam is happy the tension is gone, and he's thrilled about the make-up sex. (He's luxuriating in the double-whammy of negative and positive reinforcement.) Still, he can't shake off the vague feeling that she got the upper hand somehow. He feels undignified, but he's unsure why.
6. **Repeat.** For now, Adam is no longer the villain and has returned to idealized hero status. He's relieved, though he senses a pall over the relationship that he can't define. As a result, he's a bit more reserved than before. He polices his behavior, but eventually, inevitably, another rupture occurs. The cycle begins anew, with each iteration adding to his unease and strengthening his need to self-police.

Ben's Empty Love

Like Adam, Ben is ambitious and conscientious, though with a more brash and extroverted personality. He's self-assured, charismatic, and socially connected. Ben is a hero in the community—a firefighter, perhaps. His high profile attracted his romantic nemesis like a moth to a flame.

She loves being seen with a hero; he loves being seen with an attractive woman who reveres him. Unfortunately, like Adam, Ben is in a downward spiral that will destroy his spirit. The cycle begins here:

1. **Flattery and attention**. Ben is the center of her world. She showers him with affection, especially in public. She violates his boundaries but in a way that feels charming to him. For instance, when he asked her to stop texting him during work hours, she "playfully" sent flowers instead. She pushed past "no" as if to say she would not take a back seat, even to his job. She shows him off to friends and family. She calls him her soulmate. He feels privileged to occupy a prominent place in such a vibrant woman's life.
2. **Demands for service and commitment.** She expects that he be at her service, day or night, and she's vocal about it. She says things like "I'm depending on you" or "I need you at this event with me." He's happy to comply. He enjoys feeling important.
3. **Rupture.** Inevitably, he makes a mistake. She's disappointed. No one can meet her expectations of loyalty and constant presence. Perhaps he forgets to run one of the many errands she expects, or he's unable to be at her side during a social gathering. She doesn't hide her disappointment. She says she feels discouraged about the relationship, and she wonders aloud if she misjudged his character.
4. **Crisis.** She retreats. She doesn't cut him off completely, but she conspicuously focuses on other, more dependable

people … "people who won't let me down when I need them." Ben's "love" takes over. He works to regain her trust. He apologizes and sends flowers. He neglects his own responsibilities to help with hers. He takes her at her word that she is a dynamic, high-performing woman who requires a dynamic, high-performing man. He assures her, through word and effort, that he is trying to be that man.

5. **Resolution.** She eventually relents and trusts him again. Though she points out that the trust is tenuous, she reinstalls him to a position of prominence. She praises his efforts as if he were an employee. The sex is great again.
6. **Repeat.** Ben is once again the center of her world, though it's less rewarding with each iteration of the cycle because she's less effusive each time she forgives him. He has a vague sense he's being used, and he's irritated by her refusal to take responsibility for her mistakes. Over time, the chorus repeats, and with each verse, he becomes nervous, small, and shame-driven around her. Anxiety overtakes him whenever she punishes him by withdrawing. He feels he can't afford to disappoint her, but he's unsure how to avoid doing so. Like Adam, he learns to walk on eggshells in her presence.

Adam and Ben illustrate two patterns among many in which men devote themselves to relationships that slowly deplete their vitality. If they remain, these cycles will reduce them to husks of their once-vibrant selves. Though the details of their cycles are different, Adam and Ben might identify with the following story about a horse as told by a man I know. This might be the most important horse story you read all day, or at least one of the top three.

The man who told me this story frequently visited Scotland as a child. His extended family there owned a business delivering milk in horse-drawn carriages.

Among the horses in the stable, the family prized one in particular: the white horse whose name the man couldn't recall. This clever horse had learned his route so well that he could walk it with minimal guidance. He even knew which houses to visit. (I don't know if he could recite each customer's order. The man didn't say.)

The white horse was also unusually even-tempered. Unlike other horses, he was never stubborn or oppositional, and he didn't demand breaks. He simply hitched up each morning and did what the family expected of him.

The white horse made life easier for the family, and they loved him for it. Or so they said. Their actions showed otherwise. They gave him the heaviest workload and neglected his health. They ran him every day with little attention.

I have heard that neglected draft horses can develop debilitating bone problems. Maybe that's what killed the white horse. Whatever the cause, he died young. The family had worked him to death.

Do people train horses, or do horses train people? Any good behaviorist will tell you it's a two-way street. The less agreeable horses in the stable lived longer than the white horse, in part because they were more demanding. They had conditions. They wouldn't perform if they weren't happy.

The white horse performed unconditionally, just as Adam and Ben gave their love unconditionally. They sacrificed their composure, their dignity, their resilience, and their joy. What did they each receive in return for their commitment?

- **More chaos than composure.** Despite moments of calm and even moments when the relationships made Adam and Ben feel at peace, they each knew the next catastrophe was right around the corner. Neither could feel certain the relationship would be a source of strength during their most challenging moments.
- **Shame rather than dignity.** Each relationship required shame-based self-policing to avoid the next crisis. (It never worked.)

- **More frailty than resilience.** It's hard to feel capable or competent when the next relationship crisis is imminent, waiting to deplete us. Both relationships were demanding and erratic. The women were unaccountable and functioned poorly within their relationships.
- **Fatigue instead of joy.** Like other mistreated men, Adam and Ben would say, "When it's good, it's great." The highs in these relationships made them feel like supermen. The slot-machine, double-whammy combination of positive and negative reinforcement can put a man on top of the world … for a short while. While the highs feel great, the lows are miserable, and the in-betweens are an exhausting combination of dread and self-policing.

You already know I find little value in fighting against the mind. I certainly have not discovered the off switch for a romantic attraction to the wrong women. But we don't need an off switch. Perhaps all we need is another skill we have discussed throughout: the ability to notice what the emotional side of the mind is trying to accomplish and to overrule it.

A skilled gatekeeper may love a particular woman unconditionally, but he cannot unconditionally offer his commitment. Too much is at stake. The relationship must meet requirements, and the rational mind needs to sit at the head of the table.

It's a fantasy to believe love can conquer all. It can't. Love can't overcome abuse, mental health problems, emotional immaturity, conflicting values, or substandard character. It certainly can't overcome a relationship in which the other side refuses to function as a teammate. A man can't love a woman into being what he wants her to be. Nor can he make her return his love by giving her more of what she doesn't value, as Adam and Ben tried to do.

I once heard a story of an elderly couple in an assisted living facility. She could barely speak after a stroke, and he was nearly blind. Despite their challenges, these two made each other smile and laugh each day. They had spent decades building a life and family together. Now, they were nearing the end of their time but still enjoying intimacy, teamwork, and private jokes. It's a safe bet that any man who has read this far is interested in a similar type of love.

As troubling as the mind can be, it exists to solve problems. In most people's minds, establishing a romantic connection is immensely important. That means love is a reliable source of anxiety. Operating within a composed, mature, masculine frame for love means our emotional minds may not get the immediate gratification they demand.

As far as I can tell, men can end up tormented by love in a couple of ways.

One is to idealize love. This is the emotional mind in the driver's seat, unrestrained by practical considerations. Whether from a lack of experience or an avoidance of painful realities, the man who idealizes love is vulnerable to his romantic nemesis because he lacks the wisdom or discipline to avoid her.

The other path to torment is to demonize love or, more precisely, to demonize women. To this man, love doesn't exist or it only exists to make a man vulnerable to vicious betrayal. This is another version of the emotional mind in the driver's seat. These men feel like Tantalus, tormented by delights they believe they can never possess.

As for which is the worse position, while demonizing love may be lonely and wretched, at least it is functional. I can't deny that it locks tight the gates to the kingdom. Idealizing love errs in the opposite direction. It lets the gates swing wide open for all the wrong entrants.

Idealizing love is especially dangerous for men. It's a feminine framework. It mistakenly assumes we, as men, are entitled to unconditional love and women will meet us with a warm embrace if we idealize them. This is not the way it works for men. We are not princesses in fairy tales, breathlessly surrendering to a love that engulfs us like a warm, protective blanket.

For men, the love of a good woman can be warm and protective, but it's also a costly investment. It is a commitment for which we are responsible and from which we cannot easily step away. At least, that's what several family law attorneys have told me about their clients.

Women and children who receive the love of a capable, resourceful man are truly fortunate. Given that our devotion is such a valuable commodity, why would any man invest in the wrong woman? Our last sampling of organizing principles might shed some insight. The following traps prevent men from being calm and collected about love.

Pathways to Torment

What do you suppose is love's opposite? Is it hatred, wishing for someone's demise? Or is it indifference, not caring if they live or die? I imagine either can be true in the abstract. However, the consequences of a man's choice of commitment are far from abstract. If my observations are reliable, the opposite of romantic love is similar to torment. It's the torment of desiring what we believe we can't possess or of realizing that which we possess is poisoning us.

Love is where the emotional mind tries to assert itself at all costs. It's even willing to sacrifice our health and safety. If we're to have any agency in the presence of our impulse to love, it's vital to bring our organizing principles into the light: Who do we love, and why? What manner of relationship are we attempting to replicate with our love?

Notice how many of these organizing principles involve idealizing love and clinging to a relationship like a drowning man clings to a life preserver. As always, please stop and spend time with any that strike a chord, and we will follow these eleven principles with strategies for maintaining a calm, masculine frame for love.

An unhealthy relationship is better than no relationship.

The man operating under this principle idealizes love, but he feels unworthy of it. It's likely he has never experienced a healthy romantic connection or even seen it up close. As unhealthy as romance seems to him, the lack of it seems even worse.

This man might feel discouraged and hopeless, chanting to himself, "There are no good women." He takes what he can get. Alternatively, he might believe he is the damaged one, his mind operating under the belief that no healthy woman would want him.

This man places love on a pedestal, making standards difficult, if not impossible.

I am incomplete if I'm not in a relationship.

Left to its own devices, an anxious mind will choose security over freedom. It might even choose the security of a miserable relationship to escape the anxiety of loneliness. The man who believes loneliness is intolerable won't walk into the arms of his romantic nemesis. He will run. This organizing principle is important and deserves more attention. I will revisit it in the upcoming strategy section.

I'm obligated to love her.

We've seen previously how positive traits can be a man's downfall in the romantic arena. (Recall how the combination of conscientiousness and agreeableness can prime a man for burdensome relationships.)

That same conscientiousness can lead a good man to make unreasonable sacrifices for his culture, his community, his family, or his woman. This is the man who tolerates substandard relationships because he feels he *should*. His version of love is based on external demands.

His role models say, "You're not a man if you don't marry her."

His community says, "You need to make an honest woman of her."

His culture says, "Stop trying her on for size. Commit."

His family says, "We want grandchildren."

His girlfriend says, "If you loved me, you would marry me."

For a man with a powerful sense of duty, love and obligation are so intertwined that he doesn't even consider the need for mutual benefit. This man exists to serve. His values and purpose are secondary considerations.

That's not love; that's servitude.

I can fix anything, including this relationship.

A sunk cost is unrecoverable. Rationally, sunk costs should not factor into decisions about the future, but the loss-averse emotional mind doesn't recognize that logic. Emotional logic says, *Eliminating resources and relationships is dangerous*. Hence the common romantic blunder of remaining in a relationship merely because we have invested in it.

A 2016 study found people are "willing to invest more time in a relationship in which more time had already been invested." They also found that "men seem to be more prone to commit the sunk cost effect than women when a monetary investment was present."[83]

Some of us just can't stop ourselves from trying to fix a defective and hopeless relationship. Not only are we loath to admit our efforts were ill-spent, but we might also have a genuine affection for her. For men operating under this principle, the more effort spent toward fixing it, the more invested they feel and the likelier they are to keep trying.

In my clinical experience, entrepreneurial types are especially vulnerable to this organizing principle. They have a habit of conquering challenges and bending the world to their will. This serves them well at work, but they have a hard time seeing when it serves them poorly at home. (One psychologist who reviewed an early draft of this book urged me to underscore this point because she has seen it so many times in her own practice.)

I love her too much to watch her crumble when I leave.

This man feels obliged to stay in a relationship because she desperately clings to him. She says she loves him so much she can't

---

83 Rego, S., J. Arantes, and P. Magalhães. 2016. "Is there a Sunk Cost Effect in Committed Relationships?" *Current Psychology: Research and Reviews* 37: 508-519.

cope without him, and he believes it. (Excuse me while I retch. She survived before he came along, and she can do it again.)

This man may believe he is receiving love, but he's receiving attachment born of insecurity. He doesn't have a wife or a girlfriend; he has a dependent, and he wants to be the good guy at all costs.

Of course, sometimes it isn't about being the good guy. Some women coerce and corner their men with threats of self-harm or suicide. To repeat the point, that's when it's time to dial 911.

She's perfect, on paper.

Occasionally, when the stars align, a man meets a woman who is absolutely perfect … for someone else. She's gorgeous, sexually adventurous, fun, and spirited. Unfortunately, her life goals, her personality, or her values don't align with his.

There is a time for everything, as the saying goes: a time to plant and a time to uproot … and a time to acknowledge when a relationship is bound to become a liability. Sometimes, despite our longing for a different outcome, it's impossible for her to invest in your success, or vice versa. It may simply be a matter of incompatible values with an otherwise wonderful woman.

It's a tough pill to swallow, but infatuation is different from compatibility. That reality is invisible to an emotional mind in search of a romantic connection.

The belief that she is perfect is not an organizing principle. It's a descent into fantasy. If an organizing principle is at work here, it's that romantic relationships occupy a special realm in which the rules of common sense don't apply.

Love is worth fighting for; love can conquer all.

These sentiments are not as lovely as they sound. They have a dark side. Whereas the previous organizing principle revered romantic relationships beyond common sense, this one views romance as a cause that replaces a man's purpose.

Couples who boast that their love is worth fighting for are sometimes merely justifying their desire to remain together despite their incompatibility. Sometimes they assign an outsider to the role of antagonist in order to have a common enemy to align against. The charm of "you and me against the world" can propel attachment for a while, but drama and intrigue lose their appeal the moment either partner realizes they have better ways to spend their time.

My love can rescue her.

This man believes his love has a medicinal quality that can vanquish a woman's troubles. Whether he has watched too many romantic comedies or suffers from overconfidence, he's deluded into thinking his love is a magic elixir.

Helping our women is a noble and useful impulse in healthy relationships, but it becomes a problem when we're more invested in solving their problems than they are. That's when the relationship becomes dead weight. This is another principle that plagues hard-driving, entrepreneurial types who have difficulty tolerating defeat.

Men who believe in the healing power of their love are at particular risk for poorly considered entanglements like shacking up, getting married, or having children. *If a little love can help her,* he thinks, *a lot of love and commitment will help her even more*. Entanglements are his version of hitting the problem with a bigger hammer. Unfortunately, those solutions usually magnify the original problem while simultaneously closing avenues of escape.

She's my soulmate. I will never love again.

According to a 2013 Pew study, 69 percent of adults are skeptical of the idea that we each have one true soulmate. Interestingly, more men (31 percent) than women (26 percent) believe in soulmates. (If you're wondering, I do not believe in soulmates. I believe in maximizing the compatibility of character and values among available candidates. Call me an old romantic.)[84]

The man who believes he has discovered his soulmate will be highly resistant to the idea of relinquishing her, even if keeping

---

84 Cohn, D. 2013. *Love and Marriage*. Pew Research Center, Washington, DC. https://www.pewresearch.org/social-trends/2013/02/13/love-and-marriage/.

her means tolerating a relationship that undermines composure, dignity, resilience, or joy.

It's painful to think about leaving a woman we love and admire. The emotional mind shouts at us: *We will never replicate those special moments or her delightful quirks*. This is one occasion when the emotional mind is correct. She is unique, and so is the relationship. But here's what emotional logic doesn't tell us: if we leave, we will find other opportunities to love.

Like some other items in this section, this one is more a hormone-addled belief than a proper organizing principle. The man operating under this belief is like the proverbial monkey whose hand is trapped in a small hole because he refuses to open his fist and release the food he found there. He's so fixated on what's in his grasp that he can't see the surrounding bounty.

I fear what will fill the void if this relationship ends.

This organizing principle has little to do with a man's relationship to women. It's more about his relationship to his thoughts, feelings, and memories. To a man trying to evade his own internal experiences, a relationship can serve the same purpose as booze, porn, or any other vice that offers a temporary escape from pain.

Without the distraction of a relationship, this man is left to face his anxiety. The unhealthier the relationship, the more it distracts him from whatever he's avoiding within. This man has lost sight of the fact that we magnify our mental health problems through our efforts to escape them. If he's caught in this trap, then he must maintain that relationship, like a drug habit, to avoid the painful feelings that will fill him in her absence.

This man is prone to sacrificing his future to his relationship, just as an alcoholic sacrifices his future to drink. Fortunately, like the alcoholic, he can face his demons and emerge stronger on the other side.

Women will destroy me if I get too close.

This is the only organizing principle in this list that drives a man to avoid romantic love rather than recklessly embrace it. This man sees romance as a transaction. Women are to be enjoyed for nothing more than sex and companionship, if at all.

The man operating under this principle has no room for mutual investment, family-building, or a shared vision. He will choose women who are unavailable due to existing relationships, addictions, mental health problems, or any other arrangement that obstructs meaningful connection. This man has no skin in the game, and that's how he likes it.

Every man I have met with this organizing principle arrived here honestly. Important women mistreated them. Now the men are snake-bit and want no part of a romantic connection. These men often overlook the invisible costs of isolation—the unrealized possibilities for joy and affection, the forgone feedback and opportunities for growth, and the benefit of having another heart and mind in his corner.

Health risks are also associated with social isolation, including depression, cardiovascular disease, stroke, disability, suicide, and premature death. Married people are also slightly less likely to develop dementia than those who are unmarried or divorced. Men are more vulnerable than women to these costs of social isolation since our friend networks are more sparse.[85, 86]

In addition, a 2013 study titled *Marital Status and Survival in Patients With Cancer* found that "the survival benefit associated with marriage was larger than the published survival benefit of chemotherapy," and the effect is larger for men than for women. The authors noted that cohabiting with a romantic partner appears

---

85 Wu, Daolin, Fuwei Liu, and Shan Huang. 2022. "Assessment of the Relationship Between Living Alone and the Risk of Depression Based on Longitudinal Studies: A Systematic Review and Meta-Analysis." *Frontiers in Psychiatry* 13: 954857.

86 Vegard, S., C. E. Bowen, A. Håberg, et al. 2022. "Marital Histories and Associations with Later-Life Dementia and Mild Cognitive Impairment Risk in the HUNT4 70+ Study in Norway." *Journal of Aging and Health* 0: 1-13. The authors didn't identify the protective mechanism of marriage. They noted that the number of children was a mediating variable, but health problems, social isolation, or mental distress were not.

to confer a protective benefit similar to marriage, but living with other adults (such as a roommate) does not. [87]

Such outcomes are why I use the term "risk management" rather than "risk prevention" when discussing romantic commitment. Men who think they're eliminating risk by avoiding commitment unwittingly sign up for different risks. The oversight is understandable. Risks associated with commitment are openly discussed, but risks associated with isolation sneak up on you. It's something for the aging bachelor to guard against.

I never intend to persuade a man to seek or avoid romantic commitment. That's not my job. My only wish is for informed decision-making. As the economist Thomas Sowell said, "There are no solutions. There are only trade-offs." The costs of rejecting romantic commitment are not absent; they're simply difficult to see.

The Road to Love

Here's a message that contradicts nearly every song, movie, and TV show I have heard. It's one that violates the feminine frame that says we are at our heart's mercy: *Be intentional about love. Approach it with a calm, collected, masculine mindset.*

Throughout this book, I have drilled the message that we can't control emotional logic but we can choose where we place our time and attention. Who we lust after may be beyond our control, but where we cultivate love is entirely up to us.

Emotional logic takes a backward approach to evaluating women. It searches for the most attractive woman available and then it commands us to pursue her. *Values and character? What are those?*

The rational mind has the power and wherewithal to impose a more masculine frame for love: Identify women of outstanding character and shared values, then pursue the most attractive among them. Other women, no matter how appealing, are out of the running as romantic prospects.

---

87 Aizer, A. A., M. Chen, E. P. McCarthy, et al. 2013. "Marital Status and Survival in Patients With Cancer." *Journal of Clinical Oncology* 31: 3869-3876.

This approach rules out most women, even most of the great ones. The emotional mind might not like that, but emotion doesn't rule the gatekeeper. Here are eleven strategies for putting the rational mind in the driver's seat.

Be self-governing in the presence of women.

Some men have never been without an intimate female relationship. They went from their mothers (who ensured survival) to their girlfriends (who offered affection) to their wives (who provided intimacy and companionship).

This is only a problem when stepping away from romantic commitment feels like stepping away from food and water. If the mere thought of being without female companionship or sex creates anxiety, then it's possible your emotional mind has too much influence over your romantic decisions.

Suppose you decide to take a break from romantic commitment. What's the right amount of time to do so? The clinical psychologist in me says: Face the anxiety of isolation until the anxiety reliably recedes. Don't run toward comfort when anxiety is at its peak. Doing so reinforces the anxiety, much like acquiescing to a child during a tantrum encourages more tantrums.

Sitting with anxiety until it recedes teaches our minds that anxiety won't kill us, and it's useful to know *why* we're facing anxiety—what values we're pursuing—so we're not suffering merely for the sake of it. Suffering is easier when we do so in the service of our values. It's also vital to continue purposeful activity while anxiety is running its course. Doing so further reinforces the idea that anxiety isn't in charge.

With enough practice, we can even find humor in the way anxiety operates within us. That's when we know we have kicked anxiety's ass. That's when we're truly self-governing.

Tackling anxiety and compulsions is easier with the help of a skilled psychologist who understands behavioral principles. A skilled therapist will help you understand what's behind the anxiety so you know what you're up against, and he's familiar with tactics for overcoming it.

Why bother with breaking the compulsion to seek the comfort of women? For some men, there's no need. The fortunate ones among us can transition from mother to girlfriend to wife seamlessly and securely. If there's no problem, then there's nothing to fix.

However, if isolation from female companionship is anxiety-provoking, then you might be vulnerable to your least productive organizing principles. That's worth tackling.

Avoid relationship ambiguity.

It's thrilling when a seemingly ideal woman falls for us. The downside is that women who are in love feel compelled to sow entanglements while they're blinded by infatuation. She may think her infatuation will last forever. She may want to cook for you, clean for you, and give you the best sex of your life. You may also be tempted to believe these gifts will never change.

The wise, purposeful gatekeeper knows better. He understands that neurochemistry changes during infatuation, but it always returns to baseline and gives way to realistic appraisal. That's when the genuine relationship begins. Only then, with careful deliberation, should couples consider life-altering entanglements. Those entanglements should be a blessing, not a snare.

In the meantime, girlfriends, fiancées (or intendeds), and wives (or equivalents) are distinctly different categories with unique rights and responsibilities. You might recall this was one of the first topics in the introduction. We blur the lines at our own peril.

Check your compassion about her predicament.

Women have a shorter reproductive timeline than men (though plenty of men underestimate how quickly their own clock will run out). Yet, young women are often fed the message that they can have it all in unlimited quantities: career, family, and a life of adventure. They're told through entertainment and education that life doesn't require trade-offs.

It's truly unfortunate, but Western societies don't seem to teach women that every choice eliminates other options. I have encountered a tremendous number of women who spent their twenties and thirties doggedly pursuing careers and solo adventures, only to wake up in their late thirties and early forties, longing for family and children at the precise moment when that door is rapidly closing. That's just one undesirable outcome women face. A woman might find herself to be a single mother, an aging bachelorette, or a two-time divorcée, and it may be through no real fault of her own.

Conscientious, compassionate men often feel an overpowering urge to rescue these women from their predicaments. However, the purposeful gatekeeper understands he is not responsible for solving a problem he didn't create.

Time is your ally when vetting relationships. The gatekeeper does not surrender his future to her existential pressures—and he is skeptical about his feelings of "love" that might be laced with pity and obligation.

Sometimes the most compassionate decision is to release her as soon as it's apparent that either she or the relationship does not belong in your life. As painful as it might be, her urgency is not your emergency.

Ensure informed consent regarding life plans.

In response to the previous strategy, some men might think, *That's easy to say, but I was raised to be a "good man." Now I'm saddled with guilt and shame whenever I don't "do the right thing." How am I supposed to respond to her pressure to move the relationship forward?*

The straightforward way to manage misplaced obligations is to get ahead of them with honesty about life plans so she can decide whether she wants to take part.

If we, as men, are intentional about romantic decisions, then the women we pursue have every right to know it. I believe the proper way to respond to relationship pressure is by making sure she clearly understands what you intend to do with your life, along with perfect clarity about the vetting process using unambiguous messages like this:

"I hope our relationship works out, but it might take a couple of years to know if this is the right fit for each of us. I need time to assess the relationship, and so do you."

The point is worth repeating: Her time pressure is not your problem to solve, but that doesn't negate compassion. Compassion toward her includes impeccable honesty about values and purpose and the willingness to surrender the relationship if her timeline is incompatible with your vetting requirements.

Assess her inner circle for goodness of fit.

I knew a man who was seriously considering marrying a woman whose family was infected with hostility toward men for reasons he couldn't decipher. As a hardworking, traditional man, he was everything they despised. They were inconsiderate, dismissive, and passive-aggressive toward him. Despite his efforts to bridge the gulf, their behavior failed to improve during the two years he dated this woman.

This man loved his girlfriend, and she did not share her family's hostility toward men. Regardless, he saw no sign their hostility would ever decline. If he married this woman, he would also be marrying into her family. Their attitudes would infect the relationship and diminish his quality of life.

He was also unwilling to raise children in such a hostile environment. Since they didn't trust men, he thought it likely they would undermine his efforts as a father. And what if he had sons? Would his in-laws treat them as badly as they treated him? He wasn't willing to risk it.

He wondered whether he was being too particular. He felt awful about rejecting his girlfriend when she had done nothing wrong. In the end, he realized her family's attitude was irredeemably incompatible with his values. He also had a poor appetite for interpersonal conflict, and he knew any future with her would be rife with it. The decision was painful, but he broke up with her.

Soon after, he met a woman whose family was welcoming and well adjusted. Her values and character were a better fit, too.

Twenty years later, he has a wonderful marriage. He is close to her family, as are his children.

Love is an entirely sentimental enterprise, but the gatekeeper must access that part of his mind capable of a more pragmatic and wide-ranging view—the masculine frame for love. When we commit, we aren't merely selecting one relationship with one woman. We are entering multiple relationships, each with its own effect on us.

Stress test the relationship.

Vetting the relationship involves taking part in life fully, with her by your side. You want to ensure the two of you function as a team during stressful events. For example, traveling together is a great way to test each other's mettle. How do you function as a couple when you both are fatigued and aggravated because your flight is delayed and the airline lost your luggage?

I'm not suggesting a manipulative tactic to expose her true colors. Life will offer plenty of opportunities for her to reveal her character. I suggest honesty. Tell her you want to know how you function together. She should be just as curious. It's amazing how quickly those loving feelings can evaporate when she turns into a child at precisely the moment you need her to act like an adult. Even if behaviors don't descend to that level, sometimes couples simply have incompatible coping styles.

In any long-term romantic commitment, moments will occur when we're more committed to the relationship than to the person (because the person can be temporarily annoying, but the relationship is enduringly valuable). In a healthy relationship, those moments pass and affection returns. The crucial point is that teamwork prevails even during moments of stress or annoyance.

Be intentional about second chances.

As trite as it may sound, misunderstandings and minor conflicts are opportunities to strengthen relationships. As they say in my profession, it's not about the rupture; it's about the repair. This is a good guiding principle for romantic relationships. Mistakes matter less than how we handle them.

Suppose, for example, she gets drunk and (out of character) says regrettable words to you. Good. Now you get to see how she handles herself when she screws up. Does she own up to her mistake? How does she ensure it won't happen again?

Her responses to her mistakes offer a reasonable glimpse into your future with her. You can also set a positive tone for the relationship by owning and repairing your mistakes and by observing how she handles your apologies.

I'm sure we have all seen men who make excuses for the mistreatment they receive. Statements like "She's just having a bad day" or "I shouldn't have provoked her" relieve her of responsibility and invite an abusive dynamic to take hold. It's unacceptable. Your devotion is a privilege she should treat accordingly.

Don't lead with sex.

Too many men lose their composure over sex. They have sex too early in a relationship for their own good. They cede all power to their shortsighted emotional minds, and they relinquish their standing as a gatekeeper.

That's a mistake, and it's not a question of prudishness. In my clinical opinion, it's vital to test sexual compatibility before marriage or its equivalent. Sexual incompatibility is miserable, and it's a principal cause of divorce.

However, courtships include an order of operations. Humans have followed it for thousands of years, and it's not complicated: Let the emotional connection build before jumping into the sack. Flirt. Let desire marinate. Get to know each other. Allow the essence of the relationship to reveal itself. Enjoy the dance, then enjoy the sex.

Waiting offers advantages. Delaying sex gives both sides time to notice character while minimizing the hormonal blinders that overshadow incompatibilities. That's one reason sex is risky outside of an established, healthy relationship. It becomes an entanglement we don't want to release. Just ask any man who got married because his wife was a minx in the bedroom, only to discover she was a battle-ax in the living room.

Leading with sex increases the risk of becoming stuck with an unstable woman who concluded—justifiably—that sex signaled the beginning of a serious romantic relationship. Who can blame her?

If you're looking for one more reason to wait, here's one my father might have offered: Don't be a pussy beggar. Prioritizing sex over connection conveys weakness and shows a lack of discipline. It signals poor self-control and an unwillingness to say "no."

Sex leads to infatuation and attachment on both sides. That's what it's supposed to do, and that's why a masculine frame for love means keeping hormones on a leash.

Take charge of birth control.

While you're getting to know a woman, do not—I implore you—leave her with the responsibility of birth control. If you care about your future children and your purpose, then treat birth control as your solemn responsibility. They're your soldiers. Make sure you deploy them with intention.

Forgive the indelicacy, but should you choose early encounters with unfamiliar women, make sure that you, not her, dispose of the condom. Additionally, please know that no small number of women become "accidentally" pregnant when threatened with the loss of a relationship.

I recommend not placing the responsibility of birth control on her until 1) you have vetted her well beyond the infatuation period, and 2) you would be happy if she became pregnant.

Know how and when to break up.

Being the gatekeeper isn't always fun. One of the heaviest responsibilities, aside from disobeying our own hormones, is turning women away. Breaking up is unpleasant, but it's better to part amicably after a few months of dating than to part contentiously after a few years of marriage.

Whatever the reasons for ending relationships—I have given you plenty to consider—the gatekeeper is kindhearted enough to avoid ambiguity.

Phrases such as "I think we should break up" or "We need time apart" invite negotiation. That only increases the pain. The gatekeeper is resolute, honest, and unambiguous: "It's time to break up." This responsibility can be heartbreaking. It can even be dangerous if she is emotionally immature or mentally unhealthy. Here are a few tips to ease the exit:

- **No sex during the breakup.** You may both want to cling to the feelings you once had, but sex compromises your exit and sends a cruel mixed message. Plus, to repeat the warning, some women have a knack for getting knocked up during that last romp. The emotional mind, with all its disorienting demands and urges, has no place in the discussion when it's time to part ways.
- **Anticipate doubt.** In the aftermath of a tough decision, our minds can put us on an emotional roller coaster with thoughts ranging from *Why did I do that?* to *Why did I wait so long?* Doubt is normal. It may never disappear entirely, but it will fade, and new experiences will overshadow it.
- **Avoid isolation.** It's normal to be of a divided mind after a breakup. Even when the rational mind knows it was the right decision, the emotional mind, with its ability to make us feel mentally and physically miserable, might insist we win her back. When the mind is divided, our trusted inner circle of friends and family can help us sort out our thoughts and focus on the bigger picture.
- **Tend to your problems, and let her tend to hers.** The rescuers among us may feel compelled to be her source of comfort during the breakup. Attempting to do so creates mixed messages. Do her the kindness of allowing her to retreat to her inner circle just as you retreat to yours. If you attempt to remain friendly (as might be necessary if you share children or work or social ties), then

make an agreement, if she's willing, to allow each other time and distance to regroup and recover.

- **Anticipate the urge to rekindle.** During the breakup, she may suddenly become everything you wanted. You'll forget why you broke up. You will catch yourself rationalizing, excusing, or forgetting about your incompatibilities and destructive patterns. Ask yourself: Will the relationship truly be different, or is this newfound perfection a fantasy?
- **Know that a wedding engagement is not a contract.** This is crucial for men who have doubts when approaching the altar. An engagement is not unbreakable. It is the last opportunity to survey the relationship before exiting becomes vastly more complicated; it's the last chance to scrutinize all you will receive—both good and bad—in exchange for your commitment.

  Leaving her at the altar might feel embarrassing or cruel. You may anger friends and family (though you might be surprised by how many will rally to support you). She may feel hurt and angry, and you might be tempted to "man up" and "keep your word." The wedding might seem like an unstoppable freight train, and you simply must follow through.

  It's not true. You are allowed to slow down, take a breath, and confer with your inner circle. If breaking the engagement is the right move, then do it. Ending an engagement, and looking like the bad guy, are far less painful than ending a marriage. Heartbreak doesn't hurt forever, but divorce might.

  As a personal favor to me, please pass this message on to a friend if ever you're in the position. I have met men who would have ended their engagement if only someone had reminded them that they had the option.[88]

88 Monk, J. K., J. B. Kanter, T. B. Jamison, and L. T. Russel. 2020. "Beyond Cold Feet: Experiences of Ending Engagements and Canceling Weddings."

Leave women better than you found them.

A parting act of kindness if she's willing and capable is to have the difficult postmortem conversation about why the relationship failed. This conversation can be brief.

Sometimes men fear this will hurt women, but the truth—that values don't align or that personalities conflict—is usually more comforting than wallowing in ambiguity. For many people, the wounded heart resolves ambiguity with crushing explanations such as *I'm unlovable* or *I'm damaged goods*. Assuming she's capable of having the conversation, chances are high that the explanation you give her is less hurtful than the explanation her mind will devise in the absence of feedback.

It's also useful to hear her experience of the relationship and your behavior as the man in her life. This is precious feedback you can use in future relationships, and it gives her the opportunity to unburden herself of words she might regret not saying—both good and bad.

A larger, important reason exists. You might recall from the *Before We Begin* section that our theoretical frameworks grow stronger in the absence of feedback, even if our theoretical frameworks are dead wrong. Doing even a brief postmortem on the relationship can spare each of you from strengthening self-defeating (or self-aggrandizing) theories about yourselves. Leaving people better than you found them doesn't mean they're not hurt. It means you've helped them make sense of the experience so they aren't at the mercy of their own minds.

That optimal outcome isn't always possible. Sometimes women are too embarrassed, angry, immature, or self-destructive to en-

---

Journal of Social and Personal Relationships 37: 1-20. This research examined couples who ended relationships just prior to marriage. According to the authors, couples who took time to visualize the trajectory of the relationship were able to slow the momentum of wedding plans and navigate premarital doubts. These couples examined tough questions about where the relationship was headed. They also found that family and friends were happy to help with logistics, such as canceling vendors and informing guests.

gage in the conversation. We can't force a positive outcome. We can only offer it.

Foundational Skill: You Set the Speed Limit

We round out our list of five foundational skills for the gatekeeper with a simple injunction: You set the speed limit on the relationship. The gatekeeper doesn't bow to pressure. He knows what's at stake for himself and for the woman in question. He won't advance his level of commitment beyond what's commensurate with his understanding of her character and the quality of the relationship.

In short, no gatekeeper shacks up after a few weeks of dating, puts his fiancée on the title of his house, or adopts a puppy with his girlfriend. Speed binds us to uncertain influences over our future and our purpose.

A man can never eliminate the uncertainty. Frankly, doing so sounds boring. However, we can reduce the effect of deleterious uncertainty by gathering information over a long enough time to have a reasonable understanding of the relationship's effects.

A man's limbic system only needs a fraction of a second to decide whether she's the one, but his prefrontal cortex needs a couple of years to sort through the details. In the service of avoiding emotional catastrophes, the gatekeeper's most powerful word is:

"No."

The pressure to advance romantic commitment comes not only from her or from family and friends but also from within our own minds. I knew a man who invited a girlfriend to live with him simply because his home had air conditioning and hers did not.

It sounds silly, but his decision wasn't really about air conditioning. His real motivation was an organizing principle he had never identified or examined: *Women only value me when I'm rescuing them.* He was merely following that emotional injunction and relieving her physical discomfort.

As you may have guessed, the arrangement ended poorly. He quickly learned of her volatile temper, her incompatible values, and her inability to keep her clothes off the bathroom floor. He had to repeat the lesson learned by so many before him: moving her out is harder than moving her in.

We gatekeepers may not like saying no. We do it anyway until logic says the answer is yes.

It doesn't matter how urgent her desire.

It doesn't matter if our friends are afraid we might lose her.

It doesn't matter if our parents want grandchildren or if her biological clock is ticking.

You call the shots where your life is concerned. You determine whether the relationship brings composure, dignity, resilience, joy, and love. *You* set the speed limit.

FLIGHT CHECK

- **Intimacy.** Do you have a history of believing that you cannot be happy without a commitment to a woman? Do you feel incomplete when you don't have a relationship or under threat when you do?
- **Love.** What did your parents and other important figures teach you about love between men and women? Would an objective observer say you often settle for less than you should because you idealize love? Would they say you relinquish opportunities for intimacy by choosing women who are unhealthy or unavailable?
- **Self-determination.** Looking back, have you entangled yourself before you understood how the relationship would affect your values and your purpose? If so, what do you suppose drove those decisions? If you were to write a guidebook titled *This Is How a Woman Can Earn My Commitment*, what might it say?

The Final Word

My first job requiring a skill beyond mollifying grumpy customers or washing dishes was as a pinsetter mechanic trainee. Pinsetters are the complex machines at the back end of bowling alleys that place pins on the deck and return balls after each bowler's turn. Ours were built in the 1960s. There were eighty machines, each requiring regular maintenance and repairs.

At the front end of the bowling alley were impatient customers who were quick to complain when the machines malfunctioned, and the staff who relayed their dissatisfaction through loudspeakers mounted in the mechanics shop.

Sometimes it was a high-stress job requiring speedy problem-solving in a dangerous environment. Large machine components seemed hungry to claim a finger or a foot. Bowling pins would fly out of the machines like cannon balls. It was exciting to eighteen-year-old me.

We had eighty machines to maintain. I worked with a crew of six mechanics, all substantially older than me. Among the senior mechanics was a man I instantly admired. His name was John.

John had the bearing one imagines of Abraham Lincoln. Tall and thin, he had the impeccable haircut of a gas station attendant from a 1950s magazine advertisement. Somehow, his shirt was never grease-stained or untucked from his pressed pants. His tidiness was unheard of for a mechanic.

John was tidy in his work, too, always arranging his tools neatly before a repair and cleaning as he went. He spoke clearly and chose his words well. With a sly grin, a slow amble, and a quick wit, John carried the confidence and humility of a seasoned artisan. He approached the machines not like a mechanic but like an expert caretaker.

Where others (like me) would approach a broken machine with urgency or frustration, John approached slowly. It didn't matter how busy the lanes were or how frantic the alley manager was. John moved at his own steady pace.

When a machine broke down and the source of a problem wasn't obvious, John approached like a lanky cat stalking its prey. He watched and listened. He would climb the catwalk and observe it from different angles. He even used large screwdrivers as make-shift stethoscopes to listen for bad bearings or improperly timed actuators.

On odd, difficult-to-diagnose problems, he would try slight adjustments that eluded others. John showed me how a minor upstream refinement can have a major downstream effect in a system. Sometimes the smallest adjustment is the most elegant. John could always spot them.

How did he do it? What was his superpower? Just this: He never allowed others to pressure or agitate him. He claimed as much time as necessary to size up any situation.

John knew the value of patience and dispassionate observation, and he understood the multiplicative power of small variables and minor tweaks. He was, hands down, the slowest-moving mechanic on the team—and he was unquestionably the most efficient.

In a word, John had *finesse*. That's the word I'd like to leave with you.

Our choice of romantic commitment can have wider-ranging effects than any other decision. The man who can patiently size up a budding relationship, who understands his inner workings and vulnerabilities, who avoids basic mistakes because he will not be hounded … this man approaches his romantic decisions with finesse.

I hope this book has offered a framework in which to view romantic commitment with detachment, clarity, and nuance. It is certainly not the only framework. I hope you are already modifying these ideas to fit your circumstance and that you will add your own finesse to this set of blunt tools. Here's a quick review of our main points:

- A man's purpose is his foundation. Romantic relationships must complement that purpose.
- We all operate under wordless organizing principles that

define the way we approach relationships. We fortify ourselves against our counterproductive urges when we articulate those principles.
- The mind is divided against itself. Time and dispassionate observation are your allies in resisting the most detrimental emotional impulses.

We looked at five bare-minimum qualities of healthy relationships:

- Composure adds to our capacity for sustained, focused effort toward our values and purpose.
- Dignity supports our ability to move with confidence and maximize our range of motion in life.
- Resilience strengthens our ability to navigate challenges and solve problems.
- Joy gives us a solid foundation from which to face the world.
- Love must be grounded in shared values and mutual investment in success.

We also looked at five foundational emotional skills for establishing great relationships:

- Allowing others to experience discomfort when our decisions don't fit their agenda.
- Acting in the service of values rather than following the urge to reduce our own anxiety.
- Becoming skilled artisans of high-functioning relationships.
- Understanding our intuition as a tool for wise decision-making.
- Setting the pace at which the relationship proceeds toward commitment.

A romantic relationship almost never has a neutral effect on a man's life or his purpose. Offering his commitment to a woman of admirable character and shared values is a force multiplier. Committing himself to an unhealthy relationship—even if it's with a good woman—will cause and amplify failures. No matter how enchanting a woman might be, she has no place in the gatekeeper's life if the relationship is a liability.

I'm told pilots will miss their mark by a mile for every sixty miles flown with one degree of error. That means a rocket to the moon will miss by thousands of miles if the pilot fails to course correct. Romantic commitments don't require such exacting precision, but they may offer the most profound influence over the outcome of a man's journey. That's why, where other men rush into relationships with recklessness or desperation, the gatekeeper strolls in with wisdom and finesse.

Acknowledgments

I am eternally indebted to my trainers, my supervisors, and many people I may not name here. Special thanks go to those who graciously suffered through an early draft of this book and offered priceless feedback: Chuck Chapman, Jim Clair, Jerry Crimmins, Stephanie Foster, and Orion Taraban. To Jennifer Jas: thank you for your flawless editing and your willingness to speak up. Above all, thank you to my wife and daughter for being the bright and shiny center of my world.

About the Author

Shawn T. Smith is a licensed psychologist in Denver, Colorado. His education in psychology began as a child working at his father's bar. He later earned his doctorate in clinical psychology at the University of Denver. Shawn is the author of *Surviving Aggressive People*, *The User's Guide to the Human Mind*, and *The Tactical Guide to Women: How Men Can Manage Risk in Dating and Marriage*. You can find his latest work at ironshrink.com.